HUNGARY
IN THE LATE
EIGHTEENTH CENTURY

EAST CENTRAL EUROPEAN STUDIES

OF COLUMBIA UNIVERSITY

HUNGARY
IN THE LATE
EIGHTEENTH CENTURY

The Decline of Enlightened Despotism

BÉLA K. KIRÁLY

COLUMBIA UNIVERSITY PRESS

NEW YORK & LONDON

1969

EAST CENTRAL EUROPEAN STUDIES

OF COLUMBIA UNIVERSITY

The East Central European Studies comprise scholarly books prepared at Columbia University and published under the auspices of the Institute on East Central Europe of Columbia University. The faculty of the Institute on East Central Europe, while not assuming responsibility for the material presented or the conclusions reached by the authors, believe that these studies contribute substantially to knowledge of the area and should serve to stimulate further inquiry and research.

PREFACE

A PECULIAR PROBLEM confronts the author who is writing for English-speaking readers about a period in the history of an East Central European country that has been largely neglected by English writers and who is explaining details that are outside the scope of more general histories. To what extent should his work be descriptive, even encyclopedic, and how much of it should he devote to analysis and interpretation? There is no question that this book requires more space for descriptive passages than would be necessary in a work dealing with the same historical aspect of a Western European nation. The aim, however, has been to strike a balance by including as much description as seemed necessary for ease of understanding, while the burden of the book, it is hoped, is still on the analytical and interpretative side of the subject.

The book is intended to fill a gap in the history of Hungary in the English language. Heretofore the one available work in English on this subject was Henry Marczali's *Hungary in the Eighteenth Century.* Published in 1910, it is now largely out of date and glosses over the most numerous class in Hungarian society, the peasants. Marczali deals with some elements of government, but his treatment is not comprehensive; the present work attempts to remedy this. Above all else, however, Marczali's book is today a rarity.

To assist the reader, a Glossary defining the commoner Hungarian, Latin, and German terms has been appended. A Biographical Register contains information about the most significant names that appear in the text.

Throughout the text, the names of towns, rivers, etc., are given in the Hungarian form of the name. In Map No. 1 the present-day form of the name, where different, is given in parentheses following the Hungarian form.

It is both an honor and a pleasure to express in these pages my gratitude to my friends, colleagues, and former teachers for their great and valuable assistance. Special thanks are due to Professor Robert A. Kann for his advice on sources, methods, and interpretation and for a multiplicity of acts of kindness that in many ways facilitated the preparation of this book. Professor Henry L. Roberts, when he was still Director of the Institute on East Central Europe at Columbia University, obligingly invited me to present the manuscript for publication in this series and offered much helpful counsel on the research for the book and its drafting. Professor István Deák, currently Director of the Institute on East Central Europe, with great patience read the manuscript in all its stages of preparation; his numerous suggestions were an inestimable inspiration. Professors Peter Brock, John Lotz, and Joseph Rothschild also read substantial portions of the manuscript and gave me great encouragement. Mr. Peter Beales favored me with what most of those who write in other than their native tongue so need: syntactical editing. Mr. William F. Bernhardt, editor at Columbia University Press, did much to prune and clarify, and thus to improve, my manuscript. Mrs. Shirley Lerman typed promptly and with precision and forbearance a text peppered with foreign words. Mr. Mark Bin of *Time* magazine drew the original maps.

Among the libraries used, the most valuable, housing impressive collections of pertinent material, were the Library of Congress, the Hoover Institution on War, Revolution, and Peace, and above all the Libraries of Columbia University. Significant new material was found among the documents in the *Kriegsarchiv* and the *Haus-, Hof- und Staatsarchiv* in Vienna. In the latter, *universitäts* Professor Dr. Erika Weinzirl of the University of Salzburg, at the time a Research Archivist, was generous with her time and advice, and expedited my work.

Finally, thanks are due to the Institute on East Central Europe, Columbia University, for a grant-in-aid toward the cost of travel to Vienna, and to the Graduate Center of the City University of New York, for a research grant toward the work performed in the United States. To all these persons and institutions I wish to express my gratitude.

BÉLA K. KIRÁLY

Brooklyn College of the City
University of New York
October 23, 1968

CONTENTS

MAPS

ILLUSTRATIONS

following page 34

Hungarian prelates. Original in the National Széchényi Library, Budapest. Sándor Domanovszky, ed., *Magyar Művelődéstörténet* (Budapest: Magyar Történelmi Társulat, n.d.), IV, 429.

Hungarian lord and his servitor. Oil painting from the early eighteenth century. Original in the Hungarian National Museum, Budapest. Domanovszky, ed., *Magyar Művelődéstörténet*, IV, 292.

Bene possessionatus and peasant. Copper engraving by Townson, an English traveler. Original in the National Széchényi Library, Budapest. Domanovszky, ed., *Magyar Művelődéstörténet*, IV, 68.

Group of *honoratiori*. Fresco by Anton Maulbertsch, in the parish church of Sümeg, Hungary. Domanovszky, ed., *Magyar Művelődéstörténet*, IV, 156.

A *bocskoros nemes* plowing. Pottery of the late eighteenth century. Original in the Hungarian National Museum, Budapest. Domanovszky, ed., *Magyar Művelődéstörténet*, IV, 116.

Hungarian burgher. Original in the Historical Picture Gallery, Budapest. Domanovszky, ed., *Magyar Művelődéstörténet*, IV, 160.

Hungarian peasant in *guba* (sleeveless frieze cape). Copper engraving by J. Schaffer, late eighteenth century. Original in the Historical Picture Gallery, Budapest. Domanovszky, ed., *Magyar Művelődéstörténet*, IV, 117.

Member of the *banderium* of Fejér County. Woodprint, original in the author's possession.

Crown of St. Stephen returns to Buda from Vienna. Contemporary copper engraving. Original in the Historical Picture Gallery, Budapest. Henrik Marczali, *Magyarország története III. Károlytól a bécsi kongresszusig (1711–1815)*, in Sándor Szilágyi, *A magyar nemzet története* (Budapest: Athenaeum, 1898), Vol. VIII.

HUNGARY
IN THE LATE
EIGHTEENTH CENTURY

INTRODUCTION

THE YEAR 1790 was a time of crisis in Hungary when events, plans, proposals, and countermeasures brought to a head the turmoil within the social structure, revealed the real value and strength of the organs of government, and illuminated the aspirations and aims of Hungarians of all classes. Its brief span was like a flash of lightning in the dark: it sharply delineated the essentials of late eighteenth-century Hungary and adumbrated the upheavals that were to follow during the next century and a half. That is the reason why, when late eighteenth-century Hungarian society, government, and politics are analyzed, attention is so often focused upon that single year.

The late eighteenth century—the concern of this book—is, of course, a vague term. The descriptive sections that follow on government and on political, intellectual, social, and economic conditions are relevant to the last two decades of the century. The main phenomenon that is dealt with here is the decline of enlightened despotism and its replacement with a reactionary alliance between the Hungarian estates and the Habsburg dynasty. This retrograde development began during the last, war-wracked years of the reign of Joseph II and ended in the suppression of the Jacobin movement in 1794–95. This, then, is the period of interest, of which the Jacobin movement is an integral part. The movement itself, however, is not dealt with in this book, principally because it is adequately explored not only in Hungarian but also in English and German histories.

The crisis in 1790 was caused by the French Revolution, the still raging Turkish War, a mounting Prussian pressure on Austria, the revolt in the Austrian Netherlands, the unrest in Galicia, and the feudal revolt in royal Hungary.[1] The troubles were not of that year alone:

---

[1] The term "royal Hungary" refers to the Kingdom of Hungary, exclusive of Transylvania, Croatia and Slavonia, and the Military Frontier Zones. See Appendix A and Map No. 1.

The term "feudal revolt" has hitherto not been applied by Hungarian historians.

they had their beginnings much earlier. The last five years of the reign
of Emperor Joseph II were filled with signs of the coming storm. The
war with the Ottoman Empire[2] brought about increases in war taxes,
in enlistments, and in requisitioning by the army. The burden of these
fell, above all, on the peasantry and almost wiped out the beneficial
effect of Joseph II's abolition of serfdom.[3] The peasants who were to
have benefited most from the Josephine reforms became increasingly
disillusioned, while the privileged classes had long been dismayed by
Joseph's enlightened ordinances. The census of 1785[4] which registered
the households, dwellings, and property of all classes, including the
nobility, thoroughly alarmed the nobles, who believed it to be pre-
liminary to their taxation. It kindled hitherto smoldering discontent
into open, active, but unarmed resistance to the enlightened despotism
of Joseph II. The peasant unrest and the opposition of the nobility,
added to the Empire's other difficulties in 1790, made the year an extremely trying one, even for a man of Joseph's energy and strength of
character. With his death, on February 20, 1790,[5] these difficulties
blossomed into a full-scale political crisis for Hungary.

The crisis of 1790, its causes and the course it followed, the projects
it generated, and its repercussions afford an excellent point of reference
for an analysis of society and politics in late eighteenth-century Hungary. The diverse social classes, the Roman Catholic and Protestant
churches, the Serb, Croat, and Rumanian national minorities in 1790
all made proposals, demands, complaints; some of them even took
action. Analysis of this complex of factors leads to three conclusions
about Hungarian society at the time.

First: All the components of the crisis of Hungary's feudal society
that came to a head in the 1820s and ushered in the reform era of
1825–48 already obtained at least in embryonic form in Hungarian society of the 1790s. So, too, did the concepts which imbued the programs

---

It refers to an effort of the *bene possessionati* in 1790 to dominate the power of
the state and to restrict royal power.

[2] The war fought by Austria in alliance with Russia against the Ottoman
Empire (the Turkish-Austrian-Russian War) lasted from December 2, 1787, to
the armistice of September 23, 1790; the Peace Treaty of Sistova was signed on
August 21, 1791. A year later Russia signed a peace treaty with Turkey.

[3] The institution of serfdom was abolished by a royal rescript in 1784.

[4] Details of this remarkable census are given in Chapter I.

[5] A bulletin in the official journal of the court, the *Wiener Zeitung*, February
21, 1790, No. 16, p. 1, announced that the Emperor, born on March 13, 1741,
died on February 20, 1790, at 5:30 A.M.

Map No. 1

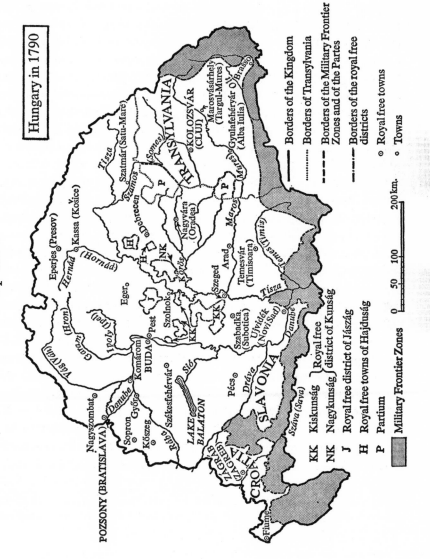

Hungary in 1790

POZSONY (BRATISLAVA)
Nagyszombat
Sopron
Kőszeg
Győr
Komárom
Rába (Raab)
Székesfehérvár
Danube
Vág (Váh)
Garam (Hron)
Ipoly (Ipel)
BUDA
Pest
Sió
LAKE BALATON
Pécs
Dráva
Eger
Szolnok
Szabadka (Subotica)
Újvidék (Novi Sad)
SLAVONIA
Száva (Sava)
CROATIA
ZÁGRÁB (ZAGREB)
Fiume
Eperjes (Presov)
Kassa (Košice)
Hernád (Hornád)
H
NK
H
Debrecen
Kőrös
Szeged
KK
KK
Arad
Danube
Tisza
Temesvár (Timisoara)
Temes (Timiş)
Szatmár (Satu-Mare)
Tisza
Szamos
Samos
Nagyvárad (Oradea)
P
P
TRANSYLVANIA
KOLOZSVÁR (CLUJ)
Maros (Mureş)
Marosvásárhely (Targul-Mures)
Gyulafehérvár (Alba Iulia)
Brassó

KK   Kiskunság ⎫ Royal free
NK   Nagykunság ⎰ district of Kunság
J   Royal free district of Jászág
H   Royal free towns of Hajdúság
P   Partium
▨   Military Frontier Zones

——— Borders of the Kingdom
········· Borders of Transylvania
– – – Borders of the Military Frontier Zones and of the Partes
–·–·– Borders of the royal free districts
⊚   Royal free towns
○   Towns

0   50   100   200 km.

of István Széchenyi and Lajos Kossuth and the bourgeois revolution of 1848.

Second: The protonationalist experiments of the Serbs, Croats, and Rumanians, the projects of the peasants, the burghers' movement, the political actions of the Roman Catholic and Protestant churches, and the activities of the pro-Habsburg aristocracy were all of secondary significance.[6] They all lent color to events, and partially affected the outcome of some, but they wielded no decisive influence over the happenings. There existed only two decisive forces: the Habsburg dynasty, with the might of its family possessions, and the *bene possessionati*, with control over the counties and the lower house of the state diet. The political crisis of 1790 centered on the headlong collision of these two forces; compromise between them achieved a complete pacification of the whole of society.

Third: The *bene possessionati* led the lesser nobility in the bid to wrest political power from the dynasty. During the eighteenth century the Habsburgs had gradually been assuming full political dominion over Hungary, a process completed by Joseph II. The gentry then initiated the feudal revolt in order to reconquer political power in the government. The effort failed. The court, and specifically Leopold II, by use of shrewd maneuvers alternating with the threat of force, cajolery, bribery, flattery, conspiracy, and even constitutional action, gained the upper hand and prevailed upon the *bene possessionati* to agree to a compromise by means of which matters were returned practically to their pre-Josephine state. The social structure of Hungary was not altered at all by the upheavals of 1790. Neither the dynasty nor the *bene possessionati* seriously envisioned any modification of the social system. Nor was there any third force powerful or inspired enough to impose a social change. In the absence of such a force, the return to the pre-Josephine social, political, and economic system went smoothly and unopposed. Since the traditional social system had to face no serious challenge, it must be considered to have been stable. And it must therefore be concluded that no real social crisis accompanied the rather serious political turmoil that beset Hungary, although such a crisis was already in the making.

[6] It is beyond the scope of this study to deal with the protonationalist movements of the non-Hungarians or with the specific variations in the society of Transylvania, Croatia and Slavonia, and the Military Frontier Zones. Investigation is concentrated on royal Hungary proper.

In analyzing the problems of the late eighteenth century, it has seemed useful to examine the various social classes separately and at length, in order to elucidate the position of society in royal Hungary, a society with a strong tendency for continuity and little evidence of change. It seemed also necessary to present a full account—the first in English—of the complex governmental system of Hungary. After a study of the society and government, attention is focused on the two main forces of change: the emergent crisis in feudal society and agriculture, and the early climax of the Hungarian intellectual revival. Only after such an analysis is an exposition of the dynamics of the late eighteenth century in order. The crux of the book is the retreat of enlightened despotism, which was the result of such variegated historical acts as the feudal revolt, the court-inspired burghers' movement, the peasant unrest, and the compromise between the court and the *bene possessionati*. All these become meaningful if viewed within the framework of the eighteenth-century history of Hungary.

For Hungary the eighteenth century began on April 30, 1711, when General János Pálffy, commander in chief of the Austrian forces and himself a Hungarian, and General Sándor Károlyi, commander in chief of the Hungarian forces, set their signatures to the Peace Treaty of Szatmár. Szatmár put an end to an eight-year war that had culminated in stalemate and compromise between the Habsburg dynasty and the Hungarian estates.[7]

The war had cost Hungary dearly. It was estimated to have taken half a million lives: 410,000 died of plague, 85,000 fell in battle.[8] It put the finishing touches to what the protracted Ottoman wars had well begun: it made of Hungary a depopulated wasteland. By 1711 the population numbered two and a half million,[9] half of what it had been during the reign of Matthias Corvinus (1458–90). In that sense, the Rákóczi war belongs to the warring past, not to the eighteenth century, since the outstanding characteristic of that century is the peaceful repopulation of Hungary.

Four essential changes marked the history of eighteenth-century Hungary: (1) repopulation and the shift of the country's economy from the periphery toward the center; (2) the foundation of a semi-modern central government; (3) an agrarian boom, which was not,

---

[7] The war of Ferenc Rákóczi (1703–11).   [8] Acsády, p. 254.
[9] *Ibid.*, p. 318.

however, accompanied by changes in the agrarian structure or by industrialization; and (4) a vigorous intellectual revival. The last two of these changes initiated a crisis in feudal society.

Repopulation was a threefold affair. The Hungarians, who had constituted the majority of the kingdom's population before the Turkish onslaught, had been decimated. Major groups of Hungarians had migrated from the lands occupied by the Turks to the peripheral areas of northern Hungary and Transylvania. After the Treaty of Szatmár the descendants of these migrants streamed back into the central, virgin lands. Many Hungarians whose ancestors had lived in those outer areas for centuries also preferred the more fertile lands of the Great Hungarian Plain and abandoned the lands of their forefathers. In the footsteps of the migrant Hungarians there followed Slovaks and Ruthenians[10] from the northern regions, and Rumanians from the eastern and southern Carpathians and other mountain areas of Transylvania.

A second migratory movement was that of the Rumanians who headed out of Walachia and Moldavia toward Transylvania and the Bánát. The virgin lands in these regions were but one of the reasons for their migration. The Phanariots' rule in the Danubian principalities was corrupt, harsh, and onerous and forced many Rumanian families to seek a more humane rule beyond the mountains in Transylvania and the Bánát.

The third phase of the repopulation of Hungary came with the conscientious Habsburg effort to resettle the country. The Habsburg court campaigned throughout Western Europe for peasants to migrate to Hungary. As a result, several settlements of Germans were established in the Transdanubian and central regions of Hungary.

These great migrations, both systematic and haphazard,[11] combined with the natural population growth to complete the repopulation of Hungary by the 1760s. According to the first modern census of the

---

[10] "In modern times the term *Ruthenians* was used in Austria-Hungary to designate the Ukrainian population of the northeast Carpathians, divided among Hungary, Austrian Poland (i.e., Galicia), and Bukovina. It thus was used in the same sense that the term *Little Russian* or *Ukrainian* was used in the Russian Empire, and no ethnical or linguistic distinction can be made between Ukrainians and Ruthenians." *The Columbia Encyclopedia* (2d ed.; New York: Columbia University Press, 1959), p. 1723.

[11] The repopulation of Hungary began with the arrival of 200,000 Serbian refugees as early as 1690. For details of the repopulation see Hóman and Szekfü, IV, 258 ff. and 441 ff.

country that took into account all the inhabitants regardless of sex, race, or religion, Hungary's population in 1788 was almost 8,500,000.[12]

As these waves of migrants massed in the Great Hungarian Plain, the heartland of the country, so too did the economic center of gravity swing toward the center.

This economic shift is illustrated by the statistics of population growth and the figures for tax receipts from the different areas of the country. The eighteenth century was in fact a time of expanding populations everywhere in the country, even in those peripheral areas from which many people migrated to the central plain. In northwestern Hungary (that is, western Slovakia) the population increased by 165 percent between 1720 and 1787, while during the same period it grew by 220 percent in the Transdanubian districts, by 352 percent in the region between the rivers Duna and Tisza, by 944 percent in the region between the rivers Tisza and the lower Maros, and by a mere 73 percent in Transylvania. The figures clearly demonstrate the relative decline of the peripheral areas compared with the growth of the central areas.[13]

Tax receipts paint the same picture. If we take as the standard of comparison the amount of *portae*[14] paid, we find that in 1720 the northwestern region (western Slovakia) paid 2,394 units, in 1780, 1,222, and in 1847 (the last year of the feudal era in Hungary), 1,434. Meanwhile, the receipts from the Great Hungarian Plain were 741 units in 1720, 1,095 in 1780, and 1,741 in 1847.[15]

The second change in eighteenth-century Hungary was the establishment of a semimodern governmental system. In general, the government that slowly emerged after Szatmár was superior in efficiency to that prior to the Rákóczi war. The basic distinction was that government offices that had formerly been run as semiprivate fiefs of divers lords were superseded by permanent offices under the crown, the officers of which were appointed by the king. The first step in that direction was the creation of the Hungarian standing army in 1715, which, in practice if not in principle, replaced the noble levy as the principle means of the country's defense. The major step, however, was the establishment in 1723 of the *Consilium regium locumtenentiale hungaricum* as the sole central executive branch of government.[16]

[12] See Appendix B.   [13] Jászi, p. 364.   [14] See p. 71.
[15] Marczali, *Hungary*, pp. 17–22.   [16] See Chapter VII for details.

The authority and scope of this institution grew gradually and reached a peak during the reign of Joseph II, who to all intents and purposes completed the centralizing and modernizing trend begun by his grandfather, Charles III of Hungary (VI as Holy Roman Emperor).

Setting up the standing army with its corps of professional officers, modern equipment, and logistics entailed high expenses of a permanent nature that had never had to be met before. The burgeoning central government offices involved ever increasing numbers of civil servants, new buildings, postal and communications services, the cost of which, too, had to be financed for the first time in Hungarian history. New, substantial government spending had to be funded.

The obvious means of solving this problem was for the Habsburgs to do what they had successfully done in their other lands: gradually introduce taxation of the nobility and clergy. This is exactly what they tried to do in Hungary also. The clergy, so dependent on the dynasty, little by little gave way, but not so the nobility. The pivotal point of the nobles' political activity was their resolute determination to keep their persons and their property exempt from taxation. In this selfish endeavor they were completely successful. As the dynasty failed to tap this jealously guarded source of income, it was constrained to resort to the age-old source of revenue, the serfs, whom it had to squeeze constantly tighter. Out of practical considerations and to some extent humanitarian sentiments, the Habsburgs attempted to limit the serfs' obligations to their lords as their obligations to the state increased. For this, most of the credit is due to Maria Theresa and Joseph II. The lords, however, resisted the dynasty's intentions with all the might at their disposal short of armed insurrection. There ensued an ever sharpening struggle between the court and the Hungarian nobility for the major share of the fruit of the serfs' labor. Thus came to an end the peaceful cooperation of the estates and the crown on serf problems, which had begun at the diet of 1608, when serf affairs were excluded from the jurisdiction of the central government (diet and king) and made the exclusive province of the county authorities, dominated by the *bene possessionati*.

The struggle between court and nobility came to a head in 1767, when Maria Theresa issued her urbarial regulations which defined the serfs' minimum landholdings and maximum obligations to lord and church. Joseph II's emancipation of the serfs in 1785 was more a symbolic than a practical measure to better their condition.

The main cause of the cut and thrust between the Habsburgs and the nobles that took place in the eighteenth century was this economic issue. Earlier Hungarian history, which was largely inspired by the gentry, set out to interpret this struggle as a valiant defense of Hungarian independence by the *bene possessionati*. While so bold an interpretation is a distortion of reality, credit has to be given to the *bene possessionati* for making sure against all odds, as a by-product of their striving to preserve their social, economic, and political domination over the whole populace, that Hungary's political and governmental system remained separate from that of the other Habsburg territories. This effort culminated during the diet of 1790–91 in the adoption of a new coronation oath, which was sworn to by Leopold II at his coronation on November 15, 1790. In part, the oath declared: "Hungary together with her annexed territories is independent and should be governed and administered according to her own laws and customs and not as other provinces are." [17] Thus the establishment of a semi-modern central government did not mean the fading away of the Hungarian state's autonomous status.

Hungary's eighteenth-century agrarian boom was unfortunately not accompanied by either an agrarian revolution or industrialization. Already in the early sixteenth century Imperial forces penetrated Hungary every year because of the long Ottoman wars. The presence in Hungary of massive foreign forces meant the presence also of many more persons to be fed, and this "imported" consumer market created a great demand for food. The Peace Treaty of Karlovce in 1699, which concluded the Ottoman wars, seemed to spell the end of this advantageous economic situation. The miserable condition of the roads and the total lack of navigable waterways made it almost impossible for Hungary to export its food surpluses to Western Europe. But the formation of the standing army only sixteen years later guaranteed that a large number of consumers would be permanently stationed in Hungary. The War of the Austrian Succession (1740–48) and the Seven Years' War (1756–63) created new and even more profitable

[17] Molnár, I, 399. The annexed territories (*terrae adnexae*) were Transylvania and Croatia and Slavonia. See Appendix A.

food markets for the landlords. These flourishing markets further swelled the earlier accumulation of capital, not, as in the West, in the market towns, but in the mansions of the lords. What was in general terms a highly beneficial development, however, meant only worse misery for the serfs because of two other factors. The landowners with their antiquated outlook considered the profits from their lands not as reinvestable capital but as a means of augmenting their own luxury. This attitude prevented the occurrence of a broad agrarian revolution on the English pattern. The second factor was that by the middle of the agrarian boom in the 1760s the repopulation of Hungary was complete. The virgin lands that could be freely settled had disappeared, and this made the serfs ever more dependent on the whims of the landowners, for there was nowhere for them to go. The serfs' exposure to lordly caprice, their need to cultivate the land on the owners' terms, led to an acceleration in their obligations to the lords and the gradual expropriation of their landholdings. Most of the land slowly became consolidated into huge manorial estates that continued to grow larger and larger.

Neither Maria Theresa's urbarial regulations nor Joseph II's emancipation edict was able to make any fundamental change in the serfs' utter dependence on the lords' will. The worsening of the serfs' condition and the absence of any industrialization in Hungary made the eighteenth century an era of great social tension and ferocious peasant revolts.

Industrialization was held back partly by the insufficiency of accumulated capital and its concentration in selfish hands, but mostly by the Habsburgs' colonial policy toward Hungary. In their hereditary lands, the Habsburgs followed a mercantilistic policy, and gradually but systematically Austria and Bohemia were industrialized under their dynastic aegis. Hungary, on the other hand, was relegated to serving as a source of raw materials for the growing industries elsewhere in the Habsburg lands. No wonder that under such conditions the seeds of economic, social, and political crisis took root so well! And it was in the last decade of the eighteenth century that those seeds began to germinate and a crisis of the whole feudal system commenced.

The fourth and last change in eighteenth-century Hungary was a cultural revival. Young noblemen returned home from the West at the end of the War of the Austrian Succession and the Seven Years' War stricken in conscience, just as their Russian counterparts would following the Napoleonic Wars. The Noble Bodyguard which Maria Theresa set up in 1765 was a perennial means for the young *bene possessionati* to spend several years in Vienna, one of contemporary Europe's most sophisticated cities. There they were exposed to the Enlightenment and later returned home as conscience-stricken as their fathers had been when they came back from the battlefields of the West. It is no surprise that the first modern Hungarian literary endeavors should have been those of members of the Hungarian Noble Bodyguard. This intellectual resurgence was imbued with progressive social thought. Joseph II's enlightened rule spurred the revival to an early climax in the 1790s.

These four changes represented immense innovations in Hungary. In fact, the eighteenth century was one of the most dynamic hundred years in the nation's entire history. The innovations, however, foreshadowed an emergent crisis for the whole of feudal society, a crisis that was already clearly apparent during the last years of the reign of Joseph II. At the root of the smoldering crisis lay the fundamental socioeconomic conflict between the great, destitute majority, the serfs, and the dominant minority, the estates.

This, then, is the framework within which the late eighteenth-century society, government, and politics of Hungary will be analyzed. The decline of enlightened despotism—which came to an end with the suppression of the Jacobin movement and the simultaneous emergence of a reactionary alliance between the dynasty and the estates—was, in all its phases, in an intimate cause-and-effect relationship with the emerging crisis of feudal society in Hungary.

Part 1

THE STRATIFICATION OF
SOCIETY IN HUNGARY

Chapter I

CONSTITUTIONAL STRUCTURE
AND STATISTICAL ASPECTS
OF SOCIETY

IN THE late eighteenth century, legally speaking, the society of Hungary was still stratified according to the stipulations of Act No. 1 of 1608,[1] which defined the political nation as consisting of four estates: the prelates, the aristocrats (*barones*), the lesser nobility, and the burghers, or citizens of the royal free towns.

The bulk of the population, having no political rights, remained outside the political framework of the nation. At the base of the social pyramid lay the mass of the peasantry, itself highly stratified; at the apex was the political nation, the estates.

An account of Hungarian society in the late eighteenth century would not be complete without an analysis of its numerical composition. For this purpose we have astonishingly correct statistics—the result of the first modern census in Hungary, ordered by Emperor Joseph II. Although inferior in comparison to modern censuses, it was, in fact, superior to others of its own day. After the sixteenth century, several censuses had been made in Hungary, but the purpose of them all was to verify the number of serfs and burghers, men capable of bearing arms or paying taxes. None was ever a comprehensive survey of the entire population. This shortcoming created a good deal of confusion in respect to the size of the population. In the

---

[1] *Corpus Juris Hungarici*, III, 25 (hereafter cited as CJH). The estates were called *status et ordines* or *Karok és Rendek*.

various sources dealing with the population of Hungary before 1786 there are numerical differences ranging in the millions.

The confusion was ended, however, by the census of Joseph II. His order to organize a census in Hungary was issued on May 1, 1784, and was addressed to Chancellor Count Ferenc Eszterházy. The order emphasized that the census was "a service for the well-being of the country." [2]

The nobles greatly resented having to submit, just like the serfs, to a registration of themselves and their houses. Most of all, they resented the participation of members of the Imperial Army in the carrying out of the census, for they did not have any control or influence over the soldiers. As a matter of fact, it was this double resentment that started the nobles' resistance to the reforms of Josph II, a resistance which culminated in the feudal revolt of 1790. The Emperor, however, was strong and decisive, ordering that "whoever resists [the execution of the census], no matter who he be, must be arrested and brought here to Vienna." [3] Thus the census was carried out. In several places, for instance, the counties of Nyitra, Pozsony, Szepes, Torna, Gömör, and Komárom, and the town of Zágráb, although no blood was shed, the military had to be used to enforce the taking of the census.[4] It is also worth noting that the rebellion of Horia and Cloşca in Transylvania, although mainly caused by the extreme exploitation of the serfs, was in part a repercussion of the census.[5]

In Hungary, the actual beginning of the census was November 1, 1784, and in Transylvania, January 20, 1785. The final results were presented to the Emperor by the *Consilium locumtenentiale* on April 4, 1786. One copy of the census remained in each community, where it was supposed to be updated annually. Joseph thereby intended to innovate a systematic registration of the population. This procedure

[2] The original of the order, *Magyar Kancellária* (Hungarian Chancellery) 4904 (1784), is reprinted in Marczali, *Magyarország története II József korában*, II, 524–26.

[3] For an account of this resistance see *ibid.*, II, 369–83.   [4] Thirring, p. 5.

[5] This rebellion will be placed in historical context in Chapter XV. The relation of the revolt to the census is this: Transylvanian Rumanians believed that the purpose of the census was the extension of the Military Frontier Zone in Transylvania. To join the imaginary new military organizations, masses of Rumanian peasants gathered in Alba Iulia. The authorities, instead of enlightening them, chased them home. Increased agitation and rebellion followed. Acsády, p. 378.

was, in fact, carried through in 1786 and 1787, the data being presented to Joseph II by the *Consilium locumtenentiale* on January 31, 1788.

Unfortunately, the process of rectification was suspended in the fall of 1787 because of the outbreak of the war with Turkey. In 1790, after the death of Joseph II, the whole affair was abandoned; and to push it into oblivion, a great deal of the local registration material was burnt as a part of the feudal revolt. In several places, the original registration documents survived; most important, the computed totals of all the communities were left intact.

In basing an analysis of Hungarian society on the data of the 1788 computations, one must first examine the validity of these statistics. It is perfectly evident that the data used came from a genuine census in Hungary. With the exception of the Military Frontier Zones, it was taken in the entire Kingdom of Hungary, including Hungary proper, Transylvania, and Croatia and Slavonia. Moreover, it covered all persons regardless of sex, age, social status, or religion—indeed a revolutionary innovation in Hungary. As might be expected, there are defects in the census. For one thing, it was not uniformly executed throughout the country; that is, it did not deal with all individuals in a given county with the same precision. The data on Jews, for example, are much less detailed than those on Christians. For another thing, the registration of the female population, while numerically accurate, lacked further classification.

The statistics of the census were sent to the Emperor via two different channels: one set of results was prepared by the Hungarian civilian members of the census commission, the other by the military members. Both were then separately correlated by the highest authorities of the two groups—the *Consilium locumtenentiale* and the *Generalkommando*[6] respectively. The totals arrived at by these authorities contain certain discrepancies, an element of the census which, more than anything else, indicates its lack of present-day precision. The following is an example of the differences between the civilian and military computations (exclusive of Transylvania):

[6] The *Generalkommando* was the highest military territorial headquarters in the Habsburg military system. *Kriegsarchiv Kanzlei Akten* (KA), No. 138 (Rote: No. 343 A.E.).

	Civilian *Computation*	*Military* *Computation*
Number of houses	1,052,352	1,053,353
Christians	6,926,025	6,933,485
Jews	75,128	75,089
Total population	7,001,153	7,008,574

While the discrepancies here are negligible, they are inexplicably greater in the registration of settlements:[7]

Towns	52	94
Mezővárosok (peasant towns)	523	548
Villages	10,922	10,776

Despite its shortcomings, the census of Joseph II and its rectifications provide a wealth of data about Hungarian society in the late eighteenth century. With this in mind, the statistics of 1788 will be utilized in an analysis of the individual social groups in Hungary.

The most interesting collection of data—the community census sheets—would have provided, had it survived, a treasure house of information for social analysis. As was stated earlier, most of these local sheets were destroyed during the feudal revolt of 1790. Yet the centrally computed data, which survived in full and which appear in appendixes B, C, and D below, are sufficient for an analysis of society. In these final computations, one finds the population divided according to thirteen categories, twelve being male social-occupational groups and the thirteenth a blanket total covering all women. The major problem in this is the arbitrary classification of the population, a method which served primarily the needs of the military authorities. The twelve social-occupational groups were as follows:

1. Clergymen
2. Nobles
3. *Honoratiori* (excluding teachers)
4. Burghers of the towns and artisans of the villages
5. Peasants possessing land, as their own property or as serf holdings
6. Heirs of burghers and of serfs with possessions
7. Individuals with other kinds of income: e.g., *zsellérek*, or landless peasants; wage-earning laborers; petty clerks; miners, coach-

[7] Thirring, p. 7, n. 15.

men, and bargemen; sons of the *honoratiori;* and Protestant and Orthodox clergy

8. Soldiers on leave from regiments of the standing army
9. Soldiers on leave from supply units of the standing army
10. Individuals suitable for military service: e.g., bachelors not included in any of the above categories; sons of those listed under No. 7
11. Sons (up to the age of 12) of burghers and of peasants with possessions not registered under No. 6
12. Sons (ages 13 to 17) of burghers and of peasants with possessions not registered under No. 6.[8]

This list is exact only in regard to the number of clergymen and male nobles, for all the other social groups are somewhat mixed, making precise numerical determination difficult. Taking this into account, one arrives at the following social-occupational stratification of the male population in the Kingdom of Hungary:

	Hungary	Transylvania	Croatia and Slavonia	Total
Clergymen	11,735	5,224	1,528	18,487
Nobles	155,519	32,316	9,782	197,617
Honoratiori	3,792	771	438	5,001
Burghers and artisans	75,358	11,740	3,996	91,094
Peasants with possessions	448,972	129,854	56,736	635,562
Heirs of burghers and of peasants with possessions	459,427	116,027	58,704	634,158
Zsellérek, etc.	734,184	159,260	59,086	952,530
Soldiers on leave from regiments	4,618	921	90	5,629
Soldiers on leave from supply units	36	1	1	38
Others (suitable for military service)	185,923	46,387	15,515	247,825

[8] *Instruktzio* (instruction) for filling out the sheets of the census. Hungarian National Archives (HNA) 1012 (1786), Conscr. No. 5, 66. Reprinted in Thirring, pp. 150–60.

	Hungary	Transylvania	Croatia and Slavonia	Total
Sons of burghers and peasants, ages 1–12	908,080	179,370	101,724	1,189,174
Sons of burghers and peasants, ages 13–17	252,064	51,877	25,127	329,068
Total male population	3,239,708	733,748	332,724	4,306,183[9]

Statistics show that in Hungary in 1788 there were more men than women, particularly in the countryside. The number of women in the towns, however, was greater than that of men. At the end of the nineteenth century (according to the census of 1890), the picture had changed, and women were in the majority all over the country, with the exception of the northwestern region (western Slovakia), where the men still outnumbered the women.[10] Exclusive of the military, the ratio between the sexes in 1788 was as follows:

	No. of Males	No. of Females	Excess of Males	No. of Females per 1000 Males
Hungary	3,280,955	3,187,372	93,583	971
Transylvania	734,843	708,528	26,315	964
Croatia and Slavonia	332,786	315,676	17,110	949
Total	4,348,584	4,211,576	137,008	968
Total population	8,560,180[11]			

Using these figures, we shall now deal individually with each social group in late eighteenth-century Hungary.

[9] According to the final computation of the census of Joseph II and its rectifications. HNA: *Locumtenentiale* 2900 (1788), Conscr. No. 8. Reprinted in Thirring, p. 56.   [10] *Ibid.*, p. 37.

[11] This total for the population in the Kingdom of Hungary is not exactly the same as the main computation of the census. (See Appendix B.) There, not counting the military, the total is 8,491,806, a difference of 68,374, or 8 percent. Discrepancies such as this occur frequently in the computations, but the slight degrees of difference do credit to the accuracy of the census rather than lessen its value.

Chapter II

THE FIRST ESTATE:
THE PRELATES

THE PRELATES[1] of Hungary held great power in the country, controlling the life of the population in general, and that of the serfs in particular, through a number of different channels. First, as leaders of the powerful Roman Catholic Church, they exercised control over the spiritual and intellectual life of the entire population: their authority extended over the religious life and the education not only of those of their own denomination but partially of non-Catholics as well. Furthermore, as the first estate of the kingdom, the prelates possessed political powers in the legislative branch of government as well as in the executive and judicial branches. Finally, as landlords, they received considerable material benefits from their own peasants. The Catholic churchmen drew urbarial benefits from all the serfs of the kingdom—Catholics, Orthodox, and Protestants alike—and there were additional fees due them on such occasions as baptism, marriage, and burial.

The political power of the first estate reached its height at the end of the seventeenth century. In the eighteenth century, with the growth of a centralized modern state, the spread of enlightened ideas, and the emergence of Febronianism and Josephinism in Hungary, the political importance of the prelates was greatly diminished.[2] They

[1] The term "prelates" refers only to high ecclesiastic officials of the Roman Catholic Church. It was they alone who constituted the first estate. Grünwald, p. 80.

[2] During the Middle Ages and the sixteenth and seventeenth centuries, the important offices of state (except that of the Palatine and a few others) were held by ecclesiastic dignitaries. The office of Royal Chancellor, which was the

played a role subordinate to that of the aristocrats, who in turn had to accept second place behind the *bene possessionati*. The decreased political power of the prelates did not, however, affect their material well-being, notwithstanding the fact that, with the rather unimportant exception of the burghers, they were the sole estate regularly but indirectly taxed by the crown.[3]

Statistical information on the prelates and the clergy in general is meager, for, while the census of Emperor Joseph II and the later rectifications give the exact number of clergymen, there is no classification according to different denominations.

The total number of clergymen, that is, priests and ministers, in the Kingdom of Hungary in 1788 was 18,487. Seemingly, the distribution of priests among the entire population was rather even, the ratio in most regions of the country being .3 to .4 percent. In Transylvania the ratio was double that. In the 14,008 villages in the Kingdom of Hungary there were 15,359 clergymen, more or less one for every village. By way of contrast, in the sixty-one towns, there were 3,128 clergymen. This figure naturally includes the large courts of prelates, the centers of religious orders, seminaries, and other schools. Because of this heavy clerical concentration in the towns, only half of the villages had parishes at all: that is to say, out of 8,742 villages analyzed, there were 4,459 parishes, of which 1,991 were Catholic, 1,274 Greek Orthodox, 1,015 Calvinist, and 179 Lutheran.[4]

An early eighteenth-century neo-Counter Reformation tried—and indeed successfully—to enhance the dominant position of the Roman Catholic Church in spiritual affairs, without making the kingdom a Catholic country, as was the goal. The efforts of Emperor Joseph II and his two predecessors to create a modern state were diametrically

---

most important of all, was always held by a Roman Catholic prelate until 1706. Thus the appointment in that year of Miklós Illésházy—a layman—as Royal Chancellor (1706–23) was an indication of a new era. In the decade which followed, three prelates held this office: Count Ádám László Erdődy, Count Imre Eszterházy, and Ádám Acsády. In 1733, Lajos Batthyány, a lay landlord, was appointed to the office, and never again was a prelate appointed. Mályusz, ed., *Sándor Lipót*, p. viii.

[3] The indirect taxation of the prelates by the state consisted of (1) their contributions to the state-controlled Church foundations, or *piae fundationes*, and (2) loans given to the crown which were never repaid. Felhő and Vörös, p. 121.

[4] According to the final computations of the census and its rectifications. Thirring, p. 60.

opposed to any possible increase of the political influence of the prelates in state affairs. The Church was expected to promote these efforts, and this was naturally the death sentence of the clergy's political influence.

Yet the prelates allied themselves, just as the aristocrats did, with the Habsburg dynasty and, in political matters, became subservient to it. The Habsburgs, on the other hand, as true and (up to Joseph's reign) militant Catholics, maintained the prestige of both the Church and its prelates. This alliance was an important force in 1790 and, indeed, for a long time thereafter.

Chapter III

THE SECOND AND THIRD ESTATES:
THE NOBILITY

IN PRINCIPLE, though not in fact, the Hungarian nobility were a homogeneous group, at least in regard to their fundamental political rights.[1] Whatever might have been the differences in their wealth and real authority, all were entitled to the basic privileges of Hungarian noblemen: the right of *habeas corpus;* the right to be subject to nobody but the legally crowned king; the right to the free ownership of their domains, to pay no taxes,[2] and to owe no service but in arms; and, finally, the *Jus resistendi*, meaning the right to resist the king should he attack the liberties and privileges warranted by the *Aurea Bulla* of Endre (Andreas) II in 1222.[3] These fundamental rights, so clearly

[1] "No lord has more nor any [lesser] nobleman fewer privileges." Verbőczi, p. 47.
  "True nobility is the product of military life and knowledge and of other spiritual and physical qualities and merits. Should our prince [king] award a castle or a town or a village or a title to any estate to any man of whatever standing for his meritorious deeds or services, that man [pending subsequent legislative action], by virtue of the prince's award, instantly becomes a genuine nobleman and is freed of all obligations of peasant status.
  "Such an award of *szabadság* [privileges] is called by us *nemesség* [nobility]. . . . Such noblemen . . . are considered to be members of the Holy Crown and are subject to no one save to the authority of their legally crowned prince [king]." *Ibid.*, p. 51.
[2] The lowest stratum of the lesser nobility was the *bocskoros nemesek* (poor nobles). These nobles during the eighteenth century were obliged by the county to pay county taxes regularly and occasionally state taxes also. Thus they could justly be called taxed nobles. Their obligation to pay taxes, however, never was enacted as a permanent obligation (prior to 1836); thereby the principle that all nobles were exempt from paying taxes—fictitious though it was—was maintained.
[3] Verbőczi, pp. 55–57. The *Jus resistendi* was abolished by Act No. 4 in

defined in the *Tripartitum* of István Verbőczi published in 1517, were for centuries conscientiously cherished by the nobility of Hungary.

In addition to the Hungarian nobles, the nobility of Croatia were also *Magyar nemesek* (Hungarian noblemen).[4] The nobility consisted of natives of the land, *nativi,* and naturalized foreigners, *indigenae.*[5]

While constitutionally the Hungarian nobility were homogeneous, in fact they were very highly stratified. Ancestry, wealth, office, court connections, and many other factors made them a variegated class. At the top were to be found the aristocrats, and at the bottom the *bocskoros nemesek* (poor noblemen).

THE SECOND ESTATE: THE ARISTOCRACY[6]

In the battle of Mohács, in 1526, and during the protracted Ottoman wars that followed, the old Hungarian aristocracy was decimated and a new one gradually emerged. That new aristocracy was a creation of the Habsburgs, dependent on and loyal to the dynasty,[7] and its

---

1687, as a reward to the Habsburg dynasty for the liberation of Buda, the ancient capital of the land. The leaders of the feudal revolt in 1790 tried unsuccessfully to reestablish the *Jus resistendi.*

[4] In addition to the Hungarian and Croatian nobility, the nobility of the Kingdom of Hungary included the *Székelyek,* the *Kunok,* the *Jászok,* and the *Hajduk.* Marczali, *Hungary,* p. 104.

[5] *Ibid.,* p. 103. One of the most distinguished "Hungarian" *indigenae* was Prince Eugene of Savoy, who received immense grants of landed property in Hungary.

[6] The term "aristocracy" denotes the highest echelon of the nobility as a social class. Constitutionally speaking, the members of the second estate, commonly called aristocrats, officially were the *Világi főrendek* (lay lords) and as such comprised the following subgroups:

I. Highest officials of the state (*Magnates regni*)
   1. *Barones regni*
     a. Major bannerets (*nagy zászlós urak*): the Palatine, the *országbiró* (lord chief justice), the Banus of Croatia and Slavonia, the *tárnokmester* (lord high treasurer)
     b. Minor bannerets (*kis zászlós urak*): two crown guards, the Count of Pozsony, the Governor of Fiume
   2. *Főispánok* (county high sheriffs)

II. Titled aristocrats: princes, counts, and barons
   Ernő Nagy, *Magyarország közjoga* (*Államjog*) [The Constitutional Law of Hungary (State Law)] (5th ed.; Budapest: Athenaeum, 1905), pp. 123, 124, 125, 127.

[7] At the maximum only ten families of the old Hungarian aristocracy still existed after the Treaty of Szatmár of 1711. Wellmann, "Az udvari ember," in Domanovszky, ed., *Magyar művelődéstörténet,* IV, 289.

influence grew substantially at the expense of the lesser nobility. The new and increasingly more powerful aristocracy played an important role not only in the political life but also in the defense of the Habsburg sector of partitioned Hungary, that is, in the northern and western crescent of the formed kingdom.

The nobility, having lost their status and land, fled from the territories occupied by the Turks. They were replaced there by the *timariotes*. The lesser noblemen, fleeing to the royal region of the land, either assumed service as officers in the mighty zone of fortifications[8] or attached themselves to the households of aristocrats as *servitori* or *familiares*. The medieval system of aristocratic households staffed with officers and officials of noble birth flourished again.

The aristocrats, assuming the military leadership of major sectors of the fortified zones, used in addition to their own *servitori* the neighboring lesser noblemen hired to serve as additional officers in their semiprivate armies. These lesser noblemen drew salaries and supplies from the lord; several of them performed lifelong service at the side of their masters. Such contractual feudal bonds were inherited by their sons. The younger generation received an education and learned manners in the lord's household. In such a system the political influence and prestige of the aristocrats grew without precedent in Hungarian society.

The castles of the aristocracy, in a kingdom where the monarch lived abroad, provided a substitute for the political, the economic, the military, and, above all, the cultural leadership the court of a national king might have offered to the nation. The castles of the aristocrats and the *servitori* dependent upon them created an interdependent society, where the aristocrats lived and worked, as well as fought and enjoyed life, together with the lesser nobility. A certain exclusiveness of the aristocracy was the result of their wealth, culture, and power, but it was limited to the needs of leadership in a rough era and served as a force of integration rather than of segregation.

---

[8] There was an immense system of fortifications on both the Habsburg and the Ottoman sides of the border, which was practically stable between the beginning of the seventeenth century and 1683. The dividing line between the Habsburg and the Ottoman zones of fortification was in general terms the line starting out at Zengg on the Adriatic, passing through Bihács, the Una River, Sziszek, Kanizsa, Keszthely, Lake Balaton, Veszprém, Komárom, Léva, Korpona, Szendrő, and Tokaj. Excellent maps of these fortifications, showing all the major fortresses, are in Hóman and Szekfü, III, 225, 257.

After the War of Liberation (1683–99), particularly after the Treaty of Szatmár in 1711, these knightly castles ceased to represent military values in the face of the modern Imperial Army and in the absence of the Turkish threat. In the eighteenth century the aristocrats abandoned their uncomfortable and henceforth useless fortresses for the sake of new, comfortable baroque castles which they built in the open fields, in groves, or on the hills. Here in their proud new homes they were physically more accessible than they had been in their forts. Socially, however, the aristocrats became permanently segregated from the rest of the people, including the lesser nobility. No longer needing the military cooperation of the lesser noblemen, they did not want to share their now greater comfort with them either. The system of *servitori,* formerly fruitful for the lord and beneficial for the lesser nobility, began to disappear because it no longer served the lords' purpose.[9]

From the sixteenth century on, the aristocracy began to distinguish itself from the rest of the nobility by titles. At the end of the Middle Ages, the Hungarian kings had already awarded the title of *gróf* (count) to some aristocrats, but the custom had not become general.[10] The Habsburgs, however, began systematically to connect the endowment of larger estates with the title of count. They also awarded that title to some members of the old landed aristocracy such as the Nádasdy, Zrinyi, Erdődy, Frangepán, and Thurzo families.[11] In the seventeenth century the Habsburgs began to award the title of count without regard to ownership or grant of landed property. From the end of the seventeenth century the justices of the kingdom came to be called *Freiherr* or *Liber baro,* after the German pattern. Already a considerable part of the Hungarian aristocracy was at that time *indigenae,* or first-generation foreigners who were awarded Hungarian citizenship by the diets in accordance with the wish of the dynasty.[12]

The highest knightly title, that of prince, was not granted as a Hungarian social rank. Prior to 1806 princely titles took the form of Prince of the Holy Roman Empire and after that date Prince of the

---

[9] Wellmann, "Az udvari ember," in Domanovszky, *Magyar művelődéstörténet,* IV, 292–95.

[10] The title of *gróf* was granted by King Béla III (1172–96) for the first time in Hungarian history when he awarded the countship of Modrus to the ancestors of the Frangepán family. Hóman and Szekfü, II, 30.

[11] *Ibid.,* III, 195, and IV, 256.   [12] Eckhart, p. 201.

Austrian Empire. The title was inherited by the first-born male heir of the family. In 1687 Palatine Pál Eszterházy[13] and in 1764 Palatine Lajos Batthyány[14] were created Princes of the Holy Roman Empire. In 1714 Emperor Charles VI named the Primate of Hungary as a Prince of the Holy Roman Empire.

At the end of the seventeenth and during the first decade of the eighteenth century the aristocrats in Hungary were Hungarian in language, culture, and sentiment. Their culture was Latinized, to be sure, but they conversed and corresponded in Hungarian. It is interesting to note that they knew very little German. This is no indication that they were uncultured; on the contrary, there were sizable libraries and Renaissance works of art in their castles. The Hungarian language was used not only in family life and social affairs but also by the highest officeholders of the land in correspondence with the counties.[15]

A great change in the status, importance, and wealth of the aristocrats began after the Treaty of Szatmár.[16] The change was due to complex factors, perhaps the most important of which was the considerable increase in the number of aristocrats. High officials and generals of the Empire and kingdom, suppliers of the army, and rich men who loaned to the *Hofkammer* or who leased or purchased for cash the landed properties of the Hungarian Chamber[17] were awarded Hungarian lordships and land.[18] These newcomers, influential, rich, or both, intermarried with the former, not-very-ancient Hungarian

---

[13] Hóman and Szekfü, IV, 256.   [14] *Ibid.*, p. 498.

[15] General Sándor Károlyi, one of the high commanders of Ferenc Rákóczi, wanted to translate a document in German captured from the Austrian enemy in 1706. However, he could not find a single man, including the aristocratic officers, among the 30,000-man corps operating beyond the Tisza River who could translate the text accurately. Grünwald, p. 93.   [16] Andics, pp. 72–76.

[17] The *Hofkammer* in Vienna, founded by Ferdinand I, controlled and augmented Imperial incomes. It supervised the provincial chambers, including the Hungarian Chamber [*Kammer, királyi kamara*] founded in 1528. Stationed in Buda and after 1540 in Pozsony, it was moved back to Buda in 1784 by Joseph II. The Hungarian Chamber administered the royal revenues (*regaliae*), without the interference of the Hungarian estates. The *regaliae* came from the incomes of mines of the salt monopoly, the minting of coins, custom duties, and the products of lands owned by the crown. Eckhart, pp. 244–47. For details, see Chapter VII.

[18] A typical case was that of Baron János Harrucken, a supplier of the army, from Linz, Austria. The *Hofkammer* owed him 26,000 florins. As compensation, Harrucken was given possession in full of the lands owned by the Chamber in Békés, Csongrád, and Arad counties. The Harrucken family became one of the richest landlords of Hungary. Szeberényi, p. 92.

aristocratic families and were integrated with them. The increase in number of these rootless foreigners within the Hungarian aristocracy started a qualitative change inside the class itself as well as in its relation to the rest of the nation.

Under the rule of Maria Theresa the knighting of *indigenae* further increased.[19] The Queen also went out of her way to lure Hungarian aristocrats to Vienna in order to bind them to her throne and court and to loosen their connections with the rest of the nation. She overwhelmed the Hungarian aristocrats, new and old, with the signs of her grace. In 1764 she founded the Hungarian Noble Bodyguard to entice the gentry and aristocratic youth to Vienna.[20] In the same year, the St. Stephen Order was founded mainly to decorate aristocrats of her Empire, Hungarians and non-Hungarians alike. The court life, the luxury of Vienna, the marriage of the Hungarian magnates with ambitious and luxury-loving Austrian and Bohemian aristocratic ladies, caused the heavy indebtedness of many of them.[21] Maria Theresa often came to their rescue and granted very large loans to Hungarian and other court aristocrats. In 1773 she gave away nine million florins of the secularized Jesuit wealth as loans to aristocrats, 2,765.400 florins having been granted, at 4 percent interest, to Hungarians.[22] Henry Marczali, the distinguished historian of that era, an apologist for,

[19] The stratification of the aristocrats of Hungary in 1778 was as follows:

	nativi	indigenae
Princes	2	18
Counts	82	69
Barons	24	160*
Total families	108	247

* Including *indigenae* of rank less than a baron.

Almanach von Ungarn 1778, quoted in Marczali, *Hungary*, p. 123, n. 1.

[20] The Hungarian Noble Bodyguard was established by the diet of 1764–65. Hóman and Szekfü, IV, 654.

[21] The aristocrats were not interested in cultivation of their lands, but rather in luxury, entertainment, and social life. This trend went so far that several serfs, instead of fulfilling their *robot* obligations on the lands, were dressed in uniforms and served as bodyguards around the castles to contribute to the splendor of their lords' households. *Memoirs of Sándor Ujfalvy of Mezőkövesd*, edited by Farkas Gyula Kolozsvár (1941), quoted in Trócsányi, p. 56.

[22] Marczali, *Hungary*, p. 125. One of the most notorious cases was that of Count Károly Zichy, who at only thirty-five years of age assumed one of the highest offices of the realm, *Országbiró* (Lord Chief Justice). He married Countess Khevenhüller, whose extravagant taste and way of life almost ruined financially that otherwise brilliant young courtier. Mályusz, ed., *Sándor Lipót*, p. 26.

rather than an antagonist of, the aristocracy, had this to say on that trend: "The enormity of the historical crime of the Hungarian aristocracy is that they ruined themselves financially in Vienna and by thus losing their independence deprived their nation of one of its principal supporters." [23]

The cumulative effect of this situation was similar to what happened to the French aristocrats in Versailles under the reign of Louis XIV. But the aristocrats of France, though transformed into courtiers, remained Frenchmen after all. In Hungary the change was twofold. The aristocrats became courtiers, to be sure, but they were also denationalized. Indebted up to their necks, they became unconditionally dependent on the mercy of the court. There began a wild hunt for offices. In 1780 the majority of the Hungarian lords were still in possession of their lands, heavily mortgaged though they were. They spent most of the year in the splendor of the Viennese court. The aristocracy not only became alienated from the rest of the nation by its customs, its dress, and its German and French language, but a real rift occurred between the civilization of the aristocracy and that of the lesser noblemen. The aristocrats, in their new homes in Vienna, assumed the way of life of the Viennese court; the lesser noblemen remained bound to their lands, their manors, or their houses in the country and remained Hungarian in their culture. The rift between the two different parts of the nobility put an end to the system of *servitori*. The aristocrats and lesser noblemen became alien to each other.[24]

It did not take long for this split to be discovered, especially by literary men and political thinkers. The denationalized aristocracy became hated and ridiculed in Hungary. In 1782 Pál Ányos, a prominent poet, addressed a poem on proper costumes to the Hungarian youth in which he ridiculed the denationalized aristocrats:

[23] Marczali, *Hungary*, p. 119. See also Niederhauser, p. 125, and Szabad, p. 36. During Maria Theresa's reign the annual incomes of the richest aristocrats in Hungary were as follows:

Prince Eszterházy	700,000 florins
Palatine Count Batthyány	450,000
Two magnates (each)	300,000
Four magnates (each)	200,000
Four magnates (each)	150,000

In that same era a bushel of wheat cost half a florin. Marczali, *Hungary*, p. 113.
[24] Mód, pp. 111–12.

> Morality favors not perfumed handkerchiefs,
> Dainty dresses and neck-kerchiefs.
> Veils, large silver buttons and leopards skins [sic],
> Are more in accord with Hungarian wishes.[25]

A few aristocrats, like Amadé, Orczy, Ráday, Széchenyi, and Dessewffy, tried to resist the general trend of their class by attempting to safeguard the use of the Hungarian language and championing patriotism among their fellow aristocrats. Their good intentions and efforts, however, were in vain. The link connecting aristocrats and the country was no longer national but only constitutional, or rather feudal. The same trend could be witnessed in Transylvania. Baron Zsigmond Kemény, another exceptional aristocrat of ardent patriotism, complained:

Under the protecting wings of victorious absolutism the exclusivity and haughtiness of the aristocracy grew by the day. . . . Their interest met in such a degree with the efforts of the anticonstitutional reaction that among the comfortable circumstances of the class system it would have been an unexpected self-denial [on their part] to think of the sufferings of the fatherland. . . . The highest offices [of the land] were distributed among the members of a very few families as an inheritance and were transferred from one generation to the next. . . . In a grotesque contrast to the privileges and the comfort of the highest stratum of the aristocracy stood the fate of the serfs, whose obligations and services were not limited by any urbarium. Those regulations introduced by Maria Theresa were considered illegal, since their promulgation [was extraconstitutional]. Therefore, they never were seriously considered as conditions to be fulfilled.[26]

István Horváth, a noted contemporary writer, wrote to Ferenc Kazinczy:

We accounted in a proper sequence for all the well-to-do landowners of the country and we did not find even a single one among them in whom sentiment, brains, patriotism, or talent could be found, though all these would be so very necessary for the promotion of the welfare of the nation.[27]

Kazinczy complained to Dániel Berzsenyi that the aristocrats both scorned the Hungarian language as that of gypsies and failed to respect the intellectuals, writers, and poets.[28]

The connection of the aristocrats with the court was close enough to isolate other elements of the nation from the dynasty. In the court their offspring received westernized and sophisticated political train-

---

[25] Translated in Marczali, *Hungary*, p. 121.   [26] Grünwald, p. 97.
[27] *Ibid.*, p. 99.   [28] *Ibid.*, p. 101.

ing and gained broad horizons in their outlook. The lesser nobility were contented with the domination of county politics, the lower house of the diet, and society. The county assembly and administration were their school in politics and an effective one indeed. Bound too greatly and too closely to the dynasty, the aristocrats expressed no characteristic ideology. They echoed that of the Habsburgs. Therefore, the aristocracy could be considered the force neither of progress nor of conservatism. When the Habsburgs were the champions of Enlightenment, so too were the aristocrats of Hungary.[29] When the pendulum swung and Emperor Francis became the embodiment of reaction, he could count on the loyal support of the aristocrats.[30]

THE THIRD ESTATE: THE LESSER NOBILITY

The early sixteenth century was the golden age of the lesser nobility. Though that stratum of the privileged had always been a heterogeneous one, in the sixteenth century it was more compact, relatively much smaller, and less variegated than it would be at the end of the eighteenth century. In referring to the sixteenth century, the term "lesser nobility" should for all intents and purposes be understood to mean the gentry,[31] a social segment which, though numerically small, would remain a fairly constant and politically important portion of the lesser nobility throughout the feudal era of Hungarian history. But as will be shown, the Ottoman wars caused not only a great influx of former commoners into the lesser nobility but also

[29] Meszlényi, p. 58.

[30] The majority of the aristocrats of Hungary were politically loyal to, economically dependent on, and in their civilization integrated into the Habsburg court life. Yet there were independent-minded aristocrats limited in number though important in their influence. Some of them were true believers in Enlightenment; the two Orczy brothers, the four Vay brothers, Péter Balogh, the two Almássy brothers, János Sztáray, the two Forgách brothers, Ferenc Darvas, Imre Beőthy, Ignácz Bezerédy, Ferenc Eszterházy, József Teleki, the four Festetich brothers, József Klobusitzky, Ferenc Barkóczy, the three Batthyány brothers, and Miklós Skerlecz. In absolute numbers this group was small. Their fundamental shortcoming was not their small number, but rather their idea to extend freedom only to the privileged classes, in the face of the absolutistic efforts of the crown. Very few among them showed a willingness to extend equal rights to the lower strata of society also. Eckhardt, pp. 143–46.

[31] The Hungarian gentry included the *bene possessionati* and the *possessionati*. These two groups of the Hungarian lesser nobility satisfied more or less the criteria of the British gentry: "People of gentle birth and breeding . . . the class immediately below the nobility." *The Oxford Universal Dictionary*, 1955, p. 786.

the general economic and political decline of that stratum. These two factors caused an extraordinary stratification within the lesser nobility.

The really influential segment of the lesser nobility was the propertied (the *possessionati*), particularly those who owned middle-sized estates (the *bene possessionati*).[32] The *possessionati* usually owned some land, which was cultivated by a few families of serfs.[33] The *bene possessionati*, owners of middle-sized estates, villages, and great numbers of serfs, were often men of learning, a great many of whom had higher education. Whereas in the sixteenth and seventeenth centuries the main profession of the nobility was still the military, in the eighteenth century the principal professions were agriculture and law practice. Only a few families of the *bene possessionati* were to be found in the individual counties. The members of these families filled key positions in the county administrations and were frequently appointed to temporary administrative functions such as the *táblabiró*.[34] Because of their wealth and education, they enjoyed political prestige and were the natural leaders of the lesser nobility in the counties.

Mention should be made here of the *honoratiori*, that branch of society comprising not noblemen but educated lawyers, engineers, physicians, and teachers. In their opinions, behavior, and political views, the *honoratiori* were much nearer to the gentry than to the taxed nobles. In the reform era of the nineteenth century this was

[32] The *bene possessionati* applied agrarian methods similar to those of the aristocrats, but their style of life was different. They lived on their estates near the serfs. During the boom in the grain market in the eighteenth-century wars, they gained much. They built empire-style manor houses, they lived well, and they wished for each other "spring rain and mild war." Their former debts were paid by the inflationary paper money. In 1811 a royal patent abolished 60 percent of their mortgage debts. Mérei, *Mezőgazdaság*, p. 99.

[33] Along with the expropriation of serf holdings, the aristocrats tried to expropriate those possessions of the lesser nobility which were squeezed between their own lands (*arrondirozás*). The *possessionati* did not produce for the market. What they produced their families consumed; therefore, the boom in the grain market harmed rather than benefited them. The increase of *arrondirozás* undermined the foundation of their existence. Pál Felsőbükki Nagy complained in the diet of 1832–36 that in Moson County, where during the end of the eighteenth century there were 300 families of lesser nobility, in 1832 there were only three, "since the main goal of the oligarchy is to apply *arrondirozás*, which means in plain Hungarian language the extirpation of the lesser nobility." M. Horváth, *Huszonöt év*, I, 386. Mérei, *Mezőgazdaság*, p. 120.

[34] See p. 112.

the stratum of society which first received the right to vote, at least in most of the county assemblies.[35]

During the eighteenth century the gentry stabilized its control of county administration. County offices were coveted positions for gentry youngsters, offering prestige and influence. The offices, mostly *nobile officium*, or positions without salary, were elective and were periodically augented.[36] Officials in active service considered their duty only part-time engagement, since, of course, they also had to manage their own estates. The landed lesser nobility were reluctant to accept national offices in the growing central governmental organs, for they preferred not to absent themselves permanently from their own lands or from the county affairs which they considered to be the basis of their political power.[37]

The *taksás nemesek* (taxed nobles) or *bocskoros nemesek* comprised those lesser nobles, privileged but not all of them landed, who either lived and worked on a single serf section[38] (*armalis* nobles), or owned and worked a small lot not larger than a serf's section (*curialis* nobles), or perhaps had once owned more land but had been expelled from their family estates by the Turks and sought refuge in royal Hungary or Transylvania (*profugus* nobles). The immense numerical growth of the *taksás* noblemen was due to the Turkish onslaught and occurred during the protracted wars in Hungary between the middle of the sixteenth century and the end of the seventeenth century. The ennoblement of common people had already begun in earnest in Hungary during the sixteenth century. There were counties where the proportion of nobles rose from 2–3 percent in the sixteenth to 25–30 percent in the seventeenth century. This phenomenal increase was due to the Hungarian royal and the Transylvanian princely practice

[35] Hóman and Szekfü, V, 322; Gárdonyi, in Domanovszky, ed., *Magyar művelődéstörténet*, IV, 312–22.

[36] The *nobile officium* became in fact jobs with very good incomes during the eighteenth century. Maria Theresa even protested because the counties were overtaxing the serfs to collect sufficient funds to pay the ever increasing number of county officials. The extra burden on the serfs this created was one of the main grievances of the peasants in 1790. See the analysis of the Szabolcs Project in Chapter XV.   [37] Hóman and Szekfü, V, 519–20.

[38] Two terms will be used below to refer to the lots of the serfs and the taxed nobles: holding and section (called also *sessio* or session). A holding denotes the landed possessions of the serfs and the taxed nobles regardless of size. A section denotes the unit of measurement of urbarial holdings. For details on the section, see Chapter V.

Hungarian prelates

Hungarian lord and his servitor

Bene possessionatus (right)
and peasant

Group of *honoratiori*

TOP LEFT:
A *bocskoros nemes* plowing

TOP RIGHT:
Hungarian burgher

RIGHT:
Hungarian peasant in *guba* (sleeveless frieze cape)

LEFT:
Member of the *banderium* of
Fejér County

BELOW:
Crown of St. Stephen returns
to Buda from Vienna

of granting nobility as an inexpensive reward for military and other services rendered to the state.[39] In most cases such distinction provided exemption from public taxes but no grant of land for the new noblemen. Their tax-exempt status, however, began to fade away during the eighteenth century. A great majority of these new nobles served the lords in their households as officers and officials (*familiares*), or else the lord rented out parcels of peasant lands to them. These lands did not become the property of the tenant noblemen. The so-called *armalis* noblemen lived off the yield of their own labor on the level of the serfs.[40] Owing to the shortage of laborers during the first part of the eighteenth century, some of the lords went so far as to seek ennoblement for fugitive serfs of other lords who took refuge on their lands. Once they had received such privilege, these fugitives could not be returned to their former lords. The new master used them as tenants,[41] extending thereby the number of miserable *armalis* noblemen.

Curialis nobles were those noblemen who did not have serfs but who owned and cultivated a lot of about the size of one serf section themselves (*nobile unius sessionis*). Whole villages flourished consisting entirely of such *curialis* nobility. As in the case of the serfs, the joint effect of geographic constriction and increasing population was such that many *curialis* noblemen had to divide their single section among their sons. Gradually numerous families were forced to live their wretched lives on one single section. The census of 1720 registered 1,228 villages exclusively populated by *curialis* noble families.[42]

Together the *armalis* and *curialis* nobles constituted the *taksás* noblemen, a term which indicates that they were taxed regularly by the counties and periodically by the state.[43] In that same group should be included the fugitives from the Ottoman-occupied territories (*profugus* nobles), some of whom settled on abandoned serf lots, living a life similar to that of the poor *armalis* and *curialis* noblemen.

During the eighteenth century several efforts were made to execute a census of the noblemen of Hungary. The censuses taken in

[39] Eckhart, p. 201.
[40] They were called *Briefadel* since they had nothing but a bit of parchment to prove their nobility. Marczali, *Hungary*, p. 104.   [41] Eckhart, p. 201.
[42] Gárdonyi, in Domanovszky, *Magyar művelődéstörténet*, IV, 320.
[43] Hóman and Szekfü, IV, 269.

1723 and 1732 were so unreliable that the government did not deem the figures serious enough for any practical consideration. When under more detailed instructions a new census was carried out during the years 1754–55 that was to enumerate separately the landowning and the landless noblemen, the different counties so variously interpreted the governmental instructions that that census also failed to yield reliable results. These questionable figures accounted for 17,963 landowners and 13,766 landless noble heads of families, as well as 825 nobles of unknown status, a total of 32,554.[44]

Basically different was the census taken during the reign of Emperor Joseph II. As was previously stated, this was the first census in Hungary worthy of the name. It listed a far greater number of nobles than could have been expected in light of the statistics of the 1754–55 census. Joseph ordered the registration of all noble males regardless of their age. In earlier censuses, nobles had to provide proof of the origin of their ennoblement. However, Joseph's instructions did not include any demand for such documentation, and this liberal handling of the problem might well account for the enormous increase in the number of those registered as nobles.[45] Most probably, former censuses failed to register the *bocskoros nemesek* as members of the lesser nobility. Yet even if this were the case, it is phenomenal that in certain localities the Josephine census recorded three to ten times as many nobles as the registrations of 1754–55 had. The total number of noble males in the Kingdom of Hungary in 1788 was as follows:

Hungary	155,519
Transylvania	32,316
Croatia and Slavonia	9,782
Total	197,617 [46]

The total number of noble males and females combined is not given in this census, for all women were registered under a single heading. Gusztav Thirring, in trying to ascertain the number of noble females, used the ratio of male to female inhabitants in the three component parts of Hungary and then applied this key to the

---

[44] Illésy, pp. 148–49.   [45] Thirring, p. 58.

[46] According to the final computations of the census and its two rectifications ordered by Emperor Joseph II. HNA: *Locumtentiale* 2900 (1788), Conscr. No. 8, reprinted *ibid.*, p. 59.

nobility. The ratio was this: in Hungary, there were 971 females for every 1000 males; in Transylvania, 964; and in Croatia and Slavonia, 949. Using these figures, Thirring arrived at the following number of noble males and females:[47]

	Hungary	Transylvania	Croatia and Slavonia	Total
Males	155,519	32,316	9,782	197,617
Females	151,009	31,152	9,368	191,529
Total	306,528	63,468	19,150	389,146

On the whole, the nobility comprised 4.8 percent of the population in Hungary and 4.4 percent in Transylvania, but the percentages naturally varied from county to county. One finds the highest ratio of nobility to the general population in the Great Hungarian Plain and on both shores of the Tisza River—8.6 percent and 6.2 percent respectively. Yet in certain isolated localities this ratio was higher still, e.g., Máramaros County, 16.6 percent; Borsod County, 15.2 percent; Szatmár County, 14.1 percent; and Szabolcs County, 13.3 percent. Interestingly enough, it was in these very territories that both the peasant unrest and the feudal revolt were most intense in 1790, thus indicating a causal relationship between the high ratio of nobles and the extreme exploitation of peasants. In territories which suffered the greatest devastation by the Ottoman occupation, the ratio of the nobility was as low as 2 to 3 percent of the population. One finds the lowest ratio in the Bánát.[48] In Torontál County, for example, the largest in this area, there were only 129 nobles in a population of 152,088—a mere .8 percent.[49]

The nobility played an extraordinary role in the towns after the Ottoman invasion as an ever increasing number of refugee nobles found shelter in the towns. Gradually, the custom of burghers seeking ennoblement became established. Yet even so, the average ratio of nobles in the towns was lower than that of nobles in the counties, the former being 3.8 percent in contrast with the 4.8 percent of the latter. There were naturally some exceptions: in the town of Komárom, 14.5 percent of the inhabitants were nobles; in Győr, 9.1 percent; in Buda and Pest, 6.2 percent. In Transylvanian towns (with the exception of the capital city of Kolozsvár, where the ratio was 8.5 percent), the ratio was on the average much lower. In Croatia, a large segment

[47] *Ibid.*   [48] *Ibid.*   [49] *Ibid.*, pp. 36, 59.

of the nobility was centered in Zágráb where it comprised 12.2 percent of the population.[50]

The Hungarian noblemen were not banned by law from commerce, industrial enterprise, or performing handicraft work, as were the French nobles, the Spanish knights, the Polish *szlachta*,[51] or the Russian *dvorianstvo*. These noblemen would have lost their nobility had they engaged in such endeavors. The Hungarian noblemen joined the priesthood and the professions; many lawyers, doctors, pharmacists, and engineers were of noble origin. Several *taksás* noblemen were also handicraftsmen, such as bootmakers, locksmiths, tailors, butchers, millers. Their culture and customs paralleled those of the serfs.

Most of the lesser nobility lived in houses built of clay with reed roofs. Even the gentry only began to build more dignified residences in the last quarter of the eighteenth century. Ferenc Kazinczy's *Memoirs* and his immense correspondence are a treasure house of contemporary description of the life of the lesser nobility. The great value of these primary sources is that their author was an enlightened intellectual champion of the most advanced ideas of his time. While remaining a member of the gentry in his sentiments, Kazinczy was cultured enough to be able, and brave enough to dare, to criticize his own class. He spent six and a half years in prison for his participation in the Martinovics conspiracy. After his release on June 28, 1801, he gradually became the intellectual dictator of Hungarian literary life, owing not to any official authority but to his own talent, which was respected all over the country.

Kazinczy gives a vivid description of the ways of life and the living

[50] Thirring, p. 60; also Gárdonyi, in Domanovszky, *Magyar Művelődéstörténet,* IV, 311. These figures are used by practically all sources, including the remarkable and already cited study of Béla Grünwald. In 1787 there were 75,000 noble families in Hungary. In 1789 in France there were no more than 26,000 to 28,000 noble families. In 1806 the nobility of Prussia consisted of 20,000 families; that of Prussian Poland, 25,000. Marczali, *Hungary,* p. 104. In 1840 there were 136,003 noble families and 500,000 noble men, women, and children altogether in Hungary. Mérei, *Mezőgazdaság,* p. 96. Contrasting that number with the eleven million total population of Hungary in that era, we may conclude that for every twenty common men there was one nobleman in Hungary. Such a high percentage of nobility did not exist in any other country of Europe at that time. In other neighboring countries the ratio was the following: for one nobleman there were 828 commoners in Bohemia, 350 in German Austria, 300 in Lombardy-Venice, 68 in Galicia. Szekfü, *Három nemzedék,* p. 74.

[51] Grünwald, pp. 121–22.

standards of the leading gentry. He wrote that his grandfather, Ferenc Bossányi,

acted with the superior air of a patriarch in his reed-covered house built of clay, his stackyard richly filled with stacks and with straw and hayricks, his vault filled with wine, his pits full of corn. He opened all these in time of want to those in need, giving them credit without interest rather than for profit.[52]

In general, the lesser nobility lived at a level of natural economy rather than of market economy.[53] They neither sold nor spent much. The labor necessary for the cultivation of their land required no cash since it was servile labor. Daughters and granddaughters wore the dresses of their mothers and grandmothers without danger of ridicule since all of them did the same. The principal pleasure of the lesser nobility was alimentary rather than intellectual.[54]

The main events in their lives concerned law suits brought against one another in real or imaginary clashes over ownership rights of land, the only property they had and dealt with.[55] If they were not involved in litigation against one another, they visited each other on such social occasions as birthdays and name days, weddings, baptisms, burials, fairs, meetings, installations of county officials, and card-playing parties. But the focus for their most sophisticated engagements was the county assembly. Here they were at home; here they felt themselves not only safe but the lords of the living and the dead. None were their equals and they were subject only to the legally crowned king. They made the county their own organization, and their tremendous involvement in county affairs made them exclusively county men. They saw nothing and were concerned with nothing happening beyond the narrow borders of their counties.[56]

The horrifying conditions of communication in Hungary made it impossible for the *bocskoros nemesek* to travel far. Having but a few beasts of burden, badly needed in cultivation of lands, they could

[52] Kazinczy, *Pályám emlékezete*, p. 24.
[53] The gentry, but particularly the *bene possessionati*, began to produce for the market as early as the middle of the eighteenth century.
[54] Grünwald, p. 108.
[55] The origin of the custom of bringing suits against each other goes back as far as the late seventeenth century. The *neo aquistica commissio*, an ominous institution of the Habsburgs, tried to expropriate as much Hungarian land as possible. Through endless suits the nobles tried to save their property, but in many cases they could not. Mód, p. 111. Marczali, *Hungary*, p. 112.
[56] Grünwald, p. 108.

not ride much beyond the limits of their own or their neighbors' property. In practice very few of them went abroad on their own.[57]

The status of women was curious. The education of the female members of the lesser nobility was grossly neglected, for their position in society as well as in the household was inferior. It is again worth while to turn to that master writer, Kazinczy, for a concise description of the status of the female in the society of the lesser nobility in late eighteenth-century Hungary. Kazinczy describes the position of his grandmother, the wife of Ferenc Bossányi, thus:

> She was the daughter rather than the servant of her husband; nor was she his mate in mastership of the house (ur-társa). She sat on his left when traveling in a coach, and when entering the house of someone else, she followed rather than preceded him. She could read, but not write, and the real world where she moved [as mistress] was her yard, the kitchen, and the pantry filled with pottery and frying pans.[58]

The members of the lesser nobility were real lords at their own manors. There the serfs, teachers, and ministers alike accepted the noble as the undisputed master. Here he felt at home. Since, however, he lacked finesse and culture, he could not make his way in a different environment. He did not like to leave that sound soil under his feet. He was accustomed to, and could not dispense with, the prestige he enjoyed at home, but which he lacked everywhere else. His character developed in that environment without the checks and balances of a broader, more cultured society where differences in talent, discipline, and diligence would have put him in his proper place and moderated his limitless self-confidence. His ill-founded but unchallenged prestige within his small circle made him rough. The Hungarian lesser noblemen lived in their petty microcosms as freely as sovereigns. It is informative again to turn to Kazinczy's description of his grandfather:

> His morals were impeccable, his thinking elevated, his sentiments fair and saintly. His only weakness was that in his fits of passion he thundered and hurled lightning around. . . . His valet and secretary suffered enormously every morning until they dressed him. Finally [his dressing completed], the thundering was over, the valet swept the sweat away from his face and left happily; the horrible work was over.[59]

The lack of knowledge of foreign lands made the lesser nobleman

[57] Ibid., p. 109.   [58] Kazinczy, Pályám emlékezete, p. 26.
[59] Ibid., p. 23.

believe that his land, his standard of living, his circumstances were second to none.[60] József Kármán wrote in 1795:

The libraries were neglected for the benefit of weapons, the humanities for the hunts, meditation was replaced by hunting with greyhounds. . . . The small lot the countryman lives on determines his whole horizon. . . . He does not know what is going on behind the borders of his village. . . . All his attention is limited to that tiny periphery in which he was born and on which he lives. Here lie the limits of all his ambitions. . . . The emptiness of the desert dominates such heads. . . . Talent lies idle; the lazy and wild way of life prevents its development. There is no opportunity to unfold it, there is no cause to put it into motion, there does not exist any ferment to bring it to a boil. The consequence of all this is superstition, ignorance, and blindness. . . .

The prestige and superiority of others are those shackles which restrain them. That man is believed to be righteous who is capable of making his neighbors believe him to be a learned and deeply thinking man; he finds in such places more blind and deeper trust [in him] than the Dalai Lama has. . . . That is the way in which a whole area follows a man of mediocre talents, like the pusillanimous sheep follow the ram.

When there is only one person who always talks without being contradicted by anyone, he will finally believe that he always has been talking wisely, and that it is impossible to contradict him. The man who sees the members of his household accepting his words like oracles easily considers them to be oracles indeed. Since he can discipline some farmhands and coward farmers, he will believe that Montesquieu and Calonne are but shadows compared to him.[61]

Gergely Édes, a sophisticated contemporary poet, complained to Ferenc Kazinczy: "For whom are we writing after all? . . . To the lords and [the lesser] nobles only the pork, the greyhound, the stud, sleeping, cursing, wrath, denunciation, the tale of valets and flatterers, bibulousness, etc., are attractive; they do not realize what true pleasure really means." [62]

That is, then, the political, economic, and social status, as well as the state of mind, of the lesser nobility of Hungary in the era under analysis. A dire picture indeed. The majority of the lesser nobility during the last quarter of the eighteenth century did not yet indicate the gallant and honorable role they were to play during the second quarter of the nineteenth century. Then, after an intellectual, political,

[60] Grünwald, p. 113.   [61] Quoted ibid., pp. 116-17.
[62] Letter of Gergely Édes to Ferenc Kazinczy, dated October 14, 1794. Quoted ibid., p. 118.

and social revival that was already in progress in 1790, the lesser nobility, in particular the gentry, became the pioneering stratum of Hungarian society, carrying out what the progressive bourgeois of the West did in their own countries: a liberal revolution. They established the first modern parliamentary government in Hungary and emancipated the serfs. That role, however, was yet to come. In the era under study, we have to deal with a narrow-minded, selfish, self-centered, uncivilized, stubborn, provincial, domineering, ruthless, wild lesser nobility. Whatever it was, that was the class which affected most substantially the lot of the serfs. However, it must be made clear that in 1790 a considerable number of the *bene possessionati* were already highly educated, civilized, and in their own way partisans of the eighteenth-century Enlightenment. What "their own way" meant, and what the political, social, and intellectual effects of the Hungarian gentry's brand of Enlightenment were, will be the subjects of chapters on the Hungarian intellectual revival and the feudal revolt.

Chapter IV

THE FOURTH ESTATE:
THE BURGHERS OF THE TOWNS
AND THE MINING CITIES

IT WAS a royal prerogative to grant the status of a royal free town to any settlement. The granting of the status of a burgher, on the other hand, was the privilege of town councils.[1] Many individuals not possessing the status of a burgher lived inside the town limits; as a matter of fact, non-burghers constituted the majority in the royal free towns.[2]

The population of the royal free towns and mining cities was divided into three groups. The lowest stratum was the most numerous; it included nonskilled laborers, servants, *zsellérek* (landless peasants), handicraftsmen possessing no shops, and the like. The majority of this group were politically inactive and did not have the privileges of the burghers. Only the middle and upper layers of inhabitants were considered burghers having the privileges of that class. In 1782 there were 352,000 inhabitants located in the royal free towns and mining cities, but out of them only about 20,000 belonged to the burgher class, a mere 5.4 percent.[3]

The middle layer of the inhabitants consisted of handicraftsmen who had their own shops, merchants, real estate owners, and the like.

---

[1] Oszetzky, pp. 16–17.

[2] Interestingly, some of the royal free towns possessed full serf villages to which the town was the landlord. For example, the town of Sopron possessed eight serf villages: Bánfalva, Balf, Kópháza, Harka, Ágfalva, Lépesfalva, Medgyes, and Kelénpatak. Jenny, p. 7.   [3] Mályusz, "Magyarországi polgárság," p. 227.

Compared to the lowest stratum, the middle layer was a small group.

Finally, the highest level of the town dwellers, the *oligarchia* (oligarchy), was a numerically negligible group, but town affairs were administered by them.[4] For this domination of town affairs, no legal or constitutional stipulation existed. The custom came into being during several generations prior to 1790. As early as the fifteenth century, city affairs in Buda were already administered by a *centumviratus*.[5] This body of one hundred men selected town officials, decided the policies of the town, and adopted new members through the decisions of its own inner council. More or less that was the way the upper layer of the burghers dominated town affairs throughout the country.[6]

The majority of town inhabitants, as far as the lower and middle strata were concerned, were non-Hungarians, mostly Germans. Hungarian nobles, fleeing from Turkish-occupied Hungary, gradually settled in the towns by permission of the town councils.[7] Many of these nobles took up handicraft work; some became merchants, joining the businesses of the burghers. The upper layer of the burghers began to assimilate themselves with this urban nobility by intermarriage, by adoption of the habits of noblemen, and by seeking ennoblement for themselves. In 1757 in the city council of Pest, eight members out of twelve were registered as *Inclyti regni Hungariae nobilis*, that is, Hungarian noblemen. At the end of the eighteenth century, the distinction between the nobles of the towns and the upper layer of the original burghers faded away for all practical purposes.[8]

While in some of the Western countries a great part of the nobility gradually adopted bourgeois customs, in Hungary the contrary happened. The richest layer of the burghers adopted the customs of the nobles, many becoming nobles themselves. The burghers in Hungary sought political influence not in a class struggle aimed against the dominant position of the nobles but by assimilation with the noble class.

Seeking for the causes of this specific Hungarian development, it is again necessary to go back to the Ottoman era of Hungarian history,

---

[4] Oszetzky, p. 51.   [5] Mályusz, "Magyarországi polgárság," p. 228.
[6] *Ibid.*   [7] Oszetzky, p. 61.
[8] Gárdonyi, in Domanovszky, ed., *Magyar művelődéstörténet*, IV, 331–32.

when the Turks severely damaged the previous political and economic status of the burghers. The first major undermining of their privileges originated in the fugitive noblemen's request to be admitted as residents into the towns. Several towns admitted them on the condition that they share the burdens of the burghers.[9] The settlement of the noblemen in the cities,[10] hitherto separate political entities, was followed by the intrusion of the authority of the county gentry. Sometimes the burghers were successful in preventing this trend.

In 1741 the delegates of the noblemen of Pest County complained to the national diet against the city council of Buda, stating that "several of the county gentry who had to participate in the county assembly [held in Buda] wanted to buy houses there, but they [the town council] were inventing all possible excuses to prevent them in that purchase." Indeed, up to the 1740s no noblemen except the members of the Royal Court of Appeal, who permanently resided in Pest, could buy houses in that town. The resolution of the diet of 1723 to set up the Royal Court of Appeal in Pest had caused an uproar there. The burghers did their best to prevent the establishment of the court in their town, lest with the court the nobles also come,[11] but they were unsuccessful.

In 1783 Joseph II transferred the central Hungarian government offices from Pozsony to Buda, making the old royal capital of medieval Hungary the national capital again. Naturally that brought a tremendous advantage to Pest and Buda, for both of them began to grow rapidly as nobles in great numbers swarmed into the twin cities. Even the burghers, fully estimating the great advantages to their business implicit in the transfer of the national capital to their towns, welcomed rather than opposed the change.[12]

During the eighteenth century the towns played a very modest role in Hungarian society. The Ottoman War and its devastations were very hard obstacles to be overcome quickly. The towns could not develop into intellectual or commercial centers. During Thököly's civil war (1675–85)[13] and the war of Ferenc Rákóczi (1703–11)[14] further

[9] Hóman and Szekfü, III, 551–60.   [10] Oszetzky, p. 76.
[11] Gárdonyi, in Domanovszky, *Magyar művelődéstörténet*, IV, 332.
[12] *Ibid.*, p. 333.
[13] Imre Thököly (1657–1705) launched a rebellion and a military campaign against the Habsburgs in alliance with Louis XIV in 1675. The rebellion became a civil war extending to Transylvania and northern Hungary. Initial

devastation occurred, and even cities never affected by the Ottoman wars were now burned to the ground. Bártfa was burned in 1680 by the units of Thököly, Lőcse by the army of Rákóczi, Szatmárnémeti by the *kurocok* as well as the *labancok* (warriors of Rákóczi and the Habsburgs respectively).[15] Similar destruction ruined several other towns.

In the census of 1720 the towns showed a miserable picture of underdevelopment. The largest towns of Hungary had the following populations: Buda, 12,324; Komárom, 8,321; Debrecen, 8,208; Pozsony, 7,943. The total population of the 39 Hungarian royal free towns was 125,015. According to the census of 1787, the number of townfolk had nearly tripled since 1720, to 352,000. In 1787 Pozsony was the most populous town with 28,737 inhabitants, and the other major towns had the following number of inhabitants: Debrecen, 25,747; Buda, 22,019. More than 10,000 people dwelled in these towns: Szeged, Pest, Győr, Sopron, Zombor, Székesfehérvár, Körmöcbánya.[16]

After the release from Ottoman occupation, the burghers of the liberated towns preferred rather to maintain their ancient privileges assured in royal patents than to acquire new ones. The reason for this was that the new patents granting town privileges, because of the neo-Counter Reformation, contained stipulations permitting burghership to Catholics only. (Indeed, the adoption of Protestants into burghership did not become legal until after the Patent of Toleration

---

successes resulted in the show of Thököly's arms in Moravia and even in Silesia. After the Peace Treaty of Nymwegen in 1678, however, the Habsburg forces were free to move from the Rhine to Hungary and the rebellion began to decline. Thököly then turned to the Porte, concluded an alliance with it, and cooperated with the Turks in the fateful campaign which began with the last siege of Vienna in 1683. With the defeat of the Ottoman forces, Thököly and his cause faded away also, leaving behind ruin and misery. Mód, pp. 63–65.

[14] Ferenc Rákóczi II (1676–1735), Prince of Transylvania, waged a war on the Habsburgs between 1703 and 1711. As long as the Habsburgs were tied down in the War of the Spanish Succession, Rákóczi achieved remarkable victories against the Habsburg forces in Hungary. The war, however, was devastating. The waste of material wealth was surpassed by the loss of human life. War casualties and the plague decimated the population of Hungary, already bled white during the Ottoman wars. Between 1708 and 1711, 310,000 people died of plague in royal Hungary and 100,000 in Transylvania: 410,000 altogether. War casualties numbered 85,000 dead—a grand total of half a million losses. In 1715 the population of Hungary was approximately 2.58 million. This indicates that the Rákóczi war cost the life of approximately one fifth of the whole population. Acsády, pp. 254 and 318.

[15] Gárdonyi, in Domanovszky, *Magyar művelődéstörténet*, IV, 325,

[16] *Ibid.*, p. 327.

of Joseph II was issued.) Hence, since the ownership of real estate in the cities was exclusively a privilege of burghers, such ownership was denied to Protestants in cities with new patents. Even in the cities of ancient privileges, where the Protestants were not banned from burghership, the counterreformation policy of the Habsburgs had the effect of checking the influence of the Protestants. A regulation of the Royal Chancellery issued in 1690 instructed the city councils to hold their council meetings, for the election of officeholders, only in the presence of a royal commissioner.[17] These agents prevented the election of Protestants to key positions even in places with Protestant majorities.

The royal commissioners sent by the Royal Chancellery were empowered substantially to interfere not only with the elections but also with other matters of town autonomy. Particularly important was economic control of the cities, maintained in order to squeeze out of them as much tax money as possible. Before the once-devastated towns could rebuild themselves and before they could stabilize their administration, the growing central government encroached too much upon their embryonic autonomy, therefore, the burghers never could develop effective self-government for themselves.[18]

The town councils were anxious to maintain high, almost puritanical, moral standards in their towns. The outward appearance of the burghers was controlled to check the spread of undue luxury. In 1708 the town council of Kassa ordered a ban on "extraordinary and indecent dressing and suits and luxury, particularly regarding women." [19] The city of Lőcse forbade housemaids to wear dresses similar to those of the burghers' ladies. But in spite of all the bans on luxury, the burghers enjoyed the exhibition of their wealth and taste. Wedding parties and ceremonies in particular were overwhelmingly luxurious. There was a general habit in larger towns of organizing pre-wedding processions, in which the jewelry and wedding dresses of brides were exhibited in carriages circling the entire town. The excesses connected with weddings went so far that in 1773 the town council of Kassa issued a regulation banning "at weddings all . . . debauchery, nasty and unclean utterances." [20] On the other

---

[17] Oszetzky, pp. 68–70.
[18] Gárdonyi, in Domanovszky, *Magyar művelődéstörténet*, IV, 328–29.
[19] *Ibid.*, p. 329.   [20] *Ibid.*, p. 330.

hand, Mátyás Bél, in a vivid description of burgher morality in the towns of northwestern Hungary, declared that the burghers of Nagyszombat were modest and peaceful men. He insisted that any disorder occurring in the town was initiated not by the burghers but by the university students.[21]

At the beginning of the eighteenth century the Hungarian towns still were walled and surrounded by trenches. The walls were so anxiously guarded that the town council of Pest on March 28, 1754, banned all underground caves or the building of cellars near them in order to safeguard their foundations. In 1772 the town walls of Pest were still intact. At that time, however, people began to build small houses near the walls. Soon the rapid growth of population eliminated the possibility of keeping the city inside the walls. The settlements overflowed the walls and gates, which gradually disappeared to make way for new dwellings and the growing traffic. The last city gate was destroyed in 1808, and with it the medieval character of Pest fully disappeared. The other towns of the land developed similarly.[22]

The rapid growth of the twin cities of Pest and Buda prevented effective city planning. Many of the new houses were built of clay and reed. In 1720, 200 out of the 375 houses in Pest were made of clay.[23] In Debrecen, according to the 1715 registration, practically all the houses were of clay. In the northern part of Hungary the houses were built of wood.[24] The dwellings of the burghers were rather simple. In the early eighteenth century in Eperjes, the following facts were registered: out of a total of 281 houses, 20 contained four rooms (very small ones, of course); 30 contained three rooms; and 51 contained two rooms. All the others had only one room. Seventy-one houses were described by the registry as "dirty shacks." These conditions changed little during the course of the century. In 1766 the town of Sopron included 622 houses, comprising 2,223 apartments. Of these houses, 159 contained one room only. In the central part of the city the majority of the houses contained four rooms.

The only town deserving that name in the early eighteenth century was the nation's capital, the city of Pozsony. The comparatively high standard of contemporary urbanism was due to the fact that Pozsony

[21] *Ibid.* [22] *Ibid.*, p. 334. [23] Hóman and Szekfü, IV, 389.
[24] Gárdonyi, in Domanovszky, *Magyar művelődéstörténet,* IV, 336.

had been the national capital since 1540, when the ancient capital city of Buda was taken by the Turks.[25] Mátyás Bél wrote in 1737 that the streets of the inner city were decorative because of the several splendid mansions, owned mostly by aristocrats, that were built there. Scarcely any aristocrats in Hungary would not have owned a house in Pozsony. The burghers, on the other hand, still did not have residences similar in style and luxury to those of the nobility. Out of the 206 houses of the inner town, 3 belonged to the state, 24 to the ecclesiastics, only 12 to burghers, and 53 to noblemen.

Naturally the cultural standards of the towns so promising in the Middle Ages declined commensurately with the economic decline of the burghers.[26] Industry remained underdeveloped in the framework of obsolete guilds. Since Austro-Bohemian industry was too strong to compete with, the guilds concentrated their energy not on industrial and commercial innovation or development but on old-fashioned prevention of outside competition. Thus guild members jealously safeguarded their trade, professional, and market monopolies as strictly as the nobles guarded their own privileges, and the two classes formed a double-edged opposition to progress and change.[27]

The towns were weak not only economically but also politically and intellectually. The royal Chamber encroached upon their financial autonomy. Owing to the nobles, the political influence of the towns decreased until it was practically nil, since all the towns of Hungary had only one collective vote in the Lower Chamber of the diet.[28] Finally, the county gradually seized power over the affairs of the towns. One of the most important steps in that direction was the practice by the county administration of expropriating the right to regulate the market price of individual productions of the towns.[29] The generally low standards of economy and education made the burghers as provincial in their outlook as the lesser nobility. The lowest and middle strata of the burghers lacked interest in political matters. Béla Grünwald, the Hungarian historian of the pre-1848 era, writes:

During the era of the French Revolution, when the feudal system was shaken all over Europe by the ideas and arms of the Frenchmen, and the effects of the Revolution were felt in Hungary also, it was not the spirit

[25] *Ibid.*, p. 339.   [26] Szádeczky, I, 129–39.   [27] *Ibid.*, p. 130.
[28] Hóman and Szekfü, V, 79.   [29] Grünwald, p. 130.

of the burghers that began to ferment. Perhaps they [the burghers] found it hard to tolerate the privileged and dominating position of the nobility, perhaps they would have preferred to eliminate them, but that disposition did not inspire the burghers to actions. The champions and martyrs of the new ideas were mostly of noble origin.[30]

The underdeveloped burgherdom of Hungary, too weak to absorb the new ideas and to struggle for their realization, their representatives too inactive in the diets, did not demand a new social system. They were silent even when a great part of the nobility was already in revolt. The burghers in Hungary were not the champions of bourgeois ideals. The serfs in Hungary, therefore, had to dispense with the alliance of the burghers, who were so formidable and effective a supporter of the cause of the serfs in the West. Yet, in 1790, parallel to the feudal revolt and the peasant unrest, there was also a burghers' movement in Hungary. One of the leading historians of that era, Elemér Mályusz, went so far as to call it "the first revolutionary movement" of the burghers of Hungary.[31] In Part IV we shall return to this movement. Suffice it to say here that Béla Grünwald was nearer to the correct evaluation of the state of mind of the burghers than Elemér Mályusz was. In 1790 the middle and lowest strata of the burghers lacked political self-consciousness, initiative, and, above all, revolutionary fervor. The upper stratum, on the other hand, many of whom were nobles themselves, sided with the *bene possessionati*.

[30] *Ibid.*, p. 131.   [31] Mályusz, "Magyarországi polgárság," p. 225.

Chapter V

THE PEASANTRY

ON THE LOWEST LEVEL of the social pyramid were the peasants. Knowing no privileges but only obligations, the serfs were exposed to the whims and economic interests of their landlords and the prelates. The utmost enormity of the serfs' position was that they had no constitutional or legal personality.

As a consequence of the Dózsa revolt of 1514, the greatest peasant uprising in the history of Hungary, the peasantry suffered heavily. One of the repercussions of the revolt was the bondage of the peasants to the soil.[1] The law creating this condition was only in force for one generation. The diet of 1547 established the serfs' right of migration (Act No. 26),[2] a basic right reenacted several times thereafter. Migration, however, was conditioned by detailed procedures, always supervised by the lords themselves. In addition to the complex procedure the law prescribed, the counties on their own authority introduced strict regulations of migration which for all intents and purposes

[1] All the privileges of the ruling classes of the land, as well as the punishment and future obligations of the peasants after the revolt, were compiled in István Verbőczi's *Tripartitum* or *Hármaskönyv*, first printed in Vienna in 1517. Regarding the new situation of the peasants, this work says: "[The peasants] possessed the privilege, after they paid the legal land rents and their debts, freely to move from their residence to anywhere else at their pleasure. However, they forfeited and lost that right forever during the last summer [1514] by their *kurucz* [crusader] conspiracy and rebellion against the whole of the nobility under the leadership of that most wicked bandit called Székely György [György Dózsa]. From now on, as perpetual serfs, they are totally subjected to their lords." (Article No. 25, sec. 2.)

The *Tripartitum* also clearly defined the right of ownership of the land, saying: "Beyond the fees and rewards for his work the peasant does not have any right whatsoever to his lord's land, excepting the right of inheritance; the full ownership of the land belongs exclusively to the landlord." (Article No. 30, par. 7.) (The 1844 edition is quoted.)   [2] CJH, II, 203.

bound the serfs fully and irrevocably to the soil. In the frenzy of the victory of the estates in the István Bocskay movement,[3] an act was promulgated changing fundamentally the legal status of serfs (Act No. 13 of 1608).[4] This law transferred the right of permission or denial of peasant migration, as well as all problems of serf-lord relations, to the authority of the counties from that of the diet. The state (king and diet alike) was excluded from interference with serf-lord relations for more than a century. This change put a legal end to the right of migration, the practical possibility of migration having been dead for a long time.

In the seventeenth century the serfs' lives became increasingly miserable when they were required to work twelve days annually on the extensive fortification system.[5] In addition, they paid taxes to the state, performed military service, and rendered services to the lord and church. The serfs also had to shoulder the domestic taxes (county taxes)[6] to a greater degree. The nobles who in the past had exclusively born that burden gradually exempted themselves from contributing to the domestic tax at all. Finally, the serfs also performed public works for the county. The burdens of the serfs were manifold indeed.

After the liberation of the heartland of Hungary from Ottoman occupation,[7] large uninhabited and uncultivated lands were available again. An enormous general migration commenced in Hungary, verging toward the center of the Great Hungarian Plain. The owners of these virgin lands offered considerable advantages to serfs who were willing to migrate to the lands and settle and cultivate them. A new stratum of contractual or tenant (*árendás* or *taksás*) serfs was thereby created. Individual groups or entire villages could conclude con-

---

[3] Between 1604 and 1606 István Bocskay waged a war of independence against the Habsburgs, the first in a series of similar wars. The leading political element in the war was the Hungarian gentry. The military potential of the Transylvanian principality supplied the necessary force. The war was a successful one. The Peace Treaty of Vienna in 1606 strengthened the religious freedom of the Protestants and the privileges of the estates.   [4] CJH, III, 30, 31.

[5] Fortifications on the Hungarian-Turkish borderlands, owing to the protracted war, had to be kept in good shape for almost a century.

[6] The domestic or county taxes covered the expenses of the county administration and the participation of the county deputies in the diets. The assessment of those taxes amounted to one fourth to one third of the *contributio*, or war tax, which was the main state tax. Marczali, *Hungary*, p. 26.

[7] The War of Liberation lasted from 1683 to 1699.

tracts with the lord. The full obligations of the village were to be paid in one sum for the whole population. That kind of contract was frequent where virgin lands were taken under cultivation. A great many German immigrants concluded such contracts before they entered the country.[8]

This system was exceptionally advantageous for the peasantry, particularly because more often than not the serfs could pay the equivalent of all their obligations in cash. Generally they were not obliged to fulfill any *robot*. Naturally, this system only existed where the value of labor was overwhelming because of the abundance of virgin lands and the shortage of workers.[9] As these conditions gradually faded away[10] the peasants began to feel the heavy hands of the lords. The landlords could disregard any and all contracts they had previously concluded, if they wished to do so. No authority existed in Hungary to take the serfs under its protection. In the diet of 1723, at the insistence of King Charles III, a pious act was passed ordering the counties to protect the serfs against the excesses of the lords. But that stipulation remained on paper only, as did Maria Theresa's royal order in 1751 to the counties "to take the tax-paying population under their special protection." [11]

No wonder that in spite of rigorous police regulations the fleeing of serfs from the jurisdiction of their lords was a very frequent occurrence in the early eighteenth century. As the no-man's-land in the Ukrainian steppes attracted the serfs of the Polish *szlachta* and the Russian *dvorianstvo* in the seventeenth and eighteenth centuries, so the virgin lands of the liberated central and southern parts of Hungary lured the Hungarian serfs. The challenge to try their luck in the abundance of land in the liberated territories was too great to resist. The estates naturally began to pass legislation to check the fleeing of the serfs and to return the fugitives. Act No. 101 of 1715[12] ordered the counties to let no serfs pass through their territory not in possession of the necessary traveling permits. This law further stipulated that the migration to the liberated territories and to Transylvania was to be prevented, if necessary, by military force. The act,

---

[8] Eckhart, p. 209; see also Niederhauser, p. 128.

[9] See the pattern of contracts offered by Prince Eszterházy in Szabad, pp. 20 ff.

[10] The resettlement on the Eszterházy estates was completed in the 1740s. Szabad, p. 23.   [11] Acsády, p. 343.   [12] CJH, IV, 517.

however, did not prevent migration. Act No. 6 of 1725[13] reiterated the ban and prohibited the migration of *taksás* serfs also, whose migration had not been banned previously. The newly established *Consilium regium locumtenentiale hungaricum*[14] organized the prevention of serf migration on a national scale. The effort to prevent internal migration was as yet only partly successful.

In addition to fleeing from the jurisdiction of the lords, there were other, very modest, means for serfs to escape from their miserable lives. Some who happened to accumulate enough funds redeemed themselves by cash from serfhood. Several of these freemen (*szabadosok*) gradually were knighted and joined the extensive group of *armalis* noblemen. At the end of the seventeenth century some freemen (*exemptus*), independent of the authority of the lord, dwelt in the villages. Thus on the fringe of the peasant class a small segment of freemen emerged.[15]

In serf-lord relationships a basic legal change occurred in the mid-eighteenth century. Serf obligations became uniform in most parts of the land after the promulgation of the urbarial regulations of Maria Theresa in 1767. All the authority for supervising the execution of her decree, however, lay in the hands of the nobles,[16] one of the interested parties. The lord was the serf's judge even in suits between the serf and the lord himself.[17] All the intentions of monarchs in the eighteenth century to ensure a better lot for the peasants were frustrated by the resistance of the nobles. Charles III, Maria Theresa, and Joseph II tried to introduce measures protecting the peasants, but such measures yielded very little amelioration of the real legal, economic, and social status of the serfs. The intentions of these rulers were primarily to expropriate a greater share of the serfs' labor for the state at the lords' expense. Hence the change from almost two centuries of concord between the crown and the estates to competition between the crown and the estates. Humanitarian intentions and a sense of justice on the

---

[13] *Ibid.*, IV, 610.

[14] The *Consilium regium locumtenentiale hungaricum*, the first Hungarian central government in the modern sense, was set up by Acts Nos. 97 to 122, in 1723. CJH, IV, 643–51.

[15] A serf might also become a freeman by marrying a lady. Niederhauser, p. 128.

[16] Grünwald, p. 144. The urbarial regulations for Translyvania were issued as late as 1846–47. Niederhauser, p. 131.   [17] Up to 1791.

part of these Habsburg rulers cannot, however, be denied: "I must serve justice to rich and poor alike. I must answer my conscience. I do not want to be damned for the sake of a few magnates and noblemen," said Maria Theresa.[18] She was aware that she could only extract a larger amount of taxes from the serfs if they lived better. "The sheep should be well fed in order to make it yield more wool and more milk," Maria Theresa said.[19] The conditions created by her urbarial regulations of 1767, codified by the diet of 1790–91, remained legally unchanged up to the emancipation of the serfs in 1848.

Maria Theresa's urbarial regulations introduced a clear definition of lord-serf relations, in principle at least.[20] One of their merits was the strict definition of the size of the serf holdings.[21] The measurement of the serfs' lots was the section (*sessio* or session). A full serf section consisted of an internal and an external portion. Throughout the country the internal portion was a small area with a building lot and vegetable gardens located inside the village limits. The external portion consisted of plowland and hayfield. The size of both differed in different parts of the country according to their fertility and the expectation of their yield. During the urbarial survey of Maria Theresa, the county commissions classified the plowlands and pastures according to their quality. The guiding principle in determining the size of a section was that one eighth of a full section should yield enough to support the serf and his family and to fulfill his obligations toward state, lord, and church.

The commissions introduced four divisions for the classification of the serf's plowlands. In each division the size of the section was differ-

[18] Szeberényi, p. 174. See also Acsády, p. 356. [19] Acsády, p. 353.
[20] The 1764–65 diet adjourned without yielding to the Queen's desire to introduce reforms of serfdom. That was the turning point of Maria Theresa's policy. The Queen took into her own hands the settlement of serf problems. She ordered Count Pál Festetics, the president of the Hugarian Royal Chamber, to prepare a draft decree, not for emancipation, but for the betterment of the serf's lot. The collection of material for the elaboration of the draft decree began in earnest all over the kingdom in 1765. An Austrian expert, Court Chancellor Raab, elaborated the final draft, which was promulgated in the form of a royal patent for Hungary on January 23, 1767, in Hungarian, Latin, and Slovak. Acsády, pp. 355, 356.
[21] The urbarial regulations for Hungary were more advantageous for serfs than were the regulations for Bohemia and Lower Austria. The Czech serfs performed six, the Lower Austrian serfs four, times more *robot* than the Hungarian serfs did. Niederhauser, p. 122.

ent. "However, all four used the same fundamental principles, the essence of which was on the one hand to determine the minimum size of the serf section and on the other hand to determine the maximum of serf obligations." [22]

The measuring unit of the plowland was the yoke (0.57 hectares or 1.42 English acres). In Mosony County, one section equaled 20–26 yokes; in Pest County, 24–30 yokes; in Sopron County, from 16 yokes up; and in Csanád County, from 36 yokes up.[23] The measuring unit of hayfields was one *kaszáló* or *falcastrum*, an area which yielded at the first mowing of the year a wagonload of hay. The size of a hayfield belonging to one serf section amounted to from 6 to 22 *falcastri*.[24]

In general the peasant class presented an extremely variegated picture of different stages of economic and social life. The highest echelon of the peasant class was that of serfs who, owning larger lots and accumulating some capital, were on the road toward ennoblement.[25] The lowest echelons were the poverty-stricken manorial farmhands and the sub-cotters (*alzsellérek* or *subinquilini*) who possessed neither land nor house. Between these limits the bonded peasants were classified into six basic categories: (1) serfs with one section or more; (2) serfs with one half a section; (3) serfs with one quarter of a section; (4) serfs with one eighth of a section; (5) *zsellérek* (cotters or *inquilini*); (6) *alzsellérek* (sub-cotters or *subinquilini*).

The *inquilini* possessed internal portions of a section with a house. They also might possess plowland and pastures but less in size than one eighth of a section. The *subinquilini* owned neither external nor internal parts of a section, nor did they own houses. They lived in the house of a serf or an *inquilinus*. A man was only considered to be a *subinquilinus* if inside another person's house he owned his own hearth.

---

[22] Acsády, p. 357.   [23] Eckhart, p. 217.   [24] *Ibid.*

[25] Recent research in Hungarian archives has shed some light on the enrichment of a small portion of Hungarian serfs. A group of Hungarian researchers (László Makkai, István N. Kiss, Éva Veress, Zsigmond Kirilly, and János Román) discovered that in Zemplen County—the target area of their research—1.2 percent of the serf families regularly, and another 8 percent occasionally, produced marketable surpluses as early as the late sixteenth century. László Makkai, ed., *Jobbágytelek és parasztgazdaság az örökös jobbágyság kialakulásának korszakában* [Serf Holdings and Peasant Farming in the Era of Incipient Perpetual Serfdom] (Budapest: Akademiai Kiadó, 1966), p. 449.

PEASANT LOCAL AUTONOMY

While a small group of freemen were emerging from among the rank and file of serfdom, former administrative privileges of the peasant communities were fading away. The peasant local autonomy that had so flourished during the Middle Ages was a thing of the past in the eighteenth century. The villages were now under the joint authoritarian rule of lord and county. Even the position of village headman (*biró*), a proud office in the past, was now a hated burden only. It amounted to being the henchman of the lord, carrying out his orders.[26]

Part of the juridical rights of the lord were executed by the *biró* and the village jurors (*esküdtek*), who also officially represented the lower echelon of police authority. The candidacy of the *biró* was the right of the lord, who nominated three persons from among whom the village elected the officer in the presence of the lord's representative. The lord supervised the official functions of the *biró*. If the *biró* did not fulfill his duties the lord could dismiss him. The *biró*-elect took an oath in the presence of the community that he would perform his duties loyally. The *biró* neither fulfilled urbarial services nor paid urbarial dues; however, he paid the customary public taxes to the state just as other serfs did. He bore his office for one year and could be reelected.

The village notary (*jegyző*) and the jurors were elected by the community without the interference of the lord, though all of them were dominated by the lord's prestige.[27] The village notary wrote the

---

[26] Eckhart, p. 207.

[27] The office of *jegyző* was rather new in Hungarian village administration. It became general in the seventeenth and eighteenth centuries with the increasing duties of the village in the collection of state taxes. As early as 1731 Tolna County made it compulsory for all the villages to elect a village notary. During Maria Theresa's reign, particularly after the promulgation of the urbarial regulations, the election of village notaries became universal all over the country. I. Szabó, *Tanulmányok*, p. 281. The system of village notaries raises a question: How was it possible for eighteenth-century Hungary to supply all its villages (there were 18,700 in 1770) with literate notaries? It should be borne in mind that in 1778 there were 5,001 *honoratiori*, men not of the nobility who had received a higher education. It can logically be assumed that the number of literate non-nobles must have been several times this—more than enough to fill all the offices of notary. More exact figures are available: in 1770 there were 4,000 elementary schools of all denominations in Hungary. Hóman and

village diary, in which all matters concerning the village were registered. He prepared the state and county tax registers, he performed the bookkeeping for the *biró*, and his books were presented to the lord at the end of the year for endorsement. The jurors were subordinate agents of the *biró*. If the *biró* was absent, one of the jurors substituted for him.

A special kind of autonomy developed in the large peasant towns of the Ottoman-occupied Great Hungarian Plain in the seventeenth century. The Ottoman authorities, in order to gain a kind of cooperation from the inhabitants in these towns, abolished the jurisdiction of the Ottoman *kadi* in civil and criminal suits and permitted the election of a town council led by a headman (*főbiró*), who was entitled to pass sentences in all civil and criminal cases. Particularly developed were the autonomous institutions of the cities of Kecskemét, Nagykőrös, and Cegléd. The efficiency of these communities caught the attention of several Hungarian researchers. István Szabó, a leading scholar of the Hungarian peasant problem, is of the opinion that

The peasant villages of the Great Hungarian Plain, which were left alone in all the aspects of their life, were obliged to solve all the problems of their self-administration during the era of coexistence [with the Turks]. We should not underestimate, in regard to the capability of the Hungarian peasants to rule themselves, the influential lessons and the spiritual heritage offered by those lonely peasant [communities] of the Great Hungarian Plain.[28]

The importance of this peasant self-rule was recognized by contemporaries also. The Hungarian kings endorsed self-rule in territories beyond the pale of Hungarian royal jurisdiction. Such double sovereignty, though a strange phenomenon, extended to other fields of human activities also. People located far from the border sometimes

---

Szekfü, IV, 528. Sámuel Tessedik, the contemporary reformer, commented: "In Békés County there are Lutheran [elementary] schools in five places; at present 14 schoolmasters are teaching in them. Some of them have to teach 200 to 300 pupils or more in a single classroom." Wellmann, *Tessedik*, p. 29. This would imply that in a single county there were some 2,800 pupils of various grades in the five schools, say 560 in each school. While it would be a mistake to extrapolate a national average from this figure, it is an indication that the elementary school system would have produced several hundred thousand literate and semiliterate men not of noble birth at this period.

[28] I. Szabó, *Tanulmányok*, p. 310.

sent royal taxes and even dues to the landlords who were located in royal Hungary.[29]

URBARIAL RELATIONS

Hungarian serfs were not tenants; however, they possessed perpetual right to the cultivation of their lot, to a certain part of the fruits of that lot, and to their own labor. Extraordinary yields such as minerals belonged to the lord. "The right of the serf penetrated only as deep into the soil as his plow did." [30] The serf did not have the right either while alive or through his will, after death, to transfer his section either in one unit or in more parts to anyone without the consent of the lord. Nor could he divide his lot among his children without the permission of the lord. If he wanted to sell his rights, he had to present the prospective purchaser to the lord to be judged as to whether he would be capable of fulfilling the urbarial duties. If there were several heirs and the holding was supposed to remain in the hands of only one of them, that man might be selected by the lord. If there were no heirs left behind by the deceased serf, the lord could dispose of the holding.[31]

The lord possessed the privilege of exchanging the holding of the serf for another lot of his manorial lands—*regulatio* (regulation or redistribution). In principle the new land the serf received had to be neither smaller nor worse than that which was taken away from him. If the exchange was not fair, the serf might demand that his lot be given back to him. Needless to say, that principle was often abused. Another rule prohibited the lord from mutually transferring two serfs to each other's lots, unless both consented.[32] The serf might not be ejected from his section unless he committed offenses so repeatedly that he could be considered corrupt beyond redemption.

The *Tripartitum* forbade the expropriation of the serf's plowland and only permitted the expropriation of the internal portion of the serf's section by the lord if the lord had several children and there was not enough space around the manor house to build houses for all of them.[33] Such an expropriation, from the mid-eighteenth century on, required royal permission acquired through the *Consilium locumtenentiale*. That office demanded detailed explanations as to why the

[29] Eckhart, p. 208.   [30] *Ibid.*, p. 214.   [31] *Ibid.*, p. 215.
[32] *Ibid.*   [33] Verbőczi, pp. 104, 105

expropriation was unavoidable. Finally, in the case of expropriation, all the investments of the serfs had to be compensated in cash.[34]

The serf might give up his lot if he could not fulfill all his obligations, but only if the lord consented and accepted the replacement the serf presented in its stead.[35] Act No. 35 of 1791[36] regulated the condition of migration. The precondition was a previous announcement of intention; the dates both for announcing and for moving were uniform and fixed nationally. Before the serf moved he had to settle his private and public obligations and pay his debts. He had to receive the permit to move from the lord and the *alispán;* without these documents no one was permitted to employ the serf. Whoever gave shelter to a fugitive serf violated public order and security and was prosecuted for doing so. He was fined 100 florins; he had to pay all the debts of the serf, and also all the cost of the legal procedures.[37]

If the serf was kidnaped, the county attorney (*ügyész*) started legal prosecution for the return of the serf. Also, he was obliged to commence legal procedures against the lord if the latter prevented a serf from leaving by not issuing the permit to move despite the issuance of such a permit by the *alispán.* Finally, the county attorney was also supposed to initiate legal procedures against the lord if he transferred the serf without the serf's consent from his estate in one county to an estate in another. The right of migration applied to individual serfs and not to full villages. If the movement of an individual serf was deemed to cause the decline of the area, or if it might cause considerable damage to the basis of taxation, the county possessed the right to ban migration.[38]

The migrating serf was entitled to sell his rights to his holding and his immovables, with the intervention of the lord. The estimation of sales values was determined by the neighbors and inhabitants of the area who, in the presence of the *szolgabiró* [39] (district magistrate), took oaths regarding the announced estimation. If none wanted to buy, the right of possession of immovables passed to the lord.[40]

---

[34] Eckhart, p. 215.

[35] The serf had to announce his intention to move on St. Michael's Day (about September 29) and he might move on St. George's Day (about March 12).

[36] CJH, V, 183.   [37] Eckhart, p. 216.   [38] *Ibid.*

[39] The *szolgabiró,* or head of the district administration, was elected by the county assembly.   [40] Eckhart, p. 216.

SPECIAL BENEFITS OF THE SERFS AND
SPECIFIC RIGHTS OF THE LORDS

The lords had to award the serfs further benefits in addition to their right to cultivate a full section or part of a section of plowland and some *falcastri* of hayfields. These special benefits were manifold. The serfs' right to use the communal pastures to graze their cattle was the most important of all. If the pasture was large enough, the cattle of the lord, of his officials, of the ministers, and of the teachers grazed there too. While the lord owned the property, the right of grazing belonged primarily to the village community. The lord was not to restrict that right by grazing an excessive number of his own cattle on these pastures. Nor was he to set aside any part of the communal pastures for grazing his own cattle exclusively. The pasture was available only for such cattle of the serf as served his own needs, as well as those which were used to perform *robot* services for the lord. The serfs were not to graze cattle on the communal pastures that they bred for commercial purposes. The serfs did not have to perform any special services for the lord as compensation for the utilization of the pastures. If, however, the serfs were to present a certain amount of butter to the lord, they might also graze milk cows on the communal pastures. The commissars of Maria Theresa, who were charged with the registration of urbarial data in the counties, determined the number of cattle the individual serfs were permitted to graze.[41]

The urbarial regulations issued by Maria Theresa in 1767 were not sufficiently clear concerning several aspects of this very important specific benefit of the serfs. Quarrels between lords and serfs were brought to an end in 1836 by the promulgation of Act No. 6,[42] which introduced a ban to exclude the lord's cattle from communal pastures. On the other hand, the lord and a majority of the serfs were assured the right to separate the communal pasture from that which was reserved for the exclusive use of the lord, if they wanted to do so. The portion to be set aside for the use of the community had to include four to twenty-two yokes of pasture land for every existing serf section. This stipulation also ensured the rights of the *inquilini* to graze

[41] *Ibid.*, pp. 218, 219.   [42] CJH, VI, 29.

their cattle on the communal pasture. For every eight *inquilini* the amount of pasture owed to one serf section was to be added to the communal pasture.

A second important special benefit was the *lignatio* (*faizás*): the right to collect wood in the lords' forests to supply the serfs' needs for timber, kindling, and maintenance of agricultural implements. (In the eighteenth century all agricultural implements were made of wood.) The serfs were obliged first to satisfy these needs by using the fallen branches and dead trunks of trees. Only if dry wood was insufficient were they entitled to cut live trees. The manorial court decided, and the county supervised, the amount, the quality, the place, and the time of wood collection by the serfs. The regulation took into account both the needs of the serfs and the conservation of the forests. The timber might be used only for the roof, the doors, the framework, and the windows of the serf's house. The serf did not have the right to collect timber for the walls or the fence of his house.[43]

As a compensation for the *lignatio* the bonded peasants were obliged to cut wood for the lord and to carry it to the manor house. The cutting of wood was primarily the obligation of the *inquilini;* the transport, that of the serfs.

Where forests were insufficient to satisfy their needs, the serfs possessed the right of cutting reeds (*nádalás*). That right also was registered in the urbarial regulations. The serf might cut reeds only for his own use and not for sale. His legitimate needs were supposed to include heating his home and covering his house. In compensation for that right the serf possessing one section of plowland had to cut and carry forty bunches of reeds to the lord's manor. The serfs possessing less plowland were obliged to supply proportionately fewer reeds.

Pannage (*makkoltatás*) was the right of the serfs to feed their pigs with mast in the lords' forests neighboring the serf communities. They paid cash compensation for that right. The general right of pannage also entitled the serfs to pick fruits, if they found them, in the forests. Gallnuts could only be collected by the serfs in the community forests; in the lords' forests they were prohibited from doing so.[44]

Educillatio was the right of the serf communities to operate pubs. If the community had vineyards the *educillatio* was open to them

[43] Eckhart, p. 218.   [44] *Ibid.*, p. 219.

between St. Michael's Day and St. George's Day. If they did not have their own vineyards their pubs could be kept in business from vintage until Christmas Day only. During the rest of the year the *educillatio* was reserved for the lord, who had the right to sell liquor throughout the year, but only if he maintained a hostel for travelers. If the serfs sold out their wine earlier than the deadline mentioned above, the lord might begin his own wine sale at that earlier date. In the community pub the village could sell wine bought from other communities. If, however, the serfs sold wine in a time reserved for the lord's business, the merchandise might be confiscated and the offender was fined to perform three days of *robot*. The individual serfs might sell their own wine at their own houses or in the community pub. The pub was leased out at auction, supervised by the representatives of the county administration. If the village was large enough, the community might run several pubs.[45]

Distilling of brandy by the serfs for themselves in their own boilers might be permitted by the lord for some dues paid in cash. These dues were collected annually.[46]

Hunting was one of the most jealously guarded rights of the lords. Act No. 18 of 1514 prohibited hunting and fowling to the serfs.[47] The implementation of this ban, however, was very difficult. In the mid-seventeenth century the serfs were still hunting and fowling widely. Act No. 22 of 1729 recodified the old ban of 1514, prohibiting the serfs to hunt, fowl, or fish, or to breed or keep hunting dogs.[48] The urbarial regulations of Maria Theresa did not eliminate these prohibitions. In general the lords had the right to hunt and fowl not only on their own manorial lands but also on the holdings of the serfs.[49] However, they were not supposed to abuse these rights. Because they were not allowed to damage the crops of the serfs, the lords were prohibited from hunting or fowling on the plowlands of the serfs until the harvest, on the hayfields until mowing, and in the vineyards until vintage. If the lords caused damage to the crops, they had to compensate for the loss. If a lord refused to do so, the serf might turn to the county attorney for legal defense and for compensation of his losses.

The lord was obliged to prevent the multiplication of wild game

[45] *Ibid.*   [46] *Ibid.*   [47] CJH, I, 683 (*Decretum Quintum*, par. 18).
[48] *Ibid.*, IV, 675.   [49] Hóman and Szekfü, II, 517, 622; IV, 484, 616.

in order to check excessive damages to crops and vineyards. If he abstained from doing so, the county might force him to fulfill that duty or as a last resort to organize extermination campaigns against the harmful game. The peasants were obliged to help the lord or the county in the extermination of the beasts of prey, participating annually in a three-day hunt. For that hunt the ammunition was supplied by the lord.

The damages caused by the game had to be compensated by the lord. The evaluation of the damages was performed by the village headmen and jurors of the area.[50] If the lord did not pay, he might be forced to do so through a legal suit commenced by the county attorney.[51]

The lord might collect customs duties and ferry duties (*telonium naulum*), or he might yield these rights to communities for certain compensations. If the serfs crossed custom lines or rivers at ferry-duty posts possessed by their own lord in the service of the same lord, they were exempt from paying dues.

The lord also might reserve for himself the right of supplying meat and maintaining butcheries for the communities (*macellum*). If the lord maintained butcheries, with sufficient capacity and supply for the whole community, the purchase of meat from any other source was prohibited. If the serf carried meat to the village from elsewhere, it was confiscated and the offender had to perform three days of *robot* as a fine.

The maintaining of mills was a right of the lord. The serf communities might not erect or operate mills. The serfs, however, could not be forced to use the lord's mills. Maria Theresa's urbarial regulations reaffirmed the lord's right of preemption, that is, the right to purchase the surplus crops and manufactured goods of his serfs. In principle, if the lord purchased the goods of the serfs on the basis of this right, he was to pay a price at the level of existing local market prices.[52]

THE SERVICES OF THE SERFS

All serfs, without regard to quality and quantity of their holdings, as well as all the house-owning *inquilini*, were obliged to pay a one-

---

[50] Eckhart, p. 227.   [51] *Ibid.*, p. 220.   [52] *Ibid.*

florin smoke (or house) fee to the lord.[53] Half of that fee had to be paid at St. George's Day, the second half at St. Michael's Day. Such dues were commonly called house taxes.

The serfs were obliged to pay extraordinary dues or *subsidiae* to ransom their lord if he was captured, as well as to celebrate his wedding or his first mass.[54] The system of *subsidium* had been in force ever since Act No. 39 of 1548 had enacted that obligation.[55] But Maria Theresa's urbarial regulations left valid only the ransom duty—which was already a fiction—abolishing all other *subsidiae*. The prelates and the lay members of the Upper Chamber were entitled to collect *subsidiae* to cover the expenses of their participation in the diets. After the promulgation of the urbarial regulations that was the only *subsidium* still collected.

Out of the crops of the holding and the breeding of cattle the serf annually paid a ninth to the lord (*kilenced*). Maria Theresa left it up to the serfs to decide whether they wanted to pay those dues in kind or in cash. At some places and times the lords rented out the collection of the tithe due to the prelates. In some of these cases the lord did not collect his own ninth and the tithe separately, but as a compensation for the payment of both together he collected only a seventh or an eighth of the annual product of the serfs. Wherever that practice had become general before Maria Theresa issued her urbarial regulations, the lord was obliged to continue this same system. The internal portions of the section were exempt from the ninth. Also exempt were the hayfields if the serfs did not possess more of them than they were entitled to have according to the urbarial regulations. If the soil produced a second crop in the same year, it was free of the ninth. Neither could the lord take a ninth of the hay eventually collected from the fallow portions of the plowlands, if and where a three-course rotation system was applied in the agriculture. The ninth was deducted from the total crop before any part of it was taken away as compensation for the hired farmhands.

As a ninth of the hemp and flax yield the lord might demand six pounds of hemp and flax thread from every full serf section, even if such plants were not grown on the land of the serf. In that case the

[53] The smoke fee originated in the Middle Ages when any structure in which a fire could be kindled was considered a human dwelling. Where there was smoke, the serf had to pay. [54] *Ibid.*, p. 221. [55] CJH, II, 204.

lord had to give raw material to the serf and his household had to spin thread from it. In short, a hidden labor obligation was introduced with the increase in growing hemp and flax in Hungary.

When the completion of the harvest was reported to the lord, he was obliged to take out his ninth in the course of one week. If he missed doing so, the serf was entitled to carry his portion home and leave the ninth of the lord at the place of harvest. The separation of the lord's ninth from the rest of the crop was performed in the presence of the village headman, two village jurors, and the lord's emissaries. They had to give receipts for the received ninth. If the number of calves born in a year was less than nine, the ninth from the cattle was collected not in kind but in cash. The lord had to take over this ninth not later than the Day of John the Baptist, but he might demand the further breeding of the cattle by the serfs up to St. Michael's Day and not any further. If, however, the calves were hurt or lost after the Day of John the Baptist, the serf could not be held responsible and was not obliged to pay for the damage or the loss.[56]

The tithe (tized) was paid by the serfs either to the bishop or to certain prelates, whoever enjoyed that feudal service to the Church. If the ecclesiastics who were entitled to collect these dues wanted to lease the right, the lord had the privilege to take the lease if he wished to do so. In some places, the lord yielded that right to the village community, which then leased it from the bishop and paid him the tithe in one sum. If the serf was not obliged to pay a ninth to the lord for any crop he produced, the Church was not entitled to demand a tithe from that crop either. Furthermore, the serf was not obliged to pay a tithe of corn, regardless of whether he did or did not pay the ninth. Nor was he obliged to carry the tithe to the residence of the bishop, or to provide food and lodging to the emissaries of the prelate who collected the tithe. The collection of the tithe had to coincide with the collection of the ninth. If anyone refused to pay the tithe he was forced to pay double.[57]

Ever since the promulgation of the serf legislaton of 1514, the serfs had had to pay gifts to the lord.[58] Maria Theresa's urbarial regulations, however, limited the maximum amount of these annual gifts to two chickens, two capons, and twelve eggs. Thirty sections jointly presented one calf as a gift. These gifts might be presented in cash,

---

[56] Eckhart, p. 221.   [57] Ibid., p. 222.   [58] CJH, I, 670 ff.

instead of in kind, excepting the calf, which had to be presented in kind in any event.

The most burdensome obligation of the serfs was the *robot*. All the serfs, the *inquilini* as well as the *subinquilini*, had to perform *robot*. The serfs, particularly handicraftsmen and merchants, might and did hire laborers to perform the *robot* in their stead. The days of *robot* depended on the quality and quantity of the soil the serf cultivated. The serf possessing a full section owed one day of *robot* weekly with draft animals or two days of *robot* (*gyalog robot*) without draft animals. A day of *robot* could also be performed through any service the serf rendered to the lord by the use of his feet, such as delivering messages or mail. The serfs possessing a half, a quarter, or an eighth of a section performed proportionately smaller amounts of *robot*. The *inquilini* rendered eighteen days of *gyalog robot* annually; the *subinquilini*, twelve days.

The day of the *robot* began at sunrise and ended at sunset. Between March and October the hours of commuting from home to the place of labor were included in the working hours of the day. In the winter months, if the time of commuting was not more than one hour, that time was not included in the working hours. The principle of *Casus nocet domino* stipulated that, if the serf had to stop his work because of bad weather or for any other cause beyond his control after he had already begun to work, he did not have to make up the lost working hours. If such stoppage occurred before noon, one half-day of *robot* was considered completed; if it occurred in the afternoon, one full day was counted as performed.[59]

In a period of one week the lord did not have the right to force the serf to perform more than two days of *gyalog robot* or one day of *robot* with draft animals. If during harvest, vintage, the collecting of hay, the cultivation of vineyards, or at any other time the lord demanded the performance of double that maximum amount, he had to leave the next week absolutely free for the serf himself. Later that regulation was changed so as to make the maximum extraordinary *robot* three days a week, only one of which might be *robot* with draft animals. Joseph II ordered that, if three days of *robot* were demanded of the serf in one week, these three days must not follow each other in an uninterrupted sequence. Among these three days one

[59] Eckhart, p. 222.

day had to be left free for the serf to enable him to take care of his own work. One quarter of the total annual *robot* obligation of the serfs had to be left for the winter season.

The lords could not demand *robot* above the maximum amount set by the urbarial regulations. If by any mistake more *robot* was performed and at the end of the year the registers revealed that mistake, the lord had to pay wages for the additional amount of work rendered to him. In no event had the lord the right to demand that the *robot* due the following year be performed during the current year. If for any reason the serf did not perform his *robot* obligation, he had to supplement it during the next year by performing the proper amount of *robot*. If the lord consciously forced the serf to render *robot* above the legal obligations, the serf might file suit against him. Whether the serf should render *robot* with or without draft animals was decided by the lord according to his needs. The serf plowed with his own plow, using either two or four oxen, according to the local habits. The local urbarial regulations prescribed the methods to be followed.[60]

The serfs owed so-called long transport duties in addition to the *robot*. Four serfs possessing one full section each, or more serfs jointly possessing lands in that amount, annually had to transport goods two days' distance in one carriage drawn by four oxen. The lord might demand the performance of that long transport whenever he wanted it, except during the main season of summer work, or when the roads were too muddy. If the span did not arrive at its destination in two days, the additional time had to be accounted for in the common *robot* duties of those who performed the long transport. All the customs or ferry dues required during the long transport had to be paid by the lord himself.[61]

THE JURISDICTION OF THE LORDS

Up to 1848, when all feudal privileges were abolished, the lord possessed extensive juridical powers over his serfs. All the serfs and

[60] Eckhart, p. 223.

[61] All the details of serf obligations and manorial jurisdiction were compiled in two early nineteenth-century works: Carolus Pfahler, *Ius Georgicum regni Hungaricae et partium eidem annexarum* (Keszthely, 1820), and Carolus Pauly, *Constitutio rei urbarialis regni Hungariae* (Vienna, 1817). Professor Ferenc Eckhart digested the contents of both these works in his book cited several times above.

inquilini, as well as the nobles cultivating serf sections (*armalis* nobles), were subjects of that jurisdiction in all matters connected with the holdings they lived on and cultivated. The manorial court (*uriszék*) had juridical authority in all legal cases originating in urbarial relations and in all clashes between the lord and peasants, or between the lord's serfs, or between the lord's serfs and individuals not under the jurisdiction of the lord. The manorial courts also had legal authority in criminal offenses in which the fine prescribed by law or by custom was at least twenty-four beatings with the stick in the case of male criminals, or twenty-four lashes in the case of female criminals, or three days' imprisonment, or, finally, more than three days of *robot.*[62]

The lord was obliged to protect the person and property of the serf. One part of his obligation was to play the role of the plaintiff in the case of one of his serfs wanting to file a civil suit against a nobleman other than his lord. In criminal and political cases, that role was played by the attorney of the lord's manorial court or by the county attorney.

The serf possessed the right to will his properties, but under two restrictions. One of these was the stipulation that the serf only possessed the full right to will properties he himself acquired. The holdings he inherited had to be inherited by his sons if he had any. If the serf died without male issue, he could only will his movables and the half of his lot he himself had acquired. The rest was inherited by the lord. The lord became the guardian of the children of the deceased serf and the properties were handled according to the will of the deceased. If there was no will, the lord either ordered the sale of the property or assigned a guardian for the property who handled it under the supervision of the lord. The lord was also obliged to ensure fair profits for the heirs from the properties they inherited.

TAXES

The nobility and the clergy (the latter at least in principle) were exempt from the payment of direct state taxes.[63] However, the government was able to introduce a kind of indirect tax hidden in the price

[62] For further details see Chapter VII, under "The Judicial Branch."
[63] Verbőczi, pp. 55–57.

of salt that was levied upon lords and peasants alike, inasmuch as salt was a commodity both serf and noble had to buy. Since the price of salt was not exposed to the interplay of supply and demand, the government could arbitrarily decide upon the price at its pleasure.

During the eighteenth century, the Habsburgs repeatedly but unsuccessfully tried to tax the soil. In the diet of 1728–29 the estates stubbornly resisted such an effort by the dynasty. The land legally was the property not of the serfs but of the privileged classes and therefore it had to remain tax-exempt: so the estates decided. Only the serfs in their person were to be taxed. The struggle ended in the full victory of the estates and the principle of *ne onus inhaereat fundo* was promulgated.[64] Maria Theresa, in her need for the help of the Hungarian estates during the desperate early years of the War of the Austrian Succession, made that principle valid for all time to come.[65] This privilege was considered by the estates the cornerstone of the constitution and one of the perpetually fundamental rights of the nobility. Joseph II vigorously challenged the concept and initiated a series of measures to tax the land of the estates, an action that was the primary cause of the feudal revolt.

The only obligation of the nobility to the state was the defense of the homeland, in the form of a *levée en masse* of the nobility (*posse comitatus,* called also *insurrectio*). The organization of the Hungarian standing army in 1715 created new government expenses to be covered by taxes. With the introduction of that system the noble levy lost its military importance; however, there was no loss at all to the national defense. In the eighteenth century, the era of well-trained, well-equipped, mobile professional armies, the noble levy was an obsolete concept. The utilization of this form of military force had become less and less frequent even before the standing army was organized. With the establishment of that army there was a serious possibility that the noble levy, the only serious contribution the noblemen rendered to the state, would not be used in the future at all. It would have been fair, therefore, if the estates, as compensation for the advantage they received, had been willing to contribute to the maintenance of the standing army.[66] They did not do so.

[64] "The land cannot and will not be taxed."
[65] Act No. 8 of 1841. Marczali, *Hungary,* p. 19.
[66] For some of the psychological aspects, the military importance, and the political "bargaining" value of the noble levy, see Wangermann, p. 53.

THE *CONTRIBUTIO*

For the maintenance of the standing army the *contributio* (war tax) was collected, the largest permanent regular tax of the land. The war tax was paid exclusively by the nonprivileged population and by the royal free towns. It increased from 2.1 million florins in 1724 to 4.4 million florins in the 1780s.[67]

The major part of the war tax was to have been paid in cash, but cash was scarce in Hungary. In 1783, for example, the Sáros County government expressed fear that the system of barter would have to be applied again. Along with several other counties, Sáros suggested unsuccessfully that the government should accept payment of taxes in kind.[68]

The diets only voted for the total of the war tax to be paid by Hungary as a whole. The amount each individual county or royal free town had to pay was determined by diet concourses headed by the Palatine. The unit of assessment was the *porta*.[69]

The *porta* was a very general unit in the assessment of taxes among the counties and royal free towns that took into account their relative tax-paying capacities. But the *porta* was not specific enough in assessing the contribution among the taxpayers of each county or free town. In order to assess the tax as fairly as possible among the taxpayers, a subunit of taxation called the *dica* was introduced. All the factors determining the actual tax-paying capacity of a subject were valued in *dicae* and then added up to determine the amount the individual had to pay.

The counties and royal free towns kept very accurate and detailed files on the tax-paying capacities of the taxpayers. The *dicalis conscriptio* registered the number of children of the taxpayers above the age of sixteen, brothers, cotters, servants, maids, animals, buildings, arable lands, meadowlands, vineyards, orchards, cabbage and

[67] Marczali, *Hungary*, p. 19; Felhő and Vörös, p. 241.

[68] Archives of the Hungarian Royal Chancellery, October 30, 1783. Quoted in Marczali, *Hungary*, p. 20.

[69] The value represented by one *porta* was changed several times. In the Middle Ages the *porta* was worth an amount of money (e.g., in 1405, thirty *dénárs*); under Matthias Corvinus it was worth a certain plot of land; in 1609 one *porta* represented twelve houses; and finally, after 1723, it was only a mathematical unit of tax assessment.

tobacco gardens, vegetable gardens and plum gardens, mills and sources of other income, such as sowing mills or taverns, furnaces, beehives, manufacturing shops, merchant shops, and incomes from communally-owned properties. The factors registered in the *dicalis conscriptio* were valued by certain codes (*clavis repartionis*) in the following way: one *dica* was equivalent to the person of the taxpayer himself, or four sons, or eight daughters, or thirty-two pigs, or forty sheep owned by the taxpayer, etc.; e.g., as a part of his total taxes, a serf with one son, four daughters, and eight pigs had to pay taxes amounting to two *dicae*.

Naturally, there were substantial differences in the estimated values of taxable items in the *dicalis* estimates of the various counties, subject to the expected value of labor. In manufacturing towns, human labor was valued higher than in exclusively rural areas. In the former, therefore, the serf's *dica* value was higher than in the latter. One serf was equivalent to one *dica* in Vas, Zala, Máramaros, and Sopron counties; one-half *dica* in Arad, Bihar, Csanád, and Győr counties; one-quarter *dica* in Fehér, Baranya, Borsod, and Heves counties; one-eighth *dica* in Esztergom, Tolna, and Trencsén counties. In areas where pastures were rich and the breeding of livestock easy and cheap, one *dica* was worth more than in poorer areas. For example, one *dica* was equivalent to eight sheep in Sáros, Szepes, and Varasd counties; sixteen sheep in Sopron and Gömör counties; fifty sheep in Bács County; sixty sheep in Csanád County; eighty sheep in Tolna County.[70]

The tax-paying capacity of all the taxpayers was added up by the royal free towns and county districts (*járások*) in summaries called *summarii*.[71] The tax-paying capacity of a county represented the total of the *summarii* of its districts. The diet concourses presided over by the Palatine took into account these *summarii* when they assessed the national total of taxes among the counties.

DOMESTIC TAXES (*CASSA DOMESTICA*)

The taxes collected to cover the county budget were called domestic taxes; they were paid by the serfs, in spite of the fact that the nobles

---

[70] Berzeviczy, pp. 174–77.   [71] Felhő and Vörös, p. 241.

were obliged by legislation enacted by Matthias Corvinus in 1486 to pay all the expenses of the county administrations. This regulation was reendorsed by Act No. 58 of 1659. The name "domestic tax" was first applied in the text of Act No. 60 of 1723. The domestic taxes covered the expenses of the county administration as well as the expenses of the delegates of the counties to the diet. They amounted to one fourth or one third of the *contributio* or war tax[72] during the first half of the eighteenth century. Then they increased so that in 1790 the domestic tax was larger than the *contributio*.

[72] Marczali, *Hungary*, p. 26.

Part II

THE GOVERNMENT AND
THE CHURCHES

Chapter VI

THE STRUCTURE OF GOVERNMENT
AND THE FOCI OF POWER

THE GOVERNMENT of royal Hungary as it existed in the late eighteenth century was a mixture of both medieval and modern institutions. The latter were the outcome of various reforms put into effect by the three most recent monarchs: Charles III (1711–40), Maria Theresa (1740–80), and Joseph II (1780–90). The most medieval institution was the judicial branch of the government; the most modern, the executive, the *Consilium regium locumtenentiale hungaricum*. Between these two extremes was a whole range of institutions, largely of medieval foundation and overlaid with a more or less modern patina.

The central governmental institutions that were to varying degrees involved in the administration of royal Hungary fell into three categories: first, the Habsburg court and the Imperial agencies with direct authority for Hungarian affairs;[1] second, the Hungarian royal govern-

---

[1] When mention is made of Vienna, or the Habsburg central authority, or those Imperial offices which had authority over Hungarian affairs, the following institutions should be borne in mind:

(1) The Habsburg court, consisting of the Habsburg family, the monarch's trusted friends, and official and unofficial advisers.

(2) The *Staatsrat*, the supreme coordinating body of the monarchy for all important political and economic matters. During and after the reign of Joseph II, the *Staatsrat* became inundated by the increasingly unimportant matters that it had to deal with. Francis I, in particular, overbureaucratized the *Staatsrat*. He divided it into four sections and established over the whole a *Konferenzrat* that gradually superseded the *Staatsrat*.

(3) The *Hof- und Staatskanzlei,* which managed the external affairs of the Empire and the affairs of the dynasty.

(4) The *Hofkriegsrat,* which was responsible for the strategic planning, training, recruiting, and equipping of the standing army, the maintenance of fortifications and defenses, and the supplying of all the armed forces. In the modern-day

ment proper; and third, the complex Habsburg military system. Only after all these came the county administrations, a peculiarly Hungarian phenomenon. The royal government and the military system, as well as the counties, will be dealt with in succeeding chapters.

At this point, however, it is necessary to consider the dual foci of political power in royal Hungary during this period. The power of the dynasty was vested in the institutions of the central government, with the exception of the diet, and, with certain qualifications, in the *Consilium regium locumtenentiale hungaricum.* The power of the lesser nobility, on the other hand, was vested in the county administrations and, above all, in the diet. The dominant center of political power, however, was Vienna, the traditional capital of the Habsburgs. In fact, the considerable power that the Habsburgs wielded over Hungary was neither entirely unconstitutional nor due only to the intentions of the dynasty. With notable skill the Habsburgs exploited the traditions of the medieval Hungarian kingdom, which had left behind it a legacy of very strong executive power vested in the crown. The Hungarian state, even as early as the Árpád dynasty,[2] had existed as a unified political entity, ruled by a strong monarch and without the type of decentralization that was associated with the feudal states of Western Europe. This tradition made it very easy for the Habsburgs to increase their power to the point of exercising virtually absolute control over several aspects of the government without violating the spirit of the Hungarian constitution, and even,

sense, its responsibilities combined those of a defense ministry with those of a general staff.

(5) The *Commerz Direktorium,* later the *Hofcommerzien Rat,* which managed the industrial and commercial affairs, and directed and supervised the economic policy, of all the Habsburg lands.

(6) The *Hofrechenkammer,* which kept detailed accounts of Habsburg financial affairs. It supervised and sought to augment the income of the dynasty. The state salt and mining monopolies and the customs bureaus were within its purview. The *Hofrechenkammer* was invariably asked to give advice on all Hungarian matters, even when other government departments were responsible for taking action on them.

(7) The *Polizeihofstelle,* which was originally set up by Leopold II. Francis I enormously extended its authority, giving to it the tasks of protecting the extant political and social system, preventing the penetration of reform ideas into the Empire, and isolating the Empire from all progressive thought. To accomplish these ends it employed censorship and a network of spies and informers. It had two agencies in Hungary, one in Buda, and one in Pozsony.

See Eckhart, pp. 235–40.

[2] The Árpáds ruled as dukes of Hungary from 892 to 1000 and as kings from 1001 to 1301.

in some instances, without transgressing the letter of the law. Not a voice was raised from the estates against the fact that the Habsburgs had sole responsibility in all matters of diplomacy, defense (including the declaration of war and conclusion of peace), tariffs, and the administration of the *regaliae*. All these the medieval kings of Hungary had considered their own personal sphere of authority; the Habsburgs followed their predecessors' practices.

With the development of a modern system of government—an evolution that began during the reign of Charles III—came a series of laws that greatly extended the king's executive power. The diet of 1715 established the crown's absolute authority over public education, thus giving it influence over the intellectual life of the country. In 1741 legislative approval was given to laws that allowed the crown to grant tax exemptions to trading enterprises, to free exports and imports from customs duties, to issue and revoke licenses to set up in trade and to collect highway tolls, and to grant and repeal the permits of the guilds. These regulations made all the burghers dependent on the royal pleasure. Needless to say, the dynasty jealously guarded its privileges under the *Tripartitum* to raise anyone it wished to the nobility; this put the nobles, too, at the monarch's disposition. And by the same token, the throne's prerogative to name archbishops and bishops gave it considerable sway over the Roman Catholic Church.

Act No. 7 of 1715 confirmed and broadened the scope of the king's position as supreme judge of the kingdom. In any case of *lèse-majesté* involving a noble, the king himself was the judge of the first instance.[3] The crown also exercised considerable power over the whole judicial system of Hungary. The interpretation of all laws in force was a royal privilege, another legacy from the Árpád dynasty. The king appointed all the judges of both chambers of the Supreme Court. In short, then, the Habsburgs had in practice complete authority over the Hungarian judiciary.

The *dicasterii* of the executive branch were answerable to the crown alone. The Habsburgs' influence also extended to the very bases of the nobles' influence, the counties, since it was the monarch who appointed the *főispánok* (high sheriffs of the counties). The throne thus had substantial authority over the actual administration of the counties, though more in theory than in fact.

[3] CJH, IV, 439.

Over and above all its other powers, the crown had the exclusive right to initiate all legislation. In addition to this fundamental authority, it was the king's prerogative to summon and prorogue the diet and to promulgate all laws.

The Habsburgs' extensive power over Hungary should not be regarded as a purely negative force that was of no benefit to the Hungarian nation. Hungary's interests were well served by Charles III, Maria Theresa, and Joseph II. It was under them that the foundations of a modern system of government were laid, that the system of education was extended and improved, and that enlightened steps were taken to improve public health and welfare by, for instance, regulating the care of orphans, the building of hospitals, and the burial of the dead according to the highest standards of contemporary hygiene. But the Habsburgs' greatest contribution to the progress of Hungarian society during the eighteenth century was the increasing protection afforded to the serfs against the nobles and prelates.

The least beneficial aspect of the rule of these three monarchs was the steady erosion of the independent status of Hungary. And the worst effect of this was Hungary's relegation to a semicolonial position, where it served as a supplier of raw materials and foodstuffs and as a ready market for the manufactured goods produced by the industries of Austria and Bohemia, which had been developed as a result of the dynasty's policy of mercantile protection.

Vienna's role in relation to Pozsony,[4] the other major seat of power in Hungary, and to the county administrations was, however, largely complementary. The greatest merit of the Hungarian nobility at this period was its persevering resistance to Vienna's gradual absorption of Hungary into the Habsburg realm as just another province. This conscientious opposition culminated in the feudal revolt of 1790, which led to the reendorsement of Hungary's position as a separate kingdom. Nevertheless, the Hungarian nobility was far from being solely a force for the good. Its opposition to Habsburg encroachment on Hungary's rights under the constitution was in fact little more than a side effect of its opposition to the abolition of obsolete feudal practices, particularly to the reforms protecting the serfs. In other

[4] The executive branch of the Hungarian government was located in Pozsony up to 1785, when Joseph II transferred it to Buda, the ancient capital of Hungary. The sessions of the diet, with a few exceptions, were called in Pozsony until 1848.

words, it was the result of an act of self-interest, an effort to safeguard the economic privileges of a single social group. The nobility's resistance to the progressive stabilization of the organs of a semimodern government was also typical of its reactionary attitudes. This practically continuous struggle between the two main sources of power in Hungary took place in the various organs of government that are described and analyzed below. The competition between these two forces was brought to a head by the feudal revolt.

The political essence of the feudal revolt was an effort by the lesser nobility, or, more precisely, the *bene possessionati*, to control the power of the state and to restrict royal power. The *bene possessionati* launched this effort from home ground, their secure base in the counties, and worked through the diet to wrest control of all the other organs of state. All the government institutions, therefore, played to some degree significant parts in the feudal revolt. Suffice it to say here that, had the lesser nobility succeeded in its aims, these institutions of government would have become far more "medievalized." But it failed and the institutions of government in royal Hungary were stabilized as they had been in 1780.

Chapter VII

INSTITUTIONS OF
THE CENTRAL GOVERNMENT
OF ROYAL HUNGARY

THE LEGISLATIVE BRANCH: THE DIET

The estates and the king together composed the diet (*országgyűlés*), the legislature of the Kingdom of Hungary. In that legislative dualism the Habsburg kings weighed more heavily than did the estates.[1] The body politic of the nation was represented in the diet by the *Karok és Rendek* (*status et ordines*), which consisted of the four estates defined by Act No. 1 of 1608:[2] the prelates; the *világi főrendek* (lay lords), commonly called aristocrats; the nobles (lesser nobility); and the citizens of the royal free towns.

The diet was divided into an Upper Chamber and a Lower Chamber, although it was considered as one body in relation to the king. In the Upper Chamber were seated the aristocrats and the diocesan bishops; in the Lower Chamber, all the other Roman Catholic prelates, the full *Judicum septemvirale*,[3] the delegates from the counties, the representatives of the royal free towns, and the deputies of the absentee aristocrats.

The king possessed the exclusive prerogative of convoking the diet —a privilege hotly contested by the feudal revolt of 1790. The invitations to the diet (*literae regales*) were issued in the king's behalf

---

[1] Legislative initiative was reserved to the king. Eckhart, p. 256.
[2] CJH, III, 25.
[3] For details, see below on the judicial branch of the Hungarian government.

by the Hungarian Court Chancellery.[4] The *literae regales* had to be issued six weeks in advance of the opening of the diet and had to include the main reason for the convocation, such as a coronation or the election of a Palatine, as well as the draft legislation handed down by the court.

Delegates were appointed by the county assemblies or the town councils, as the case might be; these bodies gave the delegates their credentials (*creditiva*) and their instructions (*instructio*), to which they had strictly to adhere. They were not, therefore, representatives in the modern sense but deputies (*ablegati*). If any question came up on which the *ablegatus* had not received instruction, he had to seek it from the assembly or council. If he did not follow his instructions, he was liable to have his credentials revoked and be replaced by a new *ablegatus*.

The sessions of both chambers were open to the public; secret sessions were seldom called. The galleries were open to anyone in "decent dress." The delegates to both chambers had to wear Hungarian costumes, military uniforms, or clerical garb.

Both chambers were presided over not by elected officials but by high officers of state. The President of the Upper Chamber was the Palatine or, in his absence, the *Országbíró* (Lord Chief Justice). In the absence of both, the *Tárnokmester* (Lord High Treasurer) presided. The Lower Chamber was presided over by the *Személynök* (*Personalis* or Chief Justice) or, in his absence, the Vice-Palatine or the *Al-Országbíró* (Deputy Lord Chief Justice).

The king's power to override the diet in legislative matters was due mostly to the fact that all legislative initiative had to come from him. Strictly speaking, the Hungarian Court Chancellery was responsible for drawing up royal draft bills, but all the court institutions, such as the *Hofkriegsrat* and the *Hofrechenkammer,* could propose legislation. If such proposals were approved by the king, the Hungarian Court Chancellery had to include them in the *literae regales*. Individual members of the diet and either chamber as a whole had the right to present requests (*postulata*) and grievances (*gravamina*), but could not draft legislation. The king's representatives, however, usually discussed the drafts of bills with the diet committees.

[4] See below on the executive branch of the Hungarian government.

The diet's work on proposed legislation began with a first reading of the draft bills at a joint session of both chambers (*sessio mixta*). The *sessio mixta* decided whether the royal drafts or the *gravamina* should be the first items on the agenda of the separate chambers. After the first reading, royal drafts were debated separately but simultaneously in both chambers.

Discussion of the *gravamina* was an important part of the work of the diet. Endless complaints were submitted, particularly against the behavior of foreign units of the standing army stationed in Hungary. The instructions of county delegates also included many grievances by individual nobles (*gravamina particularia*). The *sessio mixta* had to single out the most important grievances (*gravamina praeferentialia*) and only these were put on the agenda of both the chambers.

After the *sessio mixta* had determined the chambers' agenda, the serious work of the diet began. From the middle of the eighteenth century a strange dualism came into being in the procedure of the Lower Chamber. It grew out of the recognition that, because all the presiding officers of both chambers were appointed by, and dependent on, the crown, the king might use them to impose his will on the diet. To avoid this possibility, the Lower Chamber introduced a system of unofficial meetings of the county delegates. Today they would be called large caucuses. Later, the county delegates were joined at these unofficial meetings by the Roman Catholic prelates who sat in the Lower Chamber. The meetings were chaired not by the high officers of state but by the county delegates, one by one in alphabetical order. Here, freely and without interference from government officials and the king's confidants, the delegates discussed all the problems facing the diet. These unofficial meetings were called district (*kerület*) meetings (*sessiones circulares*). They were given this name because before 1790 they were organized in four groups representing the four districts into which Hungary was divided (Cis-Danube, Trans-Danube, Cis-Tisza, and Trans-Tisza).[5] In 1790 the meetings of the four groups were combined into one.[6]

The *sessiones circulares* decided what action to take on the legislative proposals before the diet. These decisions were binding on all the county delegates, who held an absolute majority in the Lower Chamber. Thus, it was the *sessiones circulares* that made the decisions

[5] See Map No. 2.   [6] Eckhart, pp. 263–64.

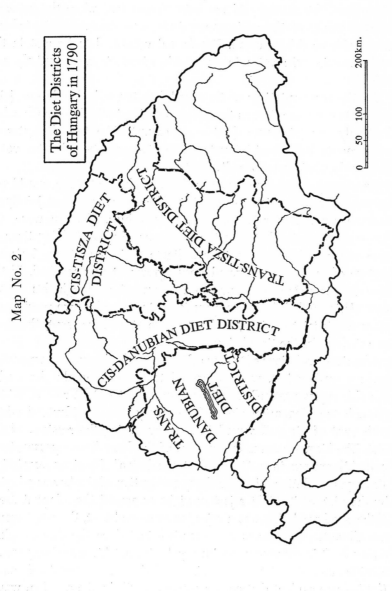

Map No. 2

The Diet Districts
of Hungary in 1790

CIS-TISZA DIET DISTRICT

TRANS-TISZA DIET DISTRICT

CIS-DANUBIAN DIET DISTRICT

TRANS-DANUBIAN DIET DISTRICT

0   50   100   200 km.

on all the legislative business before the Lower Chamber. The regular official sessions of the Lower Chamber (*sessiones regnicolares*) became pure formalities. This dual procedure of the Lower Chamber slowed down its work considerably compared with that of the Upper Chamber, where this feature did not exist. Sometimes, when the pressure of work was great, the *sessiones regnicolares* became very brief indeed, often with no debate at all. But formal votes had to be cast in the *sessio regnicolaris;* votes in the *sessio circularis* were entirely unofficial.

All the representatives of the royal free towns had only one joint vote between them, just as the prelates sitting in the Lower Chamber had only one joint vote (*votum curiatum*). The two delegates of each county had one joint vote. If the two county delegates voted differently, their vote was discounted.

As already noted, the two chambers of the diet were considered as one body in relation to the king. They were supposed jointly to endorse, amend, or reject the royal draft bills. If there were differences of opinion between the chambers, they sent delegations to each other with messages to coordinate their resolutions. This exchange of messages continued until agreement was reached. If the two chambers could not come to a compromise through this means, the Palatine called them into a *sessio mixta* under his own presidency. If even this joint session could not arrive at an agreement, the draft was shelved for the time being.

Identical resolutions of the two chambers, whether passed separately or at a *sessio mixta,* were presented to the king in the form of a "humble representation" (*humillima repraesentatio*). It was submitted through the Hungarian Court Chancellery, the president of which with most of his staff stayed in Pozsony during the sessions of the diet. The king, whatever the content of the *humillima repraesentatio,* gave his answer in a "benevolent resolution" (*benigna resolutio*). The royal resolution might be the promulgation of the law as adopted by the diet, or it might reject outright or amend the adopted draft. If the royal resolution was a rejection or amendment, the court would use all sorts of pressures and promises to induce the diet to adopt a new draft in concurrence with royal wishes. This bargaining would continue until the diet and the king settled on a compromise formula. If it became evident that no agreement was likely, the problem would be pigeonholed. When king and diet came to a full agreement, the king would promulgate the draft as a law, which became part of the unwritten Hungarian constitution and the *Corpus Juris*.[7]

A peculiar Hungarian tradition was the presence at the diet of the *Országgyűlési Ifjúság* (youth of the diet).[8] They were young aristocrats and *bene possessionati,* generally students, junior lawyers, and secretaries, who escorted the representatives. What was common to them all was their youth and conspicuously high level of education. Their expenses were paid by the counties in return for a number of services, such as attending to the delegates' correspondence, writing the minutes of caucuses, and delivering messages. The students and junior officials of government and legal offices in Poszony consorted with these county youth. Between them, they usually represented the most progressive ideas in the capital and helped both to formulate public opinion and to influence the climate of the legislature. They always crowded the galleries of the diet where they would freely express their approval or disapproval of its activities by cheering and booing.

THE JUDICIAL BRANCH

Royal Hungary was totally without any unified, general system of law that was effective for all of society. Particularism led to a wide variety of practices in different parts of the kingdom. A separate, peculiar code was in force in the kingdom proper that was quite distinct from the practices of Croatia and Slavonia. And within the kingdom itself there were different juridical methods practiced in the royal free cities, the Jász and Kun districts, the cities of the Zips, and the Hajdu towns.[9] In Transylvania there were yet three other separate judiciaries corresponding to the Hungarian counties of Transylvania, the Székely areas, and the Saxon areas. In short, the judicial branch of government was less modern and contained more substantial remnants of the Middle Ages than any other sphere.

"The ruling classes had codified the rights of the peasants in such a manner that they had no rights but to be subordinate. No peasant

[7] *Ibid.,* p. 267.
[8] The first time the youth of the diet became a political force to be reckoned with was during the diets of King Charles III. Hóman and Szekfü, V, 23. See also Marczali, *Hungary,* p. 339, n. 2.
[9] Grünwald, p. 389.

sat in judgment on his peers; their landlords were their judges." [10]
And the landlords were bound by no strict codes of precedent or
regulatory statutes, at least in practice.

As late as 1790, ownership of land automatically included the right
of jurisdiction. If a man acquired land with the right of *jus gladii*[11]
he at once acquired the power of life and death over the serfs.
Jurisdiction was still entirely the lords' private affair, not a state prerogative. Under this feudal system, the lord was always the judge,
even in cases where the serf was the plaintiff and he himself the
defendant. The lords' manorial courts (*uriszékek*) committed horrifying abuses. György Bessenyei, himself the son of a family possessing
the *jus gladii*, wrote the most devastating contemporary indictment of
the system: "The country again [after the death of Emperor Joseph II]
permits every nobleman in the land to hold a manorial court, where,
although no one may be condemned to death, he [the serf] may be
sentenced to corporal punishment, fines, or forfeiture of his property."
Bessenyei complained that, if a case was appealed to the county
court, the witnesses were either bribed or threatened so that the
lord always won the suit. A peasant, even when he was innocent,
might die in prison before his case was settled. "A few gentlemen
sitting in the county courts are brought to the verge of tears in their
bitter frustration at their inability to free an innocent man from
this arbitrariness." Bessenyei bemoaned the fact that "enacted injustices help only those who are cruel." [12]

The most harassing cases were those involving serfs in criminal
suits. The lowest courts to hear serfs' criminal cases were these same
manorial courts where the lord possessed the right of *jus gladii*. If
he did not have this authority, the court of the first instance was the
county court. Investigation of the case, however, was in the hands

[10] *Ibid.*, p. 390.
[11] *Jus gladii* was the right of the lord to exercise absolute jurisdiction, including
the power of life and death, over the inhabitants of his lands. Lords who enjoyed
the *jus gladii* were responsible only to the king. This privilege was first awarded
to Hungarian lords in the fourteenth century. Hóman and Szekfü, II, 131. The
jus gladii remained in operation until 1848. At the time of its abolition, it was
possessed by 304 individuals and 167 corporations. Grünwald, p. 395.
[12] Béla Grünwald discovered an unpublished manuscript by Bessenyei in the
Hungarian National Museum, MS 596, "Magyarországnak törvényes állása" [The
Legal Status of Hungary], written in 1804. Bessenyei's comments on the Hungarian judicial system are taken from this manuscript as quoted in Grünwald,
pp. 392–94.

of county officials who were subject to little or no legal checks or procedural regulation.[13] The use of torture was still widespread. The sentence of the county court was final and unappealable. All this, of course, put formidable power in the hands of the nobility and set the value of the serf's life at nil. The serfs' legal nonentity was a real reflection of medievalism.

The levels of jurisdiction in Hungary, starting with the highest authority, were the following:

a) The king, and in his behalf the Hungarian Court Chancellery and the *Consilium regium locumtentiale hungaricum;*

b) The *Curia regis* (a bicameral supreme court comprising the *Judicum septemvirale* [*Hétszemélyes Tábla*] and the *Tabula regia* [*Királyi Tábla*]);

c) The district courts of appeal (*kerületi bíróságok*);

d) The county courts (*megye bíróságok* or *sedriae*); and

e) The manorial courts (*uriszékek*).

The diet of 1723 introduced the system of permanent, full-time district courts of appeal and a supreme court to replace the previous system of traveling assizes.[14]

The *Judicum septemvirale* (Judiciary of Seven) had existed since 1694 and was exclusively an appeal court of last resort. It was presided over by the Palatine. Its members were the *Országbíró* (Lord Chief Justice), who presided in the absence of the Palatine; two Roman Catholic archbishops; three Roman Catholic titular bishops; six lords; and nine members of the *bene possessionati*.[15] They were chosen so that all regions of the country were represented in the court.

The *Tabula regia* (King's bench) was both the court of the nobility and the criminal court of appeal. To it were referred all cases involving the nobility that dealt with grants and ownership of land, treason, and criminal charges. For these it was a court of the first instance; but to it also were appealed criminal cases in general from the district

---

[13] That was one of the injustices the peasants protested against in 1790. See the fifth point of the Szabolcs Project, p. 223 below.

[14] Acts Nos. 24–26 of 1723. CJH, IV, 587–89.

[15] Eckhart, pp. 314–15. The two archbishops were the Primate of Hungary and the Archbishop of Kalocsa. Grünwald, p. 405. See also Marczali, *Hungary*, p. 339, n. 1. The court was founded with seven justices. Although the membership was gradually trebled, the original name referring to seven members was retained.

courts of appeal. The *Tabula regia* was presided over by the *Personalis* (*Személynök*), who had to be a member of the *bene possessionati* and who was ex officio president of the Lower Chamber of the diet,[16] in which the whole *Tabula regia* sat as a body. In addition to the *Personalis,* the members of the *Tabula regia* were two Roman Catholic prelates, two aristocrats, the Vice-Palatine, the *Al-Országbíró* (Deputy Lord Chief Justice), four professional judges, one royal attorney, four royal jurors, two jurors appointed by the Primate, and four lay jurors.[17]

Four district courts of appeal were set up by the diet of 1723 in Nagyszombat, Kőszeg, Eperjes, and Debrecen. They were in addition to the already existing court of appeal of the banus of Croatia.[18] The district courts were courts of the first instance for cases involving debt in excess of 100 florins, inheritance, and the rights of widows. They consisted of a president and five or six jurors plus reserve jurors.[19]

The county courts (*Sedria*) were courts of the first instance for all criminal cases against commoners except treason. They were also the first and last courts of appeal for the serfs' civil suits.

The manorial courts were the lowest courts. Many of them enjoyed the *jus gladii,* which gave them the right to decide the life or death of serfs without reference to any higher juridical authority and without possibility of appeal.

On March 30, 1778, the Hungarian Court Chancellery decreed that certain kinds of capital sentences could be appealed to the sovereign. "Such appeals were somewhat limited, being confined to those cases where the original courts had scruples or doubts as to the wisdom of the sentence passed." [20]

THE EXECUTIVE BRANCH

Under the medieval dualistic form of government, the crown and the estates were separate powers, coexistent rather than integrated. They had to bargain and haggle constantly like two business rivals. At the turn of the seventeenth century, a new, more modern system of government gradually evolved in Hungary and fused with the feudal

---

[16] Act No. 5 of 1764. CJH, V, 107.   [17] Eckhart, p. 317.
[18] The court of appeal of the banus possessed the same jurisdiction as the district courts of appeal.
[19] Eckhart, p. 318.   [20] Marczali, *Hungary,* p. 343.

elements of government. The new organs of government were based on the *dicasterium* system. Each *dicasterium* was responsible to the king for a specific field of administration assigned exclusively to it. As feudal dualism gave way to royal absolutism, so too did the medieval system whereby the separate spheres of administration were the semiprivate provinces of individual aristocrats run by their own retainers. The new trend was tantamount to a nationalization of state administration.

The *dicasterii* were organized into *collegia* whose members were counselors of mutually equal standing. Theirs was the task of discussing and jointly deciding everyday policy; the major decisions, however, were reserved to the king.[21] The *dicasterii*, which took their permanent shape during the reign of Charles III,[22] gave employment to the whole gamut of able society: aristocrats, lesser nobles, burghers, and specialized experts. The most important *dicasterii* were the Hungarian Court Chancellery; the *Consilium regium locumtenentiale hungaricum;* and the *Camera hungarica.*

The Hungarian Court Chancellery (*Magyar Királyi Udvari Kancellária*) was the successor of the chancelleries of the medieval Hungarian kings and had been known by this name since 1690. Like the Bohemian and Austrian chancelleries, it was an exclusive Habsburg court organ. The royal order defining its authority was issued in 1690 and remained in force until 1848, when the Chancellery was superseded by the first responsible ministry for Hungary.

The Hungarian Court Chancellery was the channel of direct communication between the person of the sovereign and the country. It issued all letters patent dealing with privileges and pardons that were the king's exclusive prerogative to grant and it dispatched all rescripts giving public authorities instructions on political or juridical matters. It was at all times in direct attendance upon the monarch and had its office located in Vienna except during sessions of the diet, when it was moved to Pozsony. The king ruled Hungary directly through the Chancellery and only indirectly through all other institutions of government. It was presided over by the chancellor, who in 1790 was Count Károly Pálffy. Of the councilors attached to the Chancellery, three were aristocrats; the rest—eleven in 1780—were drawn from the lesser nobility.

[21] Eckhart, p. 233.   [22] Marczali, *Hungary,* p. 328.

The official orders outlined the Chancellery's duties as "to thwart any attempt to impair the royal power and dignity, and rather to provide for the safeguarding of all the rights, privileges, prerogatives and exclusive power of the King, to execute the royal commands and to maintain the laws and the whole system of the country." [23] The Chancellery was to come into full session whenever it had to deal with matters affecting the royal dignity. All proposals drafted by the Chancellery had to be presented for the highest arbitration and supreme disposition of the emperor-king. In short, ultimate decisions were always left to the discretion of the sovereign.

At the same time, it was the constant duty of the Chancellery to explain the legal aspects of every royal rescript, to state whenever a royal command was at variance with existing law, to cite the articles that were infringed, and to delineate the untoward consequences that might ensue from such infringement. Hence the Chancellery was not merely a "dispatch office" but also a council of high importance. The Chancellery, in sum, was a kind of ministry not responsible to the legislative. It was in constant communication with such imperial institutions as, in particular, the *Kriegsrat*, the *Staatsrat*, the *Hof- und Staatskanzlei*, the chancelleries of Bohemia and Austria, and the *Hofrechenkammer*.

The Hungarian Court Chancellery also functioned in some respects as the Supreme Court of Appeal. It did not simply submit to the king the reports and judgments of the *Consilium locumtenentiale* or the *Curia regis* on current judicial affairs or the settlement of complaints. It analyzed such reports and judgments fully and freely and forwarded them with its own opinion for the sovereign's final decision. If the issue in question was relevant to the affairs of the imperial institutions, the Chancellery did not merely advise the appropriate institution but also "held deliberation with it in common council." [24]

Despite the wide scope of its responsibilities, however, "the influence of the Chancellery on the destinies of the nation depended not so much on its own procedure as on the decision of the sovereign to rule according to the accepted system or to go his own way. . . . The social importance of the Chancellery officials formed a glaring

[23] *Ibid.*, p. 330.   [24] *Ibid.*, p. 331.

contrast to the minimum of actual power which they enjoyed." [25]

The responsibilities of the Hungarian Court Chancellery also extended to the following:

a) It represented the Kingdom of Hungary and the subjects of the Holy Crown in relations with the Habsburg hereditary provinces. In these matters it corresponded with the Habsburg central court organs and the Bohemian and Austrian court chancelleries.

b) It administered matters requiring action stemming from the king's royal authority. These included royal mercy, appointments to ecclesiastical and lay dignities, granting titles and patents of nobility, adoptions, matters of the *indigenae,* and safe conduct.

c) It administered all those political, financial, and military matters which were royal prerogatives supposed to be dealt with by the king in person.

d) As the highest public notary office, the Chancellery was authorized to notarize contracts, wills, and legal documents.

e) Finally, the Chancellery handled the *libri regii,* the records of royal pardons. [26]

The *Consilium regium locumtenentiale hungaricum* (*Helytartótanács,* Hungarian Viceregal Council) was set up by Acts Nos. 97–122 of the 1723 diet. [27] It was presided over by the Palatine [28] and was to consist of twenty-two councilors appointed by the king from among

---

[25] *Ibid.,* p. 332.   [26] Eckhart, p. 234.   [27] CJH, IV, 643–51.

[28] A blind eye had already been turned as early as 1732 to the provision that the Palatine preside over the *Consilium.* On the death of Palatine Miklós Pálffy, the office remained vacant; instead the king appointed Prince Francis of Lorraine as Governor General of Hungary. In 1740 János Pálffy was elected Palatine, but in 1765 another Governor General was appointed, this time Prince Albrecht of Saxony, son-in-law of Maria Theresa. Between 1780 and 1783 there was neither a Palatine nor a Governor General, and the *Consilium* had to do without a permanent president. From 1783 to 1787 the *Consilium* was presided over by the *Tárnokmester,* Kristóf Niczky; and from 1787 to 1790, by Károly Zichy, the *Országbiró,* who by virtue of his office was the Palatine's lieutenant and had to sit in for him whenever he was absent from the *Consilium.* In 1790 Archduke Alexander Leopold was elected Palatine and became automatically president of the *Consilium.* After his death in 1795, his successor as Palatine and *Consilium* president was his brother, Archduke Joseph. The *Consilium* was abolished in 1848 when a ministry responsible to the Parliament was set up. Felhő and Vörös, pp. 10–15.

the prelates, aristocrats, and *bene possessionati* throughout the king-dom.[29]

The prelates, however, were generally too busy with their ecclesiastical duties and economic activities and the aristocrats with their estates to afford time to sit in the *Consilium* even though certain permanent, full-time responsibilities were theirs on paper. On the other hand, the members of the *Consilium* drawn from the lesser nobility were mostly poor and landless. From the beginning of the eighteenth century the best educated of them sought permanent employment in the organs of the state. Indeed, some of the lesser nobility had been newly created by the Habsburg monarchs in recognition of their services within the framework of the Imperial administration. The number of such professional government officials rose steadily throughout the eighteenth century just as the number of old aristocrats sitting in the *Consilium* dwindled until by 1790 it had become negligible. The old aristocracy was gradually replaced by a new aristocracy of soldiers and bureaucrats.

This new social stratum was an ideal medium for Imperial or royal service. Its members were not wealthy enough to be independent and as a consequence proved themselves the most loyal civil servants and military leaders of the Habsburgs. In the reign of Emperor Joseph II there were only nine counts and one bishop in the *Consilium,* and even they were members of the new aristocracy.[30] Act No. 101 of 1723 proclaimed that the *Consilium* was not to be subordinate to any court bureau, but that it was responsible to the king alone and should present its reports directly to him. The king was to hand down to the *Consilium* his resolutions in order of importance and in the form of rescripts or decrees.[31] Whenever the *Consilium locumtenentiale* had to communicate with neighboring provinces or states, it had to do so through the king, never directly. The law stipulated that the *Consilium* could take no decisions contrary to the

---

[29] At its foundation the *Consilium* had 22 members: 4 Roman Catholic prelates, 10 aristocrats, and 8 lesser nobles. One of the councilmen was always a Croat. The staff of the *Consilium,* which in 1784 numbered 118 officials, had grown to 268 by the year of its dissolution, 1848. Eckhart, p. 250.

[30] Felhő and Vörös, pp. 18–19.

[31] The difference between the rescript and the decree was that the former was an ordinance issued on the basis of, and in explanation of, existing law, whereas the latter was merely a writ ordering the implementation of some specific measure. Marczali, *Hungary,* p. 334, n. 1.

law of the land and had to execute the resolutions of the diet. Decisions of the *Consilium* were to be arrived at by majority vote and were unalterable.

In principle, then, the *Consilium locumtenentiale* was the executive branch of government in royal Hungary, but in practice this was not so. The Hungarian Court Chancellery dealt with all matters of substance, and since it did all the drafting of royal rescripts and decrees, it was much more of a forum for major decisions than was the *Consilium.* Any problems affecting Habsburg lands—and this term could be applied arbitrarily to any problem—could be discussed and decided by any of the court organs, and in fact were. Consequently, a great many decisions on Hungarian matters were made by the emperor's non-Hungarian advisers. The Hungarian Court Chancellery often simply communicated to the *Consilium locumtenentiale* decisions that had been reached and passed on to it by other organs. Seen in perspective, the degree to which the *Consilium locumtenentiale* could be said to govern Hungary was very limited indeed.

The *Consilium* was located in Pozsony until 1785, when Emperor Joseph II transferred it to Buda. It then continued to function in the royal capital until it was absorbed into the first ministry for Hungary.[32]

The *Consilium* was reorganized several times; the first fundamental overhaul took place in the mid-eighteenth century. At that time the increasing scope of state administration made it necessary to broaden the activities of the *Consilium.* The collective leadership of the *collegium* system was replaced by the idea of individual responsibility. Permanent committees each charged with a specific sphere of activity were set up within the framework of the *Consilium.* This specialization of endeavor enhanced the quality of the over-all work of the *Consilium.* In the mid-eighteenth century ten such permanent committees were in existence. Joseph II further reorganized these committees into departments with full-time staffs and fixed, specific areas of responsibility,[33] and increased the number of them. From his reign until 1848, the *Consilium* included the following departments: ecclesiastical foundations; ecclesiastical economy; Protestant religious affairs; Orthodox and Greek Catholic religious affairs; Jew-

[32] Eckhart, p. 250.   [33] *Ibid.*

ish affairs; public education; orphanhood; pawnbroking; health; affairs of the nobility; censorship; commerce and communications; royal free towns; county affairs; police; general administration; Jász-Kun affairs; gypsies; war taxes; and military supply. In principle, all matters of state except justice were handled by the *Consilium*.

The detailed instructions defining the authority of the *Consilium locumtenentiale* were contained in a royal rescript issued on January 20, 1724. It ordered the *Consilium* to watch over general conditions in the country, to deal with all matters that promoted the interest of the monarch and the commonweal, to preserve the rights of private persons, and to handle matters of taxation. The *Consilium* also had to supervise the enforcement in the counties and the royal free towns of all resolutions of the diet and royal rescripts. If the counties were laggard or uncooperative, it had to present the king with proposals to remedy the situation.[34]

The *Consilium* was to oversee the *főispánok*, whether they dwelt in the counties for which they were responsible or were absent, and ensure that they performed their duties properly and summoned the county assemblies in due fashion for the reelection of officials or the execution of justice. It was the responsibility of the *Consilium* to prevent county officials from oppressing the people or exploiting their labor for the officials' own ends in the guise of public works. It had to make sure that the people were levied for no more than their legal share of taxes.

The *Consilium* was to encourage private enterprise and the establishment of manufacturing settlements in underpopulated areas. If necessary, it was to invite manufacturers and merchants to move permanently into sparsely inhabited regions. It was responsible for the regulation of industry and commerce in order to protect consumers from inferior merchandise and put a stop to the sale of substandard wine. It was answerable for the upkeep of roads, bridges, and dams; the development of waterways; fire prevention; and the securing of education for children of "good family." The *Consilium* had to enforce all royal orders affecting religion, including the provisions of Act. No. 55 of 1723 which ordered the Roman Catholic prelates to dwell in their own sees. It was barred from interfering with

[34] Felhő and Vörös, p. 19.

the administration of justice but had to report to the sovereign all judicial malversation.

In the early years of its existence, the *Consilium* had tried to extend its authority yet further. For instance, it made a bid to regulate all orders emanating from the Court Chancellery, the *Kriegsrat*, and the *Camera hungarica* before they were issued to the counties and the royal free towns. This attempt, however, was nipped in the bud by the king. The *Consilium* had to be content to remain a purely executive organ under tight control from the throne.

Yet the power of the *Consilium locumtenentiale* did continue to grow in time with the rise of enlightened despotism. Its jurisdiction spread into more and more areas that under the feudal system had been outside the state's sphere of authority. Although no diet gave its endorsement, enlightened despotism came to control ever wider fields of human activity. The estates felt this most sharply in matters of serf-lord relations. They deeply resented the state's interposition in them, considering such relations to be their own exclusive concern, and railed against what they deemed to be unwarranted and unconstitutional royal interference in their affairs.[35]

Enlightened despotism extended its control into such areas as re-afforestation, pauperism, medical care for pregnant women, health regulations, and burial of the dead. These new areas of interest added to the scope of the *Consilium*'s activities.[36] A sensible increase in its power began in the 1750s and reached its peak during the reign of Joseph II.

In its nature the *Consilium* was a transition from a feudal institution to a wholly royal one. It never became a tool as fully obedient to the will of the Habsburgs as similar organs in their hereditary provinces. Whenever the prerogatives and privileges of the estates were fundamentally threatened, the *Consilium* and the Court Chancellery protested to the court. The counties, though, always distrusted the *Consilium* as an antifeudal, pro-Habsburg organ. This feeling was due, in particular, to the fact that in the 1780s the *Consilium* was dominated

[35] *Ibid.*, p. 22.

[36] During the forty-year reign of Maria Theresa, 2,340 royal decrees, patents, etc., were issued, indicating the existence already of a well-developed central bureaucracy. Its growth is clear from the fact that during the forty-three years that Francis reigned, 5,000 such royal orders were issued. Grünwald, p. 416.

by enlightened men who faithfully carried out royal instructions to protect taxpayers from the nobles. This led to a number of confrontations between the *Consilium* and the counties and individual lords and prelates. The *Consilium* toiled indefatigably to put county administration—especially tax collection—in order. This, too, met with opposition from the estates. The Protestants, for their part, looked upon the *Consilium* as a tool of Roman Catholic Vienna, especially as it strictly enforced royal regulations restricting them. Many such regulations were promulgated in the 1730s. And the form of the loyalty oath, with its specific reference to the Virgin Mary, precluded all Protestants from serving on the *Consilium* until the Patent of Toleration was issued by Joseph II. Thereafter Protestant complaints against the *Consilium* practically came to an end.

The *Consilium* was primarily a royal institution but, "as far as the regulations governing its authority permitted, it demonstrated its feudal concepts again and again by its sporadic opposition to the wishes of the king." [37] Contemporary circumstances determined how far the *Consilium* could go at any one time in expressing its feudal convictions and opposing the royal will. When Emperor Joseph II ascended the throne, he realized that the views of the individual members of the *Consilium* were so contrary to his own that the members would be incapable of implementing his orders. He therefore appointed one of his close friends and sympathizers, Count Kristóf Niczky, to preside over the *Consilium* and turn it into a bureau that would faithfully execute his reforms. Niczky was given full powers to choose his own aides; the only condition was that they had to be drawn from different regions of Hungary and had to include Protestants. This radically altered the composition of the *Consilium locumtenentiale*. Believers in the principle of enlightened despotism filled the ranks of the *Consilium* and loyally put into effect the Emperor's reforms. Even then a few voices of dissent were raised, although the reasons for them are unclear.

After Joseph II's death the feudalists gained ground again in the *Consilium*, where several members, some overtly, some covertly, supported the emergent feudal revolt. A few of them even involved themselves in republican movements. From 1795 onwards the *Con-*

---

[37] Ember, p. 8.

silium reverted to being a compliant Habsburg instrument, and remained so until its dissolution in 1848.[38]

The *Camera hungarica* (*Magyar kamara,* Hungarian Chamber) was founded by Ferdinand I in 1528. Situated at first in Buda, it was transferred to Pozsony after the fall of the former in 1541. The Chamber was the only permanent, full-time Hungarian government organ during the reigns of the first Habsburg kings of Hungary. For this reason, the first Habsburgs used it not only to administer Hungary's finances, which was its original purpose, but also to deal with political, military, and other affairs. The initial responsibility of the Chamber was the management of the *regaliae,* those royal revenues which, according to medieval Hungarian tradition, were considered direct income of the crown and were not under the supervision of the diet. These revenues consisted of the earnings from mining, the proceeds from the salt monopoly, the profits from minting coins, tariff receipts, and the returns from the landed properties of the crown.

In addition to the *regaliae,* the Hungarian Chamber in the sixteenth century also supervised the collection of the taxes voted by the diets; this responsibility was later taken over by the counties. The Chamber, moreover, was expected not only to collect the *regaliae* but also to augment them; it therefore negotiated loans for the crown whenever the *regaliae* did not yield enough to cover all the expenses of the court. It also granted parcels of crown land in settlement of unpaid royal debts. One final duty of the Hungarian Chamber was to arrange royal hunts in Hungary.[39]

It was in the Habsburg tradition to allow the financial affairs of Hungary to remain confused. To be sure, confusion in the Habsburg administration was not reserved exclusively for the management of Hungary's affairs. But whether conscious or otherwise, this confusion never permitted a clear picture to be formed of what Hungary really did contribute to the budget of the Habsburg Empire. In this respect there are different interpretations of Hungary's exact financial relationship to the rest of the Habsburg lands. One school claims that Hungary did not contribute its fair share to the budget of the Habsburg monarchy. This was the argument used by Maria Theresa, Joseph II, and their succes-

[38] Felhő and Vörös, pp. 19–23.   [39] Eckhart, p. 244.

sors to keep Hungary in colonial subjection and squeeze out of it by indirect measures what was supposedly due but not brought in by direct taxation. Another school of thought contends that through hidden channels the Habsburgs in fact collected from Hungary far more than was its fair contribution to the Habsburg budget. It adds that all the Habsburgs' complaints against the Hungarian estates were unjustified and served merely to obfuscate the Habsburgs' ruthless policy of colonization.

The latter theory tends to be borne out by the available figures. The *regaliae* collected and dispensed by the Hungarian Chamber amounted in 1780 to 5,755,988 florins, 30 percent more than the war taxes of the country. The salt monoply alone brought in 3,489,957 florins, a sum nearly as great as the war taxes voted by the diet (4,400,000 florins). The Habsburgs' income derived from gold, silver, and copper mining under direct Viennese management—and not included in the *regaliae*— was estimated at an additional four to five million florins, which were not counted as revenue from Hungary. The war taxes, in fact, were the only income recognized by the dynasty as revenue from Hungary; yet they represented barely one third of the real total receipts from the kingdom. And it might be noted at this juncture that the Habsburgs spent 1,900,000 florins a year provided by the Hungarian Chamber for the maintenance of their Viennese court alone.[40]

Already under Ferdinand I measures were introduced to mask some of the revenue derived from Hungary. One was the arrangement that made the most important customhouses on the Hungarian-Austrian border, those of Pozsony and Magyaróvár, answerable to the *Kammer* of Lower Austria in Vienna rather than subordinate to the Hungarian Chamber. The bulk of the massive Austro-Hungarian interstate commerce passed through these two customhouses. The duties collected in the process, which in fact were income from Hungary, were shown in all accounts not as Hungarian revenues but as revenues from Lower Austria. Exactly the same policy was applied to the income from the estates of five fortresses in western Hungary. These fortresses, each richly endowed with lucrative land, were Kismarton, Frak*ó, Szarvaskő, Borostyánkő, and Rohonc. Their properties included mines in Lower Hungary and land in Diósgyőr and Munkács. Once again it was the Lower Austrian Chamber that managed their revenue, which was

[40] Marczali, *Hungary,* pp. 319–20.

reserved to support the widowed Queen Mary of Hungary, Regent of the Netherlands (1531–52). The Habsburgs' substantial profits from these five fortresses came from Hungary, but were never counted as Hungarian contributions to the Habsburg budget.[41]

The Hungarian Chamber, like all the Habsburg *dicasterii*, was organized on a collegial basis. In the sixteenth and seventeenth centuries three to five councilors were collectively responsible for the Chamber's work. In the eighteenth century their number rose from ten to fourteen.

The Hungarian Chamber was constitutionally independent of the *Hofrechenkammer*, but all its reports and proposals went through the *Hofrechenkammer* to the king, and all his orders in turn to the Chamber came by way of it. Thus, though the Hungarian Chamber was independent in principle, in practice it was part and parcel of the financial system of the Habsburg lands. This subordination was patent in the system for appointing officials to the Hungarian Chamber. All appointments were a royal prerogative, in which the Hungarian diet had no say, and were made on advice to the king from the *Hofrechenkammer*.[42] That body's control over Hungary's finances was so absolute that the throne found nothing objectionable when the *Hofrechenkammer* sent instructions to local financial offices in Hungary over the Chamber's head without either its consent or its knowledge.[43] Several times the estates tried to reestablish the independence of Hungary's financial institutions, but each time to no avail. In 1569 the Hungarian diet recognized the existence of certain affairs as common and integral to the whole Habsburg domain, among them defense and finance; yet it insisted on the complete independence of the Hungarian Chamber from the *Hofrechenkammer*[44] (called the *Hofkammer* at that period). But this regulation remained just as conceived—on paper.

From the very beginning of the Habsburg era the Hungarian estates detested the Chamber. Emperor Rudolf charged it with prosecuting

---

[41] Eckhart, pp. 244–45.

[42] It must be conceded, however, that the Hungarian nobles loathed working in the Hungarian Chamber. Very seldom did they accept posts within its sphere. In 1756, for instance, there were only six Hungarian nobles serving in the Chamber. In its subordinate organs—the customhouses, salt depots, etc.—scarcely one tenth of the employees were Hungarians. The Chamber, then, was a direct instrument in the monarch's hands; it had no spirit of its own and employed a staff of "paid officials, not patriots." Marczali, *Hungary*, p. 344.

[43] Eckhart, p. 245.

[44] Act No. 38, 1569. CJH, II, 605. The act also emphasized the independent status of the Hungarian state and of Hungarian jurisdiction.

countless suits against Hungarian aristocrats, most of them Protestants, accused of high treason. The real objective behind this travesty of justice was to confiscate the lands of the aristocrats for the dynasty's benefit. The repercussions of his action were felt immediately after the estates' victory over the dynasty during the Bocskay uprising: the jubilant estates passed legislation to secure the Hungarian Chamber's independence.[45] This legislation, however, was totally ineffectual, for the actual situation went unchanged; the Chamber remained wholly subject to the *Hofrechenkammer*. In 1748 the Chamber was awarded the proud title of *Ungarische Hofkammer* (Hungarian Court Chamber).

On August 11, 1785, Joseph II merged the Hungarian Chamber with the *Consilium locumtenentiale*[46] and moved it back to its original home in Buda. But on April 30, 1791, the Chamber was once more separated from the *Consilium*.[47] It continued in existence until 1848, when it was fused into the new Hungarian Ministry of Finance under Lajos Kossuth.

[45] Act No. 5 of 1608, CJH, III, 13; Act No. 21 of 1609, CJH, III, 57; Act No. 18 of 1715, CJH, IV, 451; Act No. 8 of 1618, CJH, III, 129; Act No. 18 of 1622, CJH, III, 195.

[46] Two vice-presidencies were created, one in charge of financial affairs, one of administrative affairs. Felhő and Vörös, p. 31.

[47] *Ibid.*

Chapter VIII

MILITARY AFFAIRS

UNDER THE Hungarian constitution the Palatine was commander in chief of all the armed forces of Hungary. The Habsburgs, on the other hand, were very jealous of their privileges with respect to the army. They would brook no interference with its central command and control. This was the main reason why so often during the Habsburg period in Hungarian history the office of the Palatine lay vacant; it was not filled to prevent the Palatine from intervening in the military affairs of the Empire in general and Hungary in particular. Absolute control of the Hungarian forces became even more important to the dynasty after 1715, when the Hungarian standing army was established.[1]

From its very foundation the new standing army was under the sole command of the *Kriegsrat* in Vienna. Its supply, recruitment, quartering, mounts, food, fodder, and the everyday necessities, however, were the responsibility of the *Consilium locumtenentiale.* Hungarian military affairs were therefore under a dual authority. The purely military command, strategic planning, and troop deployment were directed by the *Kriegsrat* through six high commands (*Generalkommandos*) in the Kingdom of Hungary during the first half of the eighteenth century:[2] one for the kingdom proper, one for Transylvania, one for the Bánát, one for Slavonia, one for Croatia, and one for the Military Frontier Zones. The *Generalkammando* for the kingdom proper was stationed in Pozsony.[3]

To keep the cost of maintaining the Habsburg forces as low as pos-

---

[1] Acts Nos. 8, 21, and 59 of 1715. CJH, IV, 441, 453, 487.
[2] The *Generalkommando* system was established by Maria Theresa on October 27, 1740, by royal decree. Felhő and Vörös, p. 66.
[3] *Ibid.*, p. 67. In 1790 there were four *Generalkommandos* in Hungary.

sible, a considerable portion of the whole Habsburg army was permanently stationed in peacetime in the lands of the crown of St. Stephen. In 1740, Hungary's share in garrisoning and maintaining the army was as follows: 12 out of 52 infantry regiments were stationed in Hungary; 13 out of 18 cuirassier regiments; 7 out of 14 dragoon regiments; and 5 out of 8 hussar regiments. Thirty-seven of the army's total 92 regiments were thus stationed in Hungary.[4]

The majority of the Habsburg cavalry (25 regiments out of 40) was already stationed in Hungary during the reign of Maria Theresa. Joseph II transferred even more cavalry regiments to the kingdom. The buildings of dissolved monasteries and other ecclestiastical foundations were frequently used to house these newly arrived regiments.

THE CIVILIAN ADMINISTRATION
OF MILITARY AFFAIRS

As has been noted, while the dynasty retained command of the army, the *Consilium locumtenentiale* was responsible for its supply and other care. To discharge these duties, a provincial commissariat (*Commissariatus provincialis*) directly under the *Consilium* was set up in Hungary by the diet of 1722–23.[5] The provincial commissary was a member of the *Consilium* and always an aristocrat.

The very wide responsibilities of the *Commissariatus* included recruiting men; prosecuting deserters; granting exemptions from military service; looking after troops on furlough; caring for veterans and disabled ex-servicemen; building, equipping, and keeping up barracks; repairing fortifications; assigning recruit camps and drill grounds; billeting troops on maneuvers; purchasing horses; regulating the wearing of uniforms; quartering soldiers; victualing in kind; providing transportation for military units and supplying their mounts; paying compensation for losses occasioned by military indiscipline; compensating the civilian population for losses caused by the establishment of military settlements; and settling conflicts between the military and the civilian population.[6]

---

[4] *Ibid.*, p. 69. The cuirassier regiments were heavy cavalry; the hussars were light cavalry.

[5] The *Országos Bizottság* or *Commissariatus provincialis* was established by Act No. 100 of the diet of 1722–23. CJH, IV, 643.

[6] Felhő and Vörös, p. 100.

District commissaries (*Commissarii districtuales*) acted under the orders of the provincial commissary. The duties of the provincial and district commissaries were defined in a detailed ordinance of King Charles III which set up eight district commissariats in Hungary. These were reorganized during the reigns of Maria Theresa and Joseph II. In 1790 ten district commissariats were in existence.[7] The ten district commissaries formed a central consultative body that advised the provincial commissary. The actual work was performed by county commissaries under the supervision of the district commissaries. The county commissaries were in fact answerable to the county administrations, in whose behalf and under whose authority they acted, even though the district commissaries directed their activities.

In principle troops served for life, but usually, after twenty years' service, they could be discharged if they wished. It was not until 1830 that the period of service was reduced to ten years.[8] Generally the sole other men who could obtain a discharge were only sons and those whose special skills made them indispensable to their communities. Otherwise any soldier who applied for a discharge had to find a man to take his place in service.[9] Until 1840 recruits were forced into service by the press gang. After that time, recruits' names were drawn by lot, exclusively from among the sons of serfs. In 1787 Joseph II ordered the impressment of young Jews to work in the transportation corps.[10]

[7] The original eight district commissariats and their territories were:

Pozsony: Pozsony, Nyitra, Trencsén, Moson, Győr, and Komárom counties.

Sopron: Sopron, Vas, Zala, Somogy, and Veszprém counties.

Buda: Pest, Nógrád, Heves, Esztergom, Fejér, and Csongrád counties and the Kiskunság, Nagykunság, and Jászság.

Besztercebánya: Árva, Liptó, Turóc, Bars, Zólyom, and Hont counties.

Kassa: Abaúj, Zemplén, Sáros, Szepes, Gömör, Torna, Borsod, Ung, and Bereg counties.

Debrecen: Máramaros, Kővárvidék, Középszolnok, Szatmár, Szabolcs, and Kraszna counties.

Eszék: Baranya, Tolna, Bács, and Bodrog counties.

Szerém: Bihar, Zaránd, Arad, Csanád, Békés, and Ugocsa counties.

Several changes were made in this system. A major one was the abolition of Eszék district and its replacement by Pécs district. In 1781 a new district, the Croatian, was founded; it comprised Varasd, Kőrös, and Zágráb counties and the Fiume littoral. Felhő and Vörös, p. 68.

[8] Act No. 7, diet of 1830. CJH, V, 499.   [9] Felhő and Vörös, p. 237.

[10] *Ibid.*, p. 233.

SUPPLY OF THE STANDING ARMY

At the time of the establishment of the Hungarian standing army in 1715 there were no barracks to lodge the men and horses. They were both lodged in the houses of the civilian population. The homes and commercial buildings of the estates naturally were exempt from quartering or supplying the military.[11] The serfs and the royal free towns supplied food, lodging, and fodder for the army.[12]

The amount the taxpayer supplied in kind and services was deducted from his cash tax payments. After 1751, a code for accounting these supplies by the military—the *regulamentum*—was introduced. The *regulamentum* fixed the prices of wheat, hay, oats, and meat at the lowest possible level. Yet the Hungarians in general were patient in supplying their products to the army even at that low price.[13] In the absence of markets, the presence of the military relieved the population of surpluses they could not sell. In fact, many counties requested cavalry regiments to be stationed in their towns.[14] The supply of the army was burdensome only in nonagrarian counties.

There was a substantial difference between the price the state paid to the serfs for the food and services they rendered and their real value; this difference, of grave consequences for the serfs, was called *deperdita*.[15] The loss the serfs suffered became the object of endless quarrels, appeals, orders, and bureaucratic correspondence between the central and local governments.

The army was supplied through the *portio* system. Under this, the counties and royal free towns had to supply the garrisons stationed in their territory with a strictly defined amount of accommodation, lodging, food, fodder, and transportation. The *portio* was of three types: *portio oralis*—one pound of meat and two pounds of bread per man per day; *salganum*—firewood, light, salt, and a bed; and *portio equalis*—six pounds of oats and eight pounds of hay per horse per day and three bales of straw per horse per week.

[11] Eckhart, p. 210.   [12] Oszetzky, p. 24.
[13] Henry Marczali quotes a book, *Gespräche im Reiche der Todten zwischen Ihren Majestäten Franz I und Maria Theresia* (Vienna, 1781), p. 82, indicating that foreigners were astonished at the patience of the Hungarians in maintaining so large an army. *Hungary*, p. 28.
[14] *Ibid.*   [15] Eckhart, p. 210. See also Niederhauser, p. 132.

In some parts of Hungary these supplies could be furnished out of local produce, but in other parts the communities did not produce enough for themselves, let alone for the army units garrisoned among them. In these cases the county or royal free town was obliged to purchase and ship in the requisites from elsewhere. The *Consilium locumtenentiale* tried to ease the burden on these communities by setting up storehouses of surplus food (*domus annonaria*). There the *Consilium* stored surplus wheat bought by the state for cash and wheat supplied by the counties in partial payment of the war taxes. In time of need the *Consilium* would make loans from the stored surpluses to the counties or royal free towns. Sometimes the army's supplies were drawn straight from the storehouses. Major exports of foodstuffs to the Habsburg provinces were also made by drawing on the storehouses. The court would not only use this food to provision the army but would also sell it on the regular market at much higher prices than were credited to the Hungarian government for it. This was a practice typical of the Habsburgs' colonial exploitation of Hungary.[16]

Joseph II well intentionedly overhauled the whole system of army supply. After 1786 the entire army was supplied exclusively by the state and had no longer to depend in part on the counties and royal free towns. The cost of supplying the army was estimated to amount to half a million florins. This sum was collected from the counties, divided among them in direct proportion to the amount of *portae* that each formerly contributed. The money thus collected to supply the army was known as the *fundus deperditalis*.[17] Leopold II abolished the new system and transferred responsibility for supplying the army back to the counties and royal free towns.

---

[16] Felhő and Vörös, p. 105.   [17] *Ibid.*, pp. 232–33.

Chapter IX

THE COUNTIES

THE LOWEST constitutional units of government in Hungary were the counties (*megyék*), the royal free towns, and the royal free districts (the Jász and Kun districts, the Hajdu towns). The administrative subdivisions of the counties were the *járások* (districts), which were headed by the *főszolgabiró* (district magistrate). The *járások* were constitutionally not autonomous. Their officers were elected by the county assembly, which exercised full authority over them.

Village administrations were not part of the constitutional system of government. The villages were under the lords' jurisdiction and as such were considered to be outside the sphere of constitutional government. At the local level, county government was without question predominant; the royal free towns and royal free districts played very minor roles.[1]

The county was a very special phenomenon in the Hungarian system of government. It was an extremely powerful organ of the nobility and was dominated by the *bene possessionati*.[2] If any legal institution existed in Hungary that was more or less independent of the Habsburgs' direct domination, it was the county administration. Even the powerful enlightened despots had to reckon with the opinion of county leaders. During the eighteenth century the notion gained currency that the county was practically a self-contained, autonomous unit of the kingdom. György Bessenyei, the enlightened intellectual, wrote: "A little country, a republic, is how I envisage the county. . . . There are as many provinces and juridical units that exist independently of

---

[1] Grünwald, p. 448.

[2] The county in principle was a union of all the estates, *Nos Universitas Dominorum, Praelatorum, Baronum, Magnatum et Nobilium. Ibid.*, p. 428.

each other in the nation as there are counties into which the nation is divided." [3]

The influence and power of the counties came into being gradually. The process began during the Ottoman wars when the counties' responsibilities in connection with national defense were continually being expanded. There was an ever increasing number of defense tasks that were best carried out under the counties' direction rather than under the immediate control of the central government. Many tasks demanded a knowledge of local conditions and circumstances, and needed constant on-the-spot supervision. These included the erection of fortifications, conscription of forced labor, transporting building materials for defense works, and provisioning the local military and defense workers. Organization of such activities naturally fell to the counties and the county administrations gladly accepted the responsibility.[4]

The counties' tasks were augmented by the increase in legal suits brought as a result of the growing number of urbarial obligations imposed on the serfs in wartime conditions. Ottoman occupation of the heartland of Hungary, furthermore, made communications between the two capitals, Pozsony and Vienna, and the provinces at best hazardous, at worst impossible. The weakening of civil order and discipline as a result of the protracted wars raised the counties' police duties, for policing could scarcely be directed by the central government under such circumstances, much less performed. Throughout the Ottoman wars the central government's activities were confined almost exclusively to diplomatic, financial, and military matters. The rest of its judicial and administrative functions were relegated to the counties.

Before the foundation in 1723 of the first modern, nationwide, central organ of government in Hungary, the *Consilium locumtenentiale,* the counties were free to set up their own administrative practices, procedures, and principles affecting almost every facet of life. The counties' sphere of authority included regulation of the prices of merchandise, food, and labor; regulation of loans, interest rates, and pawnbroking; regulation of the administration of districts and villages; even regulation of juridical standards. The practices that were adopted

---

[3] Bessenyei, "Magyarország törvényes állása" [The Legal Status of Hungary], a manuscript written in 1804, discovered and quoted by Grünwald, p. 428.

[4] Eckhart, p. 268.

sometimes differed widely from one county to the next. The *Consil-ium*'s intention to coordinate and make these polymorphous regulations uniform throughout the country proved to be a laborious and lengthy enterprise.

The creation of the Hungarian standing army in 1715 enlarged yet further the counties' duties and authority. The counties assumed a considerable part of the responsibility for recruiting troops, preparing quarters for them, and supplying the army.

All the enlightened reformers from Charles III to Joseph II strength-ened the counties' authority, though for differing reasons, by giving them assignments which could be carried out by no other organs. To put into effect any substantial enlightened reform, the central govern-ment needed data, statistics, reports, registers. No health, agrarian, or welfare reforms could be introduced if such preparatory groundwork had not been completed. Once more it was only the counties that had the facilities to lay it, and so their influence and prestige grew.[5]

By the mid-eighteenth century the county administrations had be-come stable, efficient, professional, well organized, self-confident, and effective. With the recognition of these qualities grew the realization of the political potentials of the county and simultaneously the am-bitions of its leaders, the *bene possessionati*. About this time the *bene possessionati* began petitioning the central government and, more significantly yet, even defying those orders of the central government that they did not like. Their nascent self-assurance was also evidenced by another new phenomenon: a growing exchange of correspondence between counties in which political affairs and proposals for common action were discussed. Little by little the counties' burgeoning inde-pendence of action evolved into resistance to the central government, which had some effect against the Josephine reforms, especially during the Emperor's misguided Turkish War. This county resistance was the laboratory of experience that prepared the ground for the feudal revolt that erupted after Joseph II's death in 1790. It was at this time that the counties, led by the *bene possessionati*, set themselves up as the "bastions of the constitution"—a phrase dear to the nobility throughout Hungary's feudal history.

The county legislative body was the assembly (*közgyűlés*). All the nobles of the county were entitled to take part in the assembly in

[5] *Ibid.*

person. It was the high sheriff, or in his absence the deputy high sheriff, who summoned the assembly and chaired its sessions, which were open to the public. The minutes of these sessions were preserved in the county archives. At the assemblies, royal decrees, patents of nobility, government orders, and so forth were read. The assembly decided what actions were to be taken on these directives, or refused to implement them if it found them illegal under the provisions of Act No. 33 of 1545.[6]

The high sheriff was appointed by the king and acted as his lieutenant at the head of the county administration. Generally the holders of that office were aristocrats.[7] Certain aristocratic families owning extensive tracts of land in some counties received from the king the title of perpetual high sheriff (*örökös főispán*). After the liberation of central Hungary from Ottoman rule, several Roman Catholic diocesan bishops were restored to their former offices as perpetual high sheriffs. Furthermore, the Palatine was perpetual high sheriff of the County of Pest. Apart from the Palatine, there were nine ecclesiastical and fourteen lay perpetual high sheriffs in Hungary.[8] Their official title was *supremus et perpetuus comes*. Act No. 42 of 1870 abolished the office but continued the title.[9]

The key officials of the county were elected triennially at special assemblies (*Sedes restauratoria electoria*).[10] The high sheriff had the right to nominate candidates for all offices.[11] The first nominee for any office was usually the incumbent; only if he were incapacitated or too old to discharge his duties would new names be put forward.[12]

The effective head of the county administration was the deputy high sheriff. Until 1504 he was appointed by the high sheriff; thereafter his office, like those of other county officials, became elective. The deputy high sheriff had immense prestige in the county where he served. This prestige derived less from his office than from his social and economic

---

[6] CJH, II, 137. This act did not give full power to counties to reject royal orders, however.

[7] Grünwald, p. 441.   [8] Eckhart, p. 271.   [9] CJH, VII, 217.

[10] The Hungarian term for these electoral assemblies was *tisztépitőszék.*

[11] Eckhart, p. 270.

[12] The major officials were the *alispán* (deputy high sheriff), who was the actual head of the county administration, as well as the president of the county court of appeal; the *főjegyző* (county notary), head of the county hall and lieutenant to the *alispán;* the *főszolgabiró* (district magistrate), head of the district administration; the *szolgabiró,* the *főszolgabiró's* aide; and the *jurassor,* the *főszolgabiró's* legal assistant.

position. The deputy high shrievalty was restricted by law to members of the county *possessionati*—the lesser landed nobility. In practice, the office rotated among not more than three or four families, who were the richest and most powerful of the local lesser nobility. In fact, none but these oligarchs ever became candidates for the post.[13]

Two other county officials were the county notary (*főjegyző*) and the judge of the county court (*táblabiró*).[14]

The notary (*notarius*) with his staff and clerks was the head of the county hall. He read documents and resolutions before the assembly and kept the minutes of its sessions. He drafted county ordinances and regulations, and supervised the county archives and judicial documents.

The office of the *táblabirák* was something of a curiosity. To be sure, these officials were the judges of the county courts, but they could also be assigned by the assembly or county leaders to the most diverse temporary tasks—judicial, political, administrative, or whatever. The office of the *táblabirák* was reserved for those lesser nobles who had no alternative means of livelihood or were incapable of rising to any higher official ranks. There were always plenty of candidates who coveted the title of *táblabiró* but had no wish to work or earn their salary. Thus innumerable honorary *táblabirák* were appointed by the county assemblies. Toward the end of the eighteenth century there were from 100 to 500 *táblabirák* in every county in the kingdom, a national total of some 8,000 to 10,000. Every self-seeking nobleman was satisfied with a title, even if it were merely a county appointment, and the title of *táblabiró* exactly filled the bill.[15]

It was assumed, technically, that all county offices were *nobile officium*, in other words, honorary and unpaid. The fact is, though, that from the sixteenth century onwards county officials received a regular salary.[16] And over and above their salary, they also drew expenses for travel, judicial activities, and special missions. Maria Theresa herself found it necessary to protest against their too frequent salary increases.[17]

The county was the institution through which the lesser nobility

[13] Grünwald, p. 444.
[14] County notaries were regularly elected from the eighteenth century onwards. In some larger counties, deputy notaries were also elected. *Ibid.*, p. 445.
[15] Eckhart, p. 273.   [16] *Ibid.*, p. 270.   [17] *Ibid.*, and Grünwald, p. 445.

exercised social and political dominion, and was thus a considerable political force in Hungary. Its legislative importance resided in the fact that its assemblies had the right to instruct delegates to the diet. If the delegate ignored his instructions or acted without them, he could be recalled. Because of this right, it was not the diet but the county that was the real vehicle of legislative decision. Any innovation to reach the diet could come only through the county assemblies. The delegates to the diets, in fact, seldom strayed from their instructions, whatever was at issue. Thus the spirit, desires, and opinions of the counties dominated the diets.[18]

The administrative importance of the counties outweighed even their legislative role. Whatever the form of the central government, regardless of whether an enlightened or a reactionary Habsburg sat on the royal throne, the state, in the final analysis, had to govern through the counties. The Habsburgs might have absolutist and unconstitutional penchants, but they were not, after all, totalitarians. The central government might try to enforce uniform methods and fundamental reforms, but it had always to depend on the counties' cooperation. The counties moved deliberately and gradually. It was they and they alone who thwarted the radical political and social changes that the enlightened despots endeavored to introduce. It was the counties, too, which protected the landowners' economic and legal domination of the serfs.

These, then, were the reasons why the county as an institution was the most powerful force in feudal Hungary. The feudal revolt of 1790 was organized and carried out principally by the counties. Even the defeat of that revolt, however, failed to shatter the counties' stranglehold. Their influence survived the revolution of 1848 and was brought to an end only during the democratic experiment of 1945–47.

[18] Grünwald, p. 449.

Chapter X

CHURCH AFFAIRS

IT IS REMARKABLE that in the late eighteenth century religious matters still played a dominant role in political struggles as well as in literary life. This condition was caused not so much by the political influence of the prelacy as by the pervading medieval ecclesiastic aspects of the Hungarian state. Religion was still a matter of state concern, and any effort to extend religious freedom was considered primarily a political issue. Thus the ecclesiastical elements of the governmental system and the political power of the Church in the late eighteenth century can be understood only in light of the politico-religious legislation and the royal and papal decrees issued prior to that era; in particular, the Treaty of Vienna of 1606; the *Explanatio leopoldina* of 1691 and its revised form, the *Carolina resolutio* of 1731; and Emperor Joseph II's Patent of Toleration of 1781. All four were still important political factors in 1790, and some were even active from a legal standpoint.

THE TREATY OF VIENNA AND
SUPPLEMENTARY TREATIES

The Treaty of Vienna, which was concluded in 1606 between the Habsburg court and the Hungarian estates, was truly a remarkable document, for it marked the culmination of efforts to obtain an effective legal guarantee of constitutional rights for the estates in the face of royal prerogatives. In addition, it guaranteed the religious freedom of the estates. This treaty played a particularly interesting role in the events of 1790: the Protestants wanted a return to its stipulations, for they could thus gain complete political emancipation; the

Catholics wanted it wiped off the books; and the leaders of the Hungarian feudal revolt found in it a historical precedent which they used to justify their desire for a Prussian guarantee of the constitutional rights of the estates. Their hopes were based on the fact that the stipulations of the treaty had been guaranteed by a foreign power, that is, by the estates of Austria and Bohemia, including also, at the time, Silesia.

There was, however, a basic political difference between the Hungary of 1606 and that of 1790. In the former year, the powerful principality of Transylvania was still in existence and served an important function in maintaining the stipulations of the Treaty of Vienna.[1] In the latter year, Transylvania, then a Grand Principality, no longer had the power to guarantee the constitutional privileges of the Hungarian estates. Rather it was a force which could be utilized by the Habsburg court, if need be, to counter efforts and demands made by the estates of the kingdom proper.

In Transylvania a series of legislative acts had been passed that ensured freedom of religion: in 1550, molestation for religious reasons

[1] Before 1541, Transylvania was an integral part of the Kingdom of Hungary. In that year, however, a *Firman* (Decree) of the Sultan awarded it to John Sigismund of Szapolyai, the son of the deceased King John I. Geographically the separate existence of a Transylvanian state was possible because, with the fall of Buda in 1541, the Habsburgs lost the direct, year-round communication lines with Transylvania. The only roads connecting Habsburg lands with Transylvania were those which passed through northern Hungary (Slovakia), and they were impassable during the winter months. This is also the reason why those Trans-Tisza counties which lay near the Transylvanian borders and had no direct communication with the kingdom proper voted for their incorporation into Transylvania. Hence the so-called *Partes* were created. (See Map No. 1.)

In 1588 Transylvania officially became a principality. As a separate entity, the state was under the protection of the Porte. The Şeyh-ül-Islâm warned Prince Gábor Bethlen that "we shall never allow Transylvania to be unified with Hungary. Transylvania is Sultan Suliman's invention and the property of the Mighty Sultan. . . . We do not give to anybody else what belongs to us." Hóman and Szekfü, IV, 74. As long as the good will of the Porte lasted, the existence of Transylvania as a semi-independent political entity was assured. The height of Transylvanian power was reached during the reign of Gábor Bethlen (1613–29).

With the liberation of Buda in 1686, the direct military road from Hungary into the hinterland of Transylvania was opened once again, and the principality was subsequently invaded by Habsburg troops. In 1690 the *Diploma leopoldinum*, which remained in effect practically up until 1848, ordered direct administration of the principality by the Transylvanian Chancellery in Vienna. A governor was elected by the Transylvanian diet and endorsed by the king to head the local government. In 1765 Maria Theresa created the Grand Principality of Transylvania. Joseph II integrated it into the Kingdom of Hungary, but later, on his deathbed, he withdrew this regulation.

was outlawed; in 1552, the exclusion of an individual from public office because of his religious affiliation was forbidden; and the enactments of the famous Torda diet in 1564 granted an unparalleled degree of religious freedom. The Catholics, Calvinists, and Lutherans living in Transylvania were given equal rights and freedom, and when, in 1571, Unitarianism was added to these demoninations, Transylvania became the land of freedom for three nations (Hungarians, Székelys, and Saxons) and four creeds. Religious freedom was granted not only to the privileged classes but to all individuals of the three privileged nations. It is to be noted that the Orthodox Rumanians did not share this freedom.

The existence of such a high degree of religious freedom in Transylvania naturally did not pass unnoticed by the Protestants of royal Hungary, who began to press for similiar liberties. Their struggle for freedom to worship as they pleased was, at the core, related to the fight of the Hungarian estates to secure their feudal privileges. The first battle in the series of civil wars that ensued—all fought for the realization of this dual goal—resulted in a military victory for the estates in 1605 from which a political compromise with the Habsburg court followed. The stipulations of the Treaty of Vienna (1606), which granted a certain amount of religious freedom as well as feudal privileges to the estates, were codified by the diet of 1608. Religious freedom for nobles, the royal free towns, and soldiers in the fortification zones was thereby ensured.

The repercussions of the Treaty of Vienna had a notably different effect on the serfs. In so far as they were concerned, the principle of *Cuius regio eius religio* was applied. The subordination of a serf's conscience to his lord's will was but one aspect of the compromise between the dynasty and the victorious estates. All the affairs of the serfs were transferred from the authority of the king and the diet to the county administration, which was entirely controlled by the *bene possessionati*. One and a half centuries of unlimited rights of the lords to rule over their serfs then followed.

During the era of the Thirty Years' War, intermittent civil wars and new treaties, regulating religious affairs and the constitutional relationship between the monarch and the estates, followed one another. The major treaties were those of Nickolsburg (1621), Vienna (1624), Pozsony (1626), and, finally, Linz (1645). All of them reendorsed the original Treaty of Vienna and the legislation enacted by the diet of 1608. The last one, however, the Treaty of Linz, brought about a fundamental change by introducing the right of a serf to choose his own religion and by forbidding a lord to force his serfs to change their faith.[2]

With this accomplished, the long struggle for religious freedom reached a successful peak. As soon as the principality of Transylvania began to disintegrate, however, freedom of religion declined proportionately. In spite of this, the stipulations of the Treaty of Vienna and the legislation of the diet of 1608 remained integral parts of the *Corpus Juris Hungarici*—the laws of the land. It was a long, hard struggle for Habsburgs and Catholics alike to abolish them, and it was equally difficult for Protestants to maintain them: neither party was fully successful in its endeavor. Quite obviously, then, both the treaty and the legislation of the diet had a profound influence on the events of 1790.

THE *EXPLANATIO LEOPOLDINA* AND THE *CAROLINA RESOLUTIO*

The Treaty of Vienna was considered by the Habsburgs, as were all other concessions they made that were beneficial to the estates, merely as a temporary yielding to political realities of the time. Whenever they felt secure enough in Hungary to continue suppressing individual consciences, they instantly did so. This was the governing factor of Habsburg policy in dealing with *acatholici*, as non-Catholics were contemptuously called. Measures employed by the Habsburgs ranged from harsh, often bloody, restraints to more lenient restrictions. At times their policy was enforced by mere police measures; but at other times they went so far as to issue royal patents which severely restricted the religious freedom of non-Catholics. The *explanatio* and the *resolutio* may be regarded as the prototypes of such royal patents. Never endorsed by a Hungarian diet, they were at once extraconstitutional and arbitrary regulations.

After the abortive aristocratic conspiracy of Ferenc Wesselényi (1670–71), Palatine of Hungary, the Habsburgs suspended the Hun-

[2] Eckhart, p. 306.

garian constitution and launched an all-out attack on Protestantism.[3] However, in 1681, because of the Ottoman threat, the Habsburgs again felt the need to yield in their policy on religion. In the diet which met that year (one third of the delegates were Protestants), another compromise between the Habsburgs and the Hungarian estates was reached.[4] Freedom of worship for Protestants was granted, and the stipulations of the first Vienna treaty were reconfirmed. All questions dealing with religious matters were transferred back to the jurisdiction of the diet, and the royal privilege of being an arbiter in such affairs was abolished.[5]

After a major part of Hungary had been liberated and Transylvania had ceased to exist as an independent political entity, the Habsburgs quickly forgot the compromise of 1681 and began again to apply force in order to suppress freedom of religion. In 1687, by virtue of a royal decree, religious affairs were arbitrarily withdrawn from the jurisdiction of the diets and their handling was reserved as a royal prerogative.[6] In 1691 the *Explanatio leopoldina* was issued and remained in force until the issuance of its twin patent, the *Carolina resolutio,* in 1731.

The *Explanatio* arbitrarily changed the meaning of all the previous legislation concerning religion.[7] It restricted the Protestants' right of public worship. Moreover, Protestants had to celebrate Catholic holidays, and Protestant guild members had to participate in Catholic processions.

The Treaty of Szatmár (1711) promised a more respectful attitude toward laws concerning religion, and it transferred religious affairs back to the jurisdiction of the diets. It did not, however, offer Protestants any practical means of protection.[8] A few years later, in 1715, Act No. 30 went into effect, banning all discussion in the diet related to religious matters.[9] With this legislation on the books, Protestantism entered a new epoch—that of struggling to maintain its very existence. Paradoxically, although about 50 percent of the population of

---

[3] Wesselényi (the conspiracy bore his name in history) died before the conspiracy was actually revealed. Its other leading personalities were Péter Zrinyi, Ferenc Frangepán, and Ferenc Nádasdy. All three were beheaded on April 30, 1670. The following month, 9,000 troops under Montecuccoli's command invaded Hungary and two thousand people were arrested. Hóman and Szekfü, IV, 178.

[4] Eckhart, p. 307.   [5] Acts Nos. 25 and 26. CJH, IV, 67.

[6] Hermann, IV, 439.   [7] Biró *et al.*, p. 127. See also Eckhart, p. 307.

[8] Grünwald, p. 82.   [9] Marczali, *Hungary*, p. 254.

the country at this time was Protestant, and although the era between 1715 and 1780 was one of enlightened despotism, the persecution of Hungarian Protestants continued unabated.[10] In 1723 the *Consilium locumtenentiale* was organized and charged with managing all religious matters. On the question of repopulating Hungary, the *Consilium* sought to reduce the ratio of Protestants among the inhabitants.

On March 21, 1731, Charles III issued a royal decree, the *Carolina resolutio,* regulating religious affairs in Hungary. Essentially a re-endorsement of the 1681 and 1687 legislation and of the *Explanatio leopoldina,* it was intended to be a final settlement of all the Protestant problems in Hungary.

The most ominous stipulation of the *Carolina resolutio* was the introduction of the *decretalis* oath, to be administered to officials of the state. Prescribed by Verbőczi in the *Tripartitum,* it invoked the names of the Virgin Mary and the saints of the Catholic Church. Without taking such an oath, one could not be admitted to a state office, and Protestants thus were summarily excluded from these positions.[11] The restrictions imposed on Protestant schools and the severe punishment of apostates from Catholicism made the spread of Protestantism virtually impossible. Nevertheless, two Protestant churches remained in existence as religious corporations, albeit they possessed inferior rights and were forced to fight in order to survive at all.[12]

In spite of all this, it would be highly unfair to the Habsburgs to say that it was the policy of that dynasty alone—and nobody else's—to persecute the Protestants. In every respect, the Hungarian Catholic estates were equally determined to suppress Protestantism, and to that end they liberally used their majority in the diets:

The Catholic estates went further in their intolerance and persecution than did the court itself, and the Protestants placed more confidence in the

[10] Grünwald, p. 82.

[11] "The chief point on which everything turned was the *juramentum decretale,* the oath that could be taken by Catholics only—the only means of opening the way to government offices."

"In the counties also, they [Protestants] began to be excluded from all offices—even from that of *táblabiró*. Protestants who had already been elected were deposed unless they took the oath as prescribed by the Catholics." Marczali, *Hungary,* pp. 267, 268.

[12] *Ibid.,* p. 255.

monarch than they did in the diets, where they were in the minority. To escape the persecution of their fellow Hungarians, they sought the protection of the foreign dynasty.[13]

Because of the numerous regulations which affected members of the Protestant faith, they became a distinct community of political interests, a group, moreover, in which the members supported, and felt a solidarity with, each other. All their efforts were concentrated on preventing the enemy state from touching them—that is to say, on lessening its interference with their ecclesiastic and educational affairs. The persistent persecutions brought out a strong religious spirit in the Protestants, and at the same time revealed the state as an embodiment of Catholic ecclesiastical interests. This, of course, alienated the Protestants from the state.[14] Thus it is interesting to note that, during the years of suppression, Protestant spiritual and intellectual life gained in depth and devotion. Protestants produced an intellectual elite: noted theologians like György Szikszay of Debrecen and Pál Ráday, a layman, emerged; Protestant historians like Péter Bod and Mátyás Bél (the author of the *Notitia Hungariae*) were among the leading intellectuals of their era.[15]

Maria Theresa, with her rather baroque type of Catholic devotion, strictly enforced the stipulations of the *Carolina resolutio*. Her emphasis on the Catholic form of the oath of office excluded all non-Catholics from state and even county offices. The counterreformation continued. In dealing with Protestants, she followed her father's traditions, maintaining all the patents and legislations of her predecessors that restricted their religious life.

In this respect, it is important to note that although Maria Theresa was intolerant with non-Catholics she founded the *Staatsrat* and, curiously enough, staffed it with Jansenists, Gallicans, rationalists, and

---

[13] Grünwald, p. 83. (His account is slightly exaggerated.) Cardinal Mihály F. Althan, Bishop of Vác, protested against the *Carolina resolutio,* not because of its stark brutality against Protestants, but because in his view it was too mild. In the assembly of Pest County, however, the king tore the Bishop's written protest to shreds, temporarily confiscated his incomes, and ordered him to Vienna to be reprimanded. Hermann, p. 441.

[14] Grünwald, p. 86.

[15] Hermann, p. 446. The *Notitia Hungariae* is a detailed description of the counties and towns of Hungary, including information on historical, geographical, economic, and social conditions. Four volumes of this immense opus were printed; the rest survived in manuscript form. The *Notitia* was a remarkable work of high scholarly standards.

freethinkers—men like Kaunitz, Van Swieten, Ádám Kollár, and Abbot Rautenstrauch—who introduced more liberal reforms. While this enlightened spirit was not extended to religious matters and the persecution of Protestants continued, during the reign of Maria Theresa the neo-Counter Reformation exhausted itself and cleared the way for Emperor Joseph II's Patent of Toleration of 1781.

In general, however, the Protestant estates were restricted in their political rather than in their religious life. The case was different as far as the peasants were concerned. Their masters could drive them away, chastise them, or convert them by force. Moreover, Catholic proprietors, in dealing with their Lutheran serfs, greatly abused their rights. They took away the Protestants' churches; when a pastor died, they did not allow his place to be taken by another; they stripped the pastors of the land and tithes which were their only means of subsistence and forced them to pay tithes themselves; and it was no rare event for them to expel the whole population of Protestant villages.[16] In addition, Catholic priests demanded certain fees from Protestant serfs. Baptisms or burials, performed by ministers, were forbidden unless the fees had already been paid.

Protestant superintendents could not exercise their right of supervision, i.e., visitations. They were, in fact, subject to the visitations of Catholic bishops. They could not introduce books into the country unhindered. The *Consilium locumtenentiale* "had all the Heidelberg catechisms seized; and Barkóczy, while still the Bishop of Eger, had the Hungarian Bible burned in public." [17] Several Protestant colleges were degraded to the status of secondary schools—e.g., Besztercebánya, Selmec, Szatmár, and Cegléd. Those of Léva, Győr, Pápa, and Tata were confiscated altogether.

Several Protestant landowners could not resist accepting court favors and titles, and converted to Catholicism. Ferenc Batthyány, for example, could not withstand the temptation of becoming a count and so joined the Catholic Church. For the most part, however, "the bulk of the gentry could not be won over either by force or corruption. . . . In the eighteenth century, the ruling class was divided against itself and split into two antagonistic factions." [18]

In conclusion, one may say that, because of the strict enforcement of the *Carolina resolutio* and the continued suppression of Protestants

[16] Marczali, *Hungary*, p. 264.   [17] *Ibid.*, p. 265.   [18] *Ibid.*, p. 266.

during the reign of Maria Theresa, Joseph II's Patent of Toleration was insufficient to wipe out the repercussions of nearly a century of persecution. However deep the religious devotion of Maria Theresa may have been, however many instances one discovers of her having preferred religious aims to political interests, the fact remains that, in so far as Hungary was concerned, she and her administration were guided by the endeavors of the ruling party of Hungarian society, and her harshness against Hungarian Protestants was, to a great extent, an expression of that party's desires.[19] Thus, in the wake of this period, which ended with the reign of Maria Theresa, there remained a residue of internal division among the estates in matters of religion. This division, so characteristic of the political situation in 1790, had a profound influence on the events of that year.

THE PATENT OF TOLERATION
OF EMPEROR JOSEPH II

The most remarkable and enduring of the Josephine reforms was the promulgation of the Patent of Toleration by Emperor Joseph II in 1781. Although an analysis of Josephinism as a governmental doctrine would be outside the field of this study, it is necessary to discuss in brief some of Joseph's innovations as well as the antecedents of the Patent of Toleration.[20]

In 1769, Maria Theresa imposed a 20 percent tax on major ecclesiastic incomes without first consulting the Holy See. She insisted on the application of the doctrine of *Placetum regium* in regard to all documents issued by the Pope, even the *Breve*, which dissolved the Jesuit order (*Dominus ac Redemptor*) in 1773. In addition, she limited the number of ecclesiastic holidays, dissolved some monasteries, banned pilgrimages abroad, and abolished the right of asylum of the churches.[21] She reorganized the dioceses in 1776, taking considerable territory from Esztergom and forming the new dioceses of Besztercebánya, Rozsnyó, and Szepes; and from the diocese of Veszprém she created those of Székesfehérvár, Győr, and Szom-

---

[19] *Ibid.*, p. 268.
[20] "The 'revolutionary' Emperor undertook little that was entirely new in principle." Wangermann, p. 2. For an analysis of Josephinism see, in particular, Valjevac, *Der Josephinismus*, pp. 8–15.
[21] Meszlényi, p. 15.

bathely.[22] Hence, by carrying out all these actions without the consent of the Holy See, Maria Theresa, a deeply religious ruler, helped most substantially to prepare the way for Josephinism.[23]

In 1781 Joseph proclaimed the validity of *Placetum regium* in all matters, including those dealing with Church dogma.[24] He cut the ties of monastic orders with their superiors in Rome; newly appointed bishops were to take loyalty oaths to the monarch only, in which "they bound themselves to recognize the Emperor as their only legal superior and to carry out all his orders without regard to anything else." [25] Moreover, he abolished the papal *Bulla Unigenitus* in 1783.[26] He ordered that the *Bulla In Coena Domini*, which reserved the administration of several ecclesiastic punishments for the Pope, be struck from the Church books and the text sent to Vienna. The Imperial order proclaimed that "whoever refuses to remove the text from the *ritualae* and present it in Vienna shall pay a fine of fifty florins." [27] In this manner, he struck a powerful blow against the practical jurisdiction of the Pope in Hungary and simultaneously established the ideological foundation of Josephinism.

The Patent of Toleration,[28] issued on October 29, 1781, established conditions bordering on religious freedom. Most important in this respect, it abolished the *Carolina resolutio*. Groups of one hundred or more Protestant families, no matter where they lived, were allowed to build churches of their own, albeit without spires, bells, or doors opening onto the street. They were no longer obliged to observe Catholic holidays or pay fees to Catholic priests.[29] Marriage suits were transferred from the province of the Catholic ecclesiastic courts to civil courts. Mixed marriages were still conducted by Catholic priests, and while the children of a Protestant mother had to be brought up in the Catholic tradition, the sons of a Protestant father were allowed to be brought up and educated as Protestants. Today

[22] Hermann, p. 429.   [23] Meszlényi, p. 16.   [24] *Ibid.*, p. 19.
[25] *Ibid.*, p. 21. See also Hermann, p. 424.
[26] This 1713 papal bull banned 101 theses of the French Jansenist writer Paquier Quesnel (1634–1719).
[27] Hermann, p. 22. See also Meszlényi, p. 21.
[28] "Joseph II's celebrated Edict of Toleration of 1781 was regarded as inadequate by all who saw in toleration something more than a device for attracting foreign skilled craftsmen to the new industries of Austria and settlers to the wastes of Hungary." Wangermann, p. 14.
[29] Within a few years, 1,015 Protestant ecclesiastic communities were established. Hermann, p. 443.

this might seem to be a definite restriction, but in Joseph II's time it was a progressive measure indeed. In addition, the *decretalis* oath was abolished, thus opening state offices to Protestants. Even Greek Orthodoxy became an accepted, or "received," religion, and concessions were made to the Jews.

Within a few years, the reforms of the Patent of Toleration were expanded. A lord's chapel, previously open only to members of his family, was now open to anyone he cared to invite, and the jurisdiction of Catholic bishops over non-Catholics as it had formerly existed was abolished. After 1785, localities where less than one hundred Protestant families lived were permitted to have churches of their own if the county granted permission to this effect. By 1786, the building of spires and, by 1787, of doors which let onto the street was permitted.

In November, 1781, twelve Hungarian students were withdrawn from universities in Rome and Bologna; soon thereafter, on January 26, 1782, all contemplative orders in Hungary were dissolved.[30] It was to be expected that Josephinism would create a stir in Rome. Thus it was that on March 22, 1782, an alarmed Pope Pius VI arrived in Vienna with the aim of curbing the devastating reforms of Emperor Joseph II. He spent a full month there and named Archbishop Batthyány, who was Primate of Hungary at the time, a cardinal on April 19, 1782. In regard to past measures, Joseph II scarcely revoked anything at all. He consented, however, to the taking of a loyalty oath to the Pope by bishops in the future, but only after they had taken one to the king.[31]

The Pope's trip was unsuccessful, practically speaking. A few months after he had returned to Rome, an ecclesiastic commission was organized within the framework of the *Consilium regium locumtenentiale hungaricum* to centralize the administration and control of Church affairs. All matters of education were secularized. In 1784 Joseph abolished the diocesan seminaries and created, instead, state-controlled general seminaries in Pozsony, Eger, and Zágráb.[32] In the Empire between the years 1782 and 1787, 359 monasteries (276 for males, 83 for females) were abolished; of this number, 140 were in Hungary (134 for males, 6 for females).[33] The various properties of

---

[30] Meszlényi, p. 23.   [31] *Ibid.,* p. 26.   [32] Hermann, p. 422.
[33] Hermann, p. 426.

these monasteries were awarded by Joseph to the ecclesiastic foundation for the support of the parishes and the parish priests, and for the expansion of their numbers. In 1783, ecclesiastic jurisdiction over marriage suits was abolished. Liturgical books were published by the state, and the authority of papal nuncios was abolished.[34]

During his reign Joseph II issued more than six thousand patents and regulations that touched upon religious life and Church matters. With the exception of purely spiritual affairs, he heavily supervised the Church and made it virtually impossible for the clergy to communicate with Rome.[35] On January 28, 1790, all regulations which affected the Church were revoked, with, that is, the exception of the Patent of Toleration and the establishment of new parishes. Yet Dr. Meszlényi, the apologist of papal power, mournfully stated that "ecclesiastic policies during the following generations were determined by [the principles of] Josephinism, thus putting the Holy See in a position of defense." [36]

[34] Meszlényi, pp. 28, 29.   [35] Hermann, p. 435.   [36] Meszlényi, p. 30.

Part III

THE FORCES OF CHANGE

Chapter XI

THE EMERGING CRISIS
IN FEUDAL SOCIETY
AND AGRICULTURE

THE LAST FIVE YEARS of the reign of Joseph II saw the beginning of a new era for Hungary, an era which culminated in 1848 with the bourgeois nationalist revolution of Lajos Kossuth. Three main forces of change dominated this era: an emerging crisis in the feudal agricultural system and society; an early nationalism among the Hungarians and the major non-Hungarian nationalities—the Croats, Serbs, and Rumanians;[1] and an influx of enlightened ideas and the influence of the French Revolution which kindled an intellectual revival in Hungary. The cumulative effect of these forces put great stresses on the feudal system of society in the late eighteenth century.

THE PAUPERIZATION OF THE SERFS

In the eighteenth century, during the reconstruction and resettlement of Hungary up to about 1760, the serfs' lot improved, owing to a shortage of laborers. But as soon as the repopulation of the formerly uninhabited lands was complete (drastically decreasing the value of new labor), stricter contracts were offered by landowners to new tenants and the violation of existing contracts commenced.[2] The dy-

[1] Because of the complexity of the problem, the early Croat, Serb, and Rumanian nationalist movements will not be dealt with.

[2] I. Szabó, *Magyar parasztság*, p. 49. See also Mérei, *Mezőgazdaság*, p. 127. For the increasing severity of the contracts offered by Prince Eszterházy, see Szabad, pp. 28 ff.

nasty, on the other hand, began a policy of protecting the serfs in the early eighteenth century that reached a peak[3] with the promulgation of the urbarial regulations of Maria Theresa and the reforms of Joseph II.[4] The urbarial regulations, among other provisions, stipulated the maximum size for serf sections. Henceforward, the position of the serfs, who were unable to acquire new land, steadily deteriorated with the rise in population. The congestion of serfs on their ever shrinking holdings grew so great that, of those emancipated in 1848, only 17,262 possessed more than a full section, while 48,599 possessed just a full section, 43,865 possessed more than half a section, 173,119 possessed a half-section, 239,692 possessed more than a quarter-section, and 22,715 possessed less than a quarter-section.[5] The peasants' holdings dwindled to dust.

The pattern in the town of Szolnok shows this process of fragmentation of serf holdings. In the mid-eighteenth century, the predominant serf holding around the town was a quarter of a section, enough to supply a family. By 1790, the majority of serfs possessed only fractions of a section and were no longer able to provide for their families.

While the total of serf holdings did not grow, the number of bondmen increased considerably. In 1771 the number of landless peasants in Szolnok was less than half that of the landed serfs, and only one fifth of them did not possess their own house. By 1828, the ratio had increased to where there were twice as many *zsellérek* as landed serfs.[6]

In Slovak-inhabited northern Hungary, one serf section was divided up into 32, 64, or even 128 units. On one lot, small even for one fair-sized family, 30 to 40 families lived, mostly at bare subsistence level. The situation was not markedly better in the Hungarian-populated areas. It was not unusual for 3 to 5 families, that is, 20 to 25 people, to live on three quarters of a section, or about 18 yokes of land.[7]

The fragmentation of the land and the resulting pauperization of

[3] Mérei, *Mezőgazdaság*, p. 128. See also Acsády, p. 379.

[4] Joseph II abolished serfdom with a royal rescript on August 22, 1785.

[5] Mérei, *Mezőgazdaság*, p. 131.

[6] *Ibid.*, p. 132. See also Niederhauser p. 134. Interestingly enough, the economic status of the serfs located in the urbarial villages of the town of Sopron did not deteriorate between the years 1765 and 1836. Jenny, p. 11.

[7] Mérei, *Mezőgazdaság*, p. 133.

the serfs hurt both serf and lord. In some areas the lords themselves tried to prevent the fragmentation of serf holdings. But not until 1836 were the lords given authority to withhold endorsement of divisions of land, thus enabling them to arrest the process.[8]

The urbarial regulations of Maria Theresa hurt the serf in other ways, too, even though their goal was his protection. They defined the maximum number of days of *robot* to which he was subject, with the intention of preventing his being overworked. In some places, however, fewer days of *robot* were exacted than the new regulations specified. Now the lords demanded maximum *robot* in accordance with the new stipulations.

The aristocrats were generally absentee landlords. Their estates were managed by lessees or bailiffs; these middlemen now tried to squeeze from the serfs all that the lord demanded plus something for their own profit. The lords' agents were usually very corrupt. It was common practice for the bailiff to receive a low salary from the lord, ordinarily below subsistence level. He was practically forced to make his living by extortion—considered routine practice by the lords.[9]

The communal possession of serf holdings in certain parts of Hungary was also an obstacle to progress. The communal holdings were divided into individual strips of land (*dülők*) for each serf family. The holdings of one serf sometimes consisted of as many as sixty small strips of land located in widely separated parts of the village lands. The serfs had to cultivate their land according to the village pattern of rotation. This prevalence of the Russian *mir* system in some parts of Hungary discouraged individual initiative, but it gradually was abandoned everywhere, save in parts of Slavonia where it persisted up to the end of the nineteenth century.[10]

THE EXPROPRIATION OF SERF HOLDINGS

Expansion of profitable food markets in Hungary continued from the establishment of the standing army in 1715 through the major wars of the eighteenth century.[11] As a result of the expanding market,

[8] Act No. 5, 1836, CJH, VI, 18. [9] Mérei, *Mezőgazdaság*, p. 141.
[10] *Ibid.*, p. 152.
[11] The boom in the grain market reached its peak during the French Revolutionary and Napoleonic Wars. The bubble did not burst, however, with the disappearance of the good grain markets at the end of these wars. In the early 1820s

the manorial system of cultivation became dominant in the country and brought in its wake fresh disaster for the serfs: a new wave of expropriation of their lands. Expropriation of serf holdings and their consolidation into large manorial estates took various forms in different regions of the country.[12]

The landlord could simply confiscate the serfs' holdings outright; if the serf became ill or his draft animals died, his holding was taken on the excuse that he could not fulfill his *robot* obligations. Communal hayfields or parts of them were plowed and attached to manorial lands. All the lots which the serfs cultivated prior to the promulgation of the urbarial regulations and which were in excess of the maximum serf holdings defined in the edict were confiscated (*maradványföldek*). If the serf moved, his holding was expropriated. Vineyards were exchanged for barren lands (*regulatio*).[13] Finally, cleared lands (*irtványföldek*) were simply taken away from the serfs.

In general, the Habsburgs opposed this trend. One main reason for their opposition was the fact that manorial estates were tax-exempt;[14] the increase of manorial lands at the expense of urbarial lands naturally reduced the total of lands taxed by the state.

Confiscation of cleared lands is the method of expropriation that warrants the most attention. With years of hard labor, serfs were still able to extend their holdings after the completion of resettlement in the mid-eighteenth century by clearing forests and scrubland and by draining swampland. The cleared land provided large areas of additional arable land in various parts of the country, especially in the Hanság,[15] the area around the villages of Csorna, Farád, and

---

a boom in the wool market became even more profitable. In 1846–47 Hungarian grain exports to Austria yielded 9.1 million florins, while wool exports to Austria brought in 17.1 million florins. Mérei, *Mezőgazdaság*, p. 25. Prince Eszterházy, the owner of the largest landed property in Hungary, sold more grain produced by serfs on their own lots than grain from his manorial lands. That was true even in the year 1810, during the grain market boom. This landlord's income from selling timber was two and a half times more, and from selling wine two and one-fourth times more, than his income from selling grain. Szabad, p. 24.

[12] Szántó, pp. 45–49.

[13] Hetényi, p. 57; Niederhauser, p. 129.

[14] The tremendous increase in expropriations during the Napoleonic Wars is indicated in a complaint filed with the *Staatsrat* in 1828 stating that in Bács County alone 8,000 yokes of serfs' holdings had been confiscated up to that year. Mérei, *Mezőgazdaság*, p. 17.

[15] A former swampland.

Bősárkány in Sopron County. At the town of Gyula in Békés County, serfs cleared reeds, drained swamps, and increased arable land from 57,929 yokes to 238,964 between 1773 and 1847.[16]

Ownership of cleared lands was a source of endless contention. The lords maintained that it was their privilege to exchange the lands for parts of their manorial lands (*regulatio*) on condition that the lot given in exchange was of equal quality. In principle, the serf could retain his cleared lands even if he gave away his urbarial holdings.[17] The serf had the right to dispose of the cleared lands, exchanging or mortgaging them, under the sole proviso that he report any such changes to the lord or his bailiff and record them in the land register. For the possession of cleared lands the serf owed no *robot* and paid no taxes. As an acknowledgment of the lord's property rights, however, the serf paid a nominal clearing fee (*irtásdíj*).[18] The serf was also free to sell or dispose of the crops he collected from the cleared lands as he wished.

These advantages were a great incentive to the serfs and resulted in the clearing of vast tracts of land. During the thirty odd years between the end of resettlement and 1790, there was a mass movement to clear barren lands. Many serfs left their homes and migrated to places where clearing work was still possible. Some cotters thus came to own arable land. Settlements, especially in western Hungary, gained in both land and population as a result of clearing, most notably the towns of Kapuvár, Csorna, Nagycenk, Lövő, Sopron, and Köves in Sopron County. The social consequences of this movement were considerable. It offered livelihood for many in an era of decreasing work opportunity; it made well-to-do farmers richer; it gave land to the landless cotters; it created a group of free renters among the peasants.

The expropriations reversed this trend. The extent of expropriations can be seen from how much territory two leading aristocratic families gained from the cleared lands of their serfs:[19]

---

[16] At the early stages of the resettlement the increase was as follows: plowland increased from 1.0 million to 1.6 million yokes between 1715 and 1720 (60 percent); cleared lands increased during the same period from 29.273 yokes to 43.540 yokes (48 percent). Acsády, p. 318.

For the location of Sopron and Békés counties see Map No. 3.

[17] Mérei, *Mezőgazdaság*, p. 137.

[18] *Ibid.*, p. 138.

[19] *Ibid.*, p. 139. See also Szántó, pp. 60–65.

Landowners	Plowland	Expropriated Cleared Land (in yokes)	Percentage Gain
Eszterházy family	17,200	8,000	47
Széchenyi family	9,500	7,000	70

The expropriation of cleared lands robbed the serfs in the Transdanubian part of Hungary alone of more than 20,000 yokes of arable land. Several former cotters lost all of their possessions. In several cases military force was used to carry out the expropriations. In a number of instances, lands were taken away without any compensation. The bulk of expropriation took place between 1790 and 1830, with a peak in 1793. It was one of the most notorious acts of the Hungarian aristocracy. The lords' intention, naturally, was to reestablish full property rights in areas where these rights were becoming indistinct or even lost. Another reason for the expropriations was that the landlords had more labor available following the urbarial regulations of 1767 and the cleared lands presented an opportunity to put this extra labor force to useful work.

Expropriations caused much resentment and tension. To pacify the serfs, some lords suspended expropriations between 1793 and 1825, and even returned some of the land already taken. Yet of the twenty-five villages owned by the Eszterházy family in Sopron County, eleven lost all their cleared lands. The Széchenyis appropriated the cleared lands of all their villages.[20]

Parts of the expropriated lands were rented back to the peasants and parts of them were returned to the serfs as urbarial holdings. The urbarial fees and services were considerably higher than the fees paid for cleared lands, and so the lords' income increased. This transaction was not completely to the disadvantage of the serfs for two reasons. First, the urbarial holdings became irretrievable possessions of the serfs; second, the fees and services were regulated and so were not excessive, at least in principle. To bypass both these consequences, the lords in most cases merely rented the expropriated cleared lands to the peasants. Then the lord could charge the peasants exorbitant rents. Furthermore, these lots were retrievable and the lord could cancel the lease any time he wished. Since land to let was scarce, the peasants rented it even under such disadvantageous conditions.

[20] Wellmann, "Mezőgazdaság," pp. 690 ff. See also Éble, pp. 16–18.

This system increased the number of free tenants. The distribution of expropriated cleared land in Sopron County is shown in the following table:[21]

Landowners	Total of Expropriated Cleared Lands (in yokes)	Expropriated Land Retained by Lords as Manorial Estates		Expropriated Land Rented Out to Serfs	
		Yokes	Percent	Yokes	Percent
Eszterházy family	11,070	8,000	72	3,070	28
Széchenyi family	7,800	7,700	98	100	2
Bishop of Győr	2,801	371	13	2,430	87
Others	3,000	1,800	60	1,200	40

The increasing expropriations, combined with the population growth, created a new phenomenon among the serfs: the number of landless peasants greatly increased and that of landed serfs decreased. The ratio between landed serfs and landless peasants was as follows:[22]

Year	Landed Serfs	Landless Peasants
1767 (the year of the urbarial regulations)	100	46
1828	100	104
1848	100	147

Thus, in eighty years a great part of the peasantry became landless. Fundamental changes in the structure of the peasantry had already occurred by 1790, easing the way toward this new phenomenon. Many serfs had been fully or partially removed from their former holdings, and thereby a large mobile labor force emerged for the first time in Hungarian history. Legally, however, these landless peasants remained bound to their lords, exposed to his whim, and in the absence of any simultaneous industrialization this new group of landless peasants could find no employment in the towns.

The expropriation of serf holdings was not the only means of increasing the lords' marketable produce.[23] The *robot* services and

---

[21] Soós, pp. 45–48.
[22] Mérei, *Mezőgazdaság*, pp. 7–8. On the Festetics estates the ratio of *zsellérek* among the bonded peasants increased between 1768 and 1848 as follows: Keszthely manor, 300 percent; Kemend manor, 240 percent. Szántó, p. 124. For further details see Spira, ed., pp. 271–76.
[23] Szántó, pp. 50–56.

the payments in kind which they exacted were also increased. This
trend became more and more marked, culminating in the 1790s. One
might have expected these new and unjust steps by the lords, this
peak of exploitation of the serfs, to have generated revolutionary
conditions. But no peasant revolt materialized in 1790. Such meager
stirrings as did occur will be discussed in Chapter XV.

THE LOW YIELD OF SERF HOLDINGS AND
LACK OF PURCHASING POWER

Grave difficulties were caused by the extensive and ever increasing
robot, which consumed much of the time and energy the serfs sorely
needed on their own lots. Communal pastures were often used by the
lords' cattle, in defiance of the law, leaving the serfs' cattle without
grass. The fact that the lords retained property rights over the
land prevented the serfs from acquiring credit for investment in their
holdings. The cumulative effect of all these inequities was to eliminate
the possibility of capital growth for the peasant.

Agrarian booms created only temporary advantages for lord and
peasant. Steady progress in agriculture would have been possible
had permanent markets only been available, but in peacetime the
Austrian market absorbed but a small portion of the Hungarian surplus. The quality of Hungarian produce was relatively low and it
could not compete with better and cheaper produce; meanwhile, the
internal market remained static. Peasants who might have been consumers lost their purchasing power in the course of the steady process
of pauperization. Lack of regular external and internal markets was
one of the main reasons for the retardation of industry and lack of
employment opportunities.

The backwardness of industry was partly the cause, partly the effect
of the still existing medieval guild system. The guilds were dominated
by small craftsmen jealously guarding their privileges with no wish for
modernization or large-scale production. The underdeveloped state
of industry is clear from the fact that as late as 1846 only one seventh
of the population was engaged in any form of industrial work. At
the end of the eighteenth century, burghers and artisans numbered
only 91,094, 2 percent of the total male population.[24]

[24] Mérei, *Mezőgazdaság,* p. 8.

Under such conditions, the purchasing power of the whole population was very low. Unsold agricultural surpluses were stored in the lords' granaries, while the mass of peasants, victims of expropriation, were dying of starvation and epidemics.[25] One exception was the Bánság of Temes (*Temesi Bánság*). Although as deficient in land communciations as other parts of the country, it had the advantage of water communications on the Tisza and Duna rivers. Waterways led from Temesvár, through the Béga Canal[26] to the Tisza, Duna, and Száva rivers; from the Száva grain was carried by road into Austria.

THE ROBOT SYSTEM: AN OBSTACLE
TO MODERN AGRICULTURE

Maria Theresa's urbarial regulations prescribed the *robot* obligation for all serfs. After the promulgation of the regulations, the lords exacted *robot* from many peasants who had not performed it before. This was particularly mortifying for contractual serfs, freed men who were previously exempt. Naturally, the more the *robot* was enforced, the less efficient and productive it became.[27]

A prime reason for the low productivity of serf labor was that the peasants used their own primitive everyday tools to perform their *robot*. To overcome this, a few lords began to purchase tools. And on a small scale they began to hire labor, especially for the execution of certain agricultural tasks which needed more care than mass serf labor could yield.[28]

As the feudal system of serf-rendered services to the lords had grown, a complex of material, legal, technical, financial, and emotional elements had created a peculiar human interdependence between man and master. These abstruse psychological ties evolved even between absentee lords and their serfs. But by 1790, any direct relationship between lord and peasant had become a thing of the past. The aristocrats living in Vienna had little or no contact with their serfs. Most of the lesser nobles who lived near the peasants looked on them as their "subjects," or even as an "untouchable" caste. The aristocrats, in general, believed that they were entitled to use the

[25] *Ibid.*, p. 11.
[26] The Béga Canal was built during Maria Theresa's reign.
[27] Spira, pp. 283–87.   [28] Mérei, *Mezőgazdaság*, p. 9.

serfs' labor as they pleased. The contemporary liberal intellectual, Gergely Berzeviczy, wrote:

The landlord looks on him [the serf] as a tool necessary to cultivate his lands and as a chattel which he inherited from his parents, or purchased, or acquired as a reward. He demands that the serf pay dues and perform *robot* for him and regards [the serf] as one with whom he can deal as his self-interest dictates.[29]

The major psychological repercussion of the lords' unbridled power and growing arbitrariness over the serfs was an unbounded distrust of the lords by the serfs. These mutually negative attitudes created a basic obstacle to normal labor relations. According to Berzeviczy:

The peasant shows an inborn distrust toward all of his superiors, even toward those who are not responsible for his plight, and believes that he is entitled to extract benefits by craft from those who because of their superior status enjoy so many advantages over him. This attitude stems from two sources: it either originates in ignorance or in the suspicion that he [the serf] is face to face with evil intent. This latter source of distrust has been borne out by experience. Distrust also exists toward all the administrative and judicial authorities. After all, who make up the authorities? The masters of the serfs and individuals connected with them [the masters] by a series of ties.

All innovations, particularly those initiated by the lords, are hated by the peasants; they oppose them stubbornly because they are aware that the interests of the lords are contrary to their own. Serfs suspect [innovations] as instruments of the lords' intent to increase their own advantages at the expense of those of the serfs.[30]

Thus even when the lord tried to bring in improvements, serf resistance lessened their efficiency. The *robot* which the lords exacted so rigidly was perhaps the most formidable obstacle to innovation or progress. The lords tried to counter the low yield of *robot* by increasing the amount of it gradually, especially during the boom years. At different places and different times, the lords' demands were so high that the serfs had no time to cultivate their own holdings. The more control and force the lords and their supervisors introduced, the less they gained from the work of the serfs. Berzeviczy writes:

When the time for urgent labor arrives on the land of the lords, it also comes to the holdings of the peasants. They [the serfs] try to avoid the unpaid labor [*robot*], but because it must be done, they send to fulfill the *robot* the weakest members of their families, those whom they use

[29] Berzeviczy, p. 142.   [30] *Ibid.*, p. 151.

to fetch [drinking] water for them when they work on their own holdings. If the supervisor objects, the serfs quote the law [which does not specify which member of the family is to perform *robot*] or claim that the whole family is ill or busy with some other public work. This is also true in the case of plowing when serfs come to *robot* with their weakest draft animals and worst plow and other tools with which no substantial or good work can be perfomed. . . . If the serf ordered to perform *robot* owns two plows, two hoes, two scythes, two axes, etc., one can be sure that he will take with him for the work to be done for the lord that which is worse, weaker, more worn.[31]

Count Károly Zichy complained:

My estate is in a most advantageous situation, in the vicinity of four towns; my villages are on the bank of the Danube River, near the busiest roads; my bailiffs are good; the soil is of the first quality; and yet all my income is spent on administration. I can only retain income derived from the 11,000 sheep on my manorial lands. What can I expect from the weak draft animals, bad plows, and wooden carriages of the serfs? [32]

Serfs usually arrived late to perform *robot*, worked slowly, took as many breaks as possible.[33] If they had to use their draft animals, they worked even slower in order to save the animals' strength for their own work. Serf labor of this kind could not answer the quantitative and qualitative demands of cultivation.[34] Quality and quantity of production did not increase in ratio to the growth in size of manorial lands but decreased relatively in face of the lords' growing demands.[35]

THE GROWING INDEBTEDNESS OF THE LANDLORDS

The incipient crisis of the feudal system cut short the anticipated substantial increase in the income of the landlords. While their income did not increase, the luxury of their living did. Consequently the aristocrats began to borrow money to keep up their standard of living, but not to modernize their lands. One method of borrowing was to sell their crops before harvest at a price usually much below market values. The aristocrats also began raising money by mortgaging property. By 1790, total mortgage debts of the landlords in Pest

[31] *Ibid.*, p. 147.   [32] Mérei, *Mezőgazdaság*, p. 41.   [33] Szántó, pp. 146–56.
[34] Pál Királyi, *Robot és dézsma* (Pest, 1845), pp. 257–58. Quoted in Mérei, *Mezőgazdaság*, p. 27.
[35] Mérei, *Mezőgazdaság*, p. 24.

County alone amounted to 598,000 florins. In the two biggest counties, debt fluctuation between 1790 and 1820 was as follows:[36]

County	Loans Mortgaged	Loans Repaid	Debts Remaining Mortgaged after 1820
	(in millions of florins)		
Pest	4	1.4	2.6
Baranya	1.6	0.5	1.1

The massive indebtedness of the feudal ruling class spelled the beginning of its decline even during the era of economic boom. The limited extra income gained by the lords through the extension of their manorial lands and the increase of *robot* was spent on their ever increasing luxuries and interest payments on loans. Only a negligible part of the lords' income went to agricultural investment, and thus the entire agrarian system remained based on a foundation of serf *robot* with its constantly decreasing efficiency and quality. Hungarian agriculture served only one purpose: to maintain the high living standards of the nobility. It was never considered the base of an economy producing reinvestable capital.

There existed, however, a rather primitive sort of investment in the form of *melioratio,* which meant the purchase of breeding stock and the building of indispensable structures such as stables. But *melioratio* never became significant in improving techniques of production and in increasing the quality and value of products. For example, the 720,000 yokes of the Eszterházy lands produced a net income of 800,000 to 1,700,000 florins annually—a mere 1 to 2 florins per yoke, even in the early nineteenth century.[37]

The prerequisite for the introduction of new methods in agriculture was a change in the general outlook of the ruling classes. Thus, aristocrats would have to become agrarian entrepreneurs, hiring educated and knowledgeable agronomists, streamlining management, introducing capitalist methods—considering the land as capital, observing market demands, making profitable investments—all basic conditions for the improvement of agriculture. No such measures occurred to the Hungarian landowners in the 1790s.

Contradictory as it may seem, the disintegration of Hungarian feudal society began during the boom era of the French Revolution

---

[36] Ungár, p. 43. See also Mérei, *Mezőgazdaság,* p. 24.
[37] Mérei, *Mezőgazdaság,* p. 34.

and the Napoleonic Wars. The effect of the wartime boom was twofold: it ruined the debt-ridden landowners who would not change their obsolete agrarian methods, and it propelled those who could and did change them into a new class of agrarian capitalists. The bankrupt nobles were absorbed into the newly emerging petit bourgeois class.[38]

The entail system prevented the landlords from borrowing sufficient amounts of money to undertake large-scale investments. During the first part of the nineteenth century, however, the entail system was eased considerably. Unfortunately, the resultant greater ease of borrowing merely enabled the lords to run further into debt to cover personal expenses rather than for investment purposes. Changes in the entail system led only to spiraling debts and interest payments, as shown by the following figures (in florins) for the two largest counties:

	Borrowed	Repaid	Standing Debt
Pest County			
Up to 1790	not known	not known	598,000
1790–1820	4,038,758	1,426,362	2,633,260
1820–32	6,873,404	1,885,238	4,988,166
Baranya County			
Up to 1790	789,313	203,104	586,200
1790–1820	1,649,192	567,278	1,081,914
1820–32	1,993,597	82,366	1,911,231

The decline of the grain market after the French wars accelerated the indebtedness of the landowners. Even the boom in the wool market could not save them. By the middle of the nineteenth century the personal indebtedness of Hungarian landowners amounted to 300 million florins, a debt that incurred an annual interest of 18 million florins. Many of the impoverished lords were obliged to earn their livelihood by work. They retained their feudal philosophy but lost their feudal status.

AGRARIAN INNOVATORS AND REFORMERS

With a few, isolated exceptions, the whole Hungarian agricultural system was in a state of stagnation. In those rare instances, however, ingenuity and innovations produced some noteworthy successes. But

[38] *Ibid.*, p. 41.

in most of these cases, progress was only in the sphere of agricultural methods; the social system was carefully preserved without change. The innovators were still feudal-minded men of the twilight era of the eighteenth century, not reformist precursors of the social, economic, and political advances that were to burgeon in the nineteenth century. Particularly successful agricultural experiments were made by Count Csekonics, superintendent of the state stud farm at Mezőhegyes; the local landowner at Rákoskeresztur, west of Buda; Colonel Ágoston Lázár in the village of Écska on the Béga Canal; Count Antal Amadé of Görzsöny in the Transdanubian region; and Baron Lilien of Ercsi, west of Buda.[39]

Nevertheless there was a smaller group of men who sought not only technical innovations in agricultural methods and reforms in the economic life of the countryside but also a complete social and economic overhaul of the whole of society. These men can indeed be seen as harbingers of the nineteenth-century reform generation of Széchenyi and Kossuth. Above all it was Sámuel Tessedik, the Evangelical pastor of the village of Szarvas, who was the most prominent agricultural reformer of his day.[40] The direct continuation of his work was undertaken by Gergely Berzeviczy, the major part of whose ideas belongs to the nineteenth century. Berzeviczy, in fact, functions as a bridge connecting the work of Tessedik with the activities of the reformers of the next century.

The first group of innovators introduced many new methods beneficial to agriculture. They drained marshes, erected dams to reclaim land for agriculture, planted trees, built breweries and distilleries, bred fine cattle, established the cultivation of tobacco, had canals and ditches dug, and by fertilization created areas of rich arable land. Baron Lilien, furthermore, brought in new fodder crops and potatoes, and was the first man to use threshing and cultivating machines.

The most important effect of all these innovations was on the *robot* system. It was not that there was any intention or attempt to abolish or reduce it, but the innovative landlords exacted their serfs' *robot* fairly and strictly in accordance with the law. Since the serfs knew precisely what they had to do and what their rewards would

[39] Hóman and Szekfü, V, 221, and Mérei, *Mezőgazdaság,* pp. 42 ff.
[40] Balázs, *Magyarország,* II, 615–16.

be, they worked with far greater efficiency than elsewhere. The landlords hired well-trained and educated bailiffs, and paid them well. As a result these agents were men who knew their jobs well, were free of corruption, and extracted no illegal fees from the serfs.

Substantial gains accrued to landlord and serfs alike. In the disaster years of 1794 and 1795, when extraordinarily bad weather caused nationwide food shortages, and even famine here and there, these innovators harvested produce to spare.[41] Count Amadé's returns in 1788 amounted to 10,000 florins; by 1809 they had risen to 800,000 florins.[42] Baron Lilien invested half a million florins in his estate during the first fifteen years of ownership, but his profits were such that he became one of the richest men in the country.[43]

Under the influence of utilitarianism and, to a lesser extent, the Physiocrats, Sámuel Tessedik, on the other hand, instituted reforms of a very different character. By his own toil and that of his hired laborers, he created a veritable paradise out of the lands that were the benefice of the pastorship of Szarvas. He introduced a tremendous variety of innovations: he planted new fodder crops and established orchards on land that for generations had been considered barren; he made vegetable gardens; he altered the concept of animal husbandry by stabling his animals for part of the year instead of keeping them in the fields the year round, as was the local custom; he began systematic fertilization and at the same time gave up the antiquated three-crop rotation system; he planted acacia trees after discovering that they required little water and were very effective in binding shifting, sandy soil and enabling it to be brought under the plow. (When he first arrived in Szarvas, there was just one acacia tree in the whole parish; by the time he died, there were 100,000.)[44] By such means, Tessedik, like other innovators, managed to make his land handsomely profitable.

But Tessedik's technical methods were secondary to his other activities, and it was the latter that made him a reformer of national stature. He founded Hungary's first school of economics, the Ex-

---

[41] In 1794 the townsmen of Rákoskeresztur were short neither of food nor of fodder. Mérei, Mezőgazdaság, p. 47.

[42] Entry in the diary of the Palatine Archduke Joseph for September 22, 1809. Domanovszky, ed., József, II, 640.

[43] Mérei, Mezőgazdaság, p. 53.

[44] Wellmann, Tessedik, p. 81. See also Hóman and Szekfü, IV, 525–26.

perimental Economic Institute,[45] in Szarvas; he published an impressive number of books and pamphlets in German and Hungarian, campaigning for national economic, social, and political reform; and, finally, he persuaded his parishioners to adopt new agricultural practices similar to his own.

His most remarkable achievement was without doubt the Experimental Economic Institute. It was founded in 1780, flourished through the last decade of the century, and was forced to close its doors in 1806. It was a school for the unprivileged and declared war on obsolete agrarian methods. Its basic aims were to spread knowledge of economics, to fight superstitious practices, to educate men to think, and to train intelligent and able farmers, craftsmen, tradesmen, teachers, and housekeepers.[46] The languages of instruction reflected the distribution of nationalities in the area: Hungarian, Slovak, and German were used. Teachers were recruited from Buda, Sopron, Pozsony, and Vienna, and primarily for their information a library was stocked with 725 books.[47] In the early 1790s, 991 students were enrolled at the Institute, a figure that is an outstanding indication of success in its own right.

The most striking, nay, revolutionary, aspect of the pupils' education was the complete disregard for the Jesuitic scholasticism that prevailed everywhere else. The students were taught realistic subjects such as natural science, the principles of good health, meteorology, and national and local geography and history. The other main features of the teaching were its complete secularism and the coordination of practical agriculture and handicrafts with theoretical education. The peasant pupils progressed so rapidly in their learning that a visiting dignitary, a representative in the gentry-dominated administration of Békés County, Councilor Lehotczky, felt compelled to comment caustically on the young serfs: "Now these bastards know more than we do." [48]

Sámuel Tessedik received recognition and high awards from the enlightened despots. Joseph II gave him a portrait of himself and the gold *Virtute et Exemplo* medal in 1787. Leopold II received him in audience several times. In 1796, however, one year after the suppression of the Jacobin movement in Hungary, the Institute was

[45] Gyakorlati Gazdasági Intézet.   [46] Wellmann, *Tessedik*, pp. 96–97.
[47] *Ibid.*, p. 103.   [48] *Ibid.*, p. 110.

closed. It was too much out of step with reviving feudal sentiment. Yet, though the Habsburgs' enlightened views had evaporated and reaction had set in everywhere, the court still could not afford to neglect a man who, though socially dangerous, had made such important contributions to agriculture, especially when his innovations were of so much value to the Empire's efforts in the French Revolutionary Wars. In 1798 Tessedik was therefore awarded the gold *Lege et Fide* medal, and one year later it was decided to reopen the Institute. This time, however, the school was run on a different basis. The victorious reactionary forces would not tolerate its being a place of learning for mere peasant youths; the pupils were now bailiffs selected and sent there by the landlords. Where formerly there had been nearly a thousand students, there were now only twenty or thirty—a clear sign of the disfavor of the court and the estates. In 1806 all state support was cut off and the Institute finally vanished.

It would be less than fair to attribute the Institute's closure solely to the court's determination to suppress the school and muzzle Tessedik's other activities. There were hostile forces nearer at hand. The peasants had lost interest in educating their children, for it had become crystal-clear to them that, as the forces of reaction gained strength, their chances of social progress, so real during the era of enlightened despotism, had dwindled to nothing. The landed gentry resented the activities of both Tessedik himself and his school as meddling in serf affairs, which, since Tessedik was not a member of the estates, he had no right doing. The well-to-do peasantry also resented Tessedik because they dominated village administration and he exposed their corruption. Churchmen resented Tessedik because his achievements pricked their consciences for being too lax to do the same, so they condemned him for degrading himself by working with his own hands and for neglecting his pastoral duties. And so Tessedik found himself under attack on many fronts at once, a battle which in the short run he lost—but not in the long run, for some of the tradition set by his school was perpetuated in the Georgicon, the agrarian academy of Keszthely founded by György Festetics in 1797. Tessedik was consulted and his opinions heeded, but he declined the offer to become superintendent of the new institution. Unlike the Institute with its focus on peasant youth, the Academy was established to train bailiffs, drawn from the *bocskoros nemesek* or other sectors of society that could fill the office, to manage the lords' estates. Another bailiffs' school was founded in 1801 by Kristóf Nákó, lord of Nagyszentmiklós in Torontál County. This school was set up exactly according to plans elaborated by Tessedik. It was in these two schools that Tessedik's traditions survived the demise of his own Institute— not the social traditions, but his ideas on the dissemination of agricultural knowledge.

As a result of Tessedik's innovations, Szarvas village underwent a radical change. The villagers consumed a more balanced diet because of the availability of fruit and vegetables, they built larger, better-ventilated houses, they wore cleaner clothing, and their health improved.[49] They grew produce for sale and the markets of Buda and Pest were filled with fresh fruit and vegetables from Szarvas and its neighborhood. The whole peasant way of life in Szarvas became more decent and dignified than it had been before Tessedik's arrival.

An agrarian revolution in the English style was foreshadowed by Tessedik's efforts, as well as in his treatises. The most noteworthy of these was *Der Landmann in Ungarn, was er ist, und was er seyn könnte, nebst einem Plane von einem regulirten Dorfe,* published in 1784 and in a Hungarian translation in 1786. Tessedik's tracts urged an end to the thousand-year-old system of three-field rotation and the adoption of intensive cultivation of the land, using new crops and fertilization. This, he argued, should be tied in with intensive methods of animal husbandry, such as stall-feeding cattle with the newly introduced fodder crops and turnips. Tessedik suggested raising industrial crops, such as sugar beets, maize, and oilseeds, and breeding silkworms. He put great stress on drawing up careful plans for building healthy, modern villages. He put forward proposals for revolutionarily transforming the social, economic, and political status of the serfs. "Freedom [of the peasants] and ownership [by them of the land]" were his watchwords. He pointed out how the state would be able to collect more taxes by such a reform and how the whole nation would benefit from the peasants' increased well-being.[50] The reforms he proposed did not aim to redress wrongs within the framework of a feudal society but envisioned the creation of a new society of free citizens—a revolutionary change. But he did not want this change brought about by violent means; he wanted it realized through the

[49] *Ibid.,* p. 87.   [50] *Ibid.,* p. 47.

cooperation of the privileged. His vision, then, was the highly utopian one of a revolution by consent. Both the means and the end were outside the realm of possibility. The problem had to await the advent of the reform generation of the nineteenth century.

Chapter XII

THE HUNGARIAN INTELLECTUAL
REVIVAL IN 1790

HUNGARIAN literary historians call the era which began in the last quarter of the eighteenth century and which reached an early climax in 1790 the Era of Revival (*felújulás*).[1] The ideology of the revival was a fusion of the ideas of the French Enlightenment with the mentality of the Hungarian nobility. Naturally, that amalgam resulted in a rather strange ideology. Ferenc Kazinczy, who later became the literary "dictator" of Hungarian intellectual life, began in 1790 to promote the ideas of the Enlightenment with the publication of *Orpheus*, the first Hungarian magazine of literary criticism. In the first issue he wrote, "I made determined efforts to tear the bloody dagger out of the hand of superstition and to tear the mask off its horrifying face."[2]

The first wave of the Hungarian revival was composed exclusively of Voltairean writers, the Hungarian "Guardists,"[3] led by Bessenyei.[4] Their struggle for Hungarian intellectual progress was closely tied to a struggle against the authority of the Catholic Church. The leading personalities of the Hungarian militant anticlerical movement were János Fekete, Mihály Sztáray, Sándor Szacsvay, and János Laczkovics —two aristocrats, a lesser noble, and a captain of hussars respectively.

[1] Szerb, p. 215.
[2] *Ibid.*, p. 218. For the arrival of the Enlightenment in Hungary see Silagi, p. 22; Sugar, pp. 331 ff.; Waldapfel, pp. 15 ff.
[3] The writers of the Hungarian Noble Bodyguard.
[4] Lajos Némedi, "Bessenyei György és a német felvilágosodás" [György Bessenyei and the German Enlightenment], *Egri Pedagógiai Főiskola Évkönyve*, 1960, pp. 261 ff.

The majority of the Hungarian intellectuals stood solidly behind these noisy agitators—for agitators they were.

The well-educated Protestant intellectuals, in particular, supported the Enlightenment. To them, the Patent of Toleration of Emperor Joseph II meant the opportunity to practice their religion without interference. But even more important, it opened up to them political and administrative positions in the government from which they had hitherto been excluded. In 1790 they tried to achieve full political emancipation through the spread of the Enlightenment. In Hungary, the struggle for Protestant political emancipation showed interesting regional differences. The eastern regions of royal Hungary, which were mostly Protestant, accepted the Enlightenment; the primarily Catholic West—the Dunántúl (Transdanubian districts)—which felt its privileges threatened, resisted the Enlightenment.[5]

The main channels through which the ideas of the revival were spread were the press and pamphlets. The activists of the revival emphasized the importance of modernizing the Hungarian language.[6] To this end, first efforts were made in 1790 to establish a Hungarian academy of sciences and a Hungarian national theater, modeled on the Comédie Française. The Enlightenment endowed intellectual life, as well as the written and spoken Hungarian language, with a high degree of social respectability hitherto unknown in Hungary.

In the Hungarian revival three strata of society played important roles: the aristocracy, the *bene possessionati,* and the burghers and *honoratiori.* The aristocrats, as we have seen, became courtiers during the eighteenth century. Many of them could no longer even speak Hungarian. However, they had not lagged culturally; rather, they had kept abreast of Western learning, but their culture had lost its national character. Their language was primarily French, the common language of the thinkers of the Enlightenment, educated men, and the courts of Europe. Nineteenth-century reformers and the coming of nationalism condemned the aristocracy for its lack of national character. Time, however, has shown this condemnation to be largely unwarranted.

These "denationalized" aristocrats were, during most of the eight-

---

[5] Szerb, p. 218.
[6] Silagi, pp. 58–64; Pintér, *A magyar irodalom története Bessenyei György fellépésétől,* pp. 376 ff.; Marczali, *Országgyülés,* I, 341 ff.

eenth century, the only links through which Western civilization was channeled toward Hungary. The mission took on particular importance since the lesser nobility turned completely inward and severed its former proud cultural connections with the West. The isolation of the lesser nobles, however, was not entirely of their own doing, but was forced upon them in part by state censorship. The only Hungarians who were to some extent free of the rigors of Maria Theresa's censorship were the courtiers in Vienna. Only they managed to remain in touch with the mainstream of Western civilization, and many of them became adherents of the Enlightenment. The denationalized aristocracy thus became the seedbed for the Hungarian cultural and political revival.[7]

The main current of Hungarian Enlightenment flowed through Vienna. Maria Theresa was hostile to the Enlightenment, yet her court was packed with its thinkers, men such as Kaunitz, Van Swieten, and Sonnenfels, to name the more outstanding. The most important first Hungarian representatives of the Enlightenment at the Theresan court were Mihály Sztáray and Count János Fekete, both devoted disciples of Voltaire. Fekete was in frequent correspondence with Voltaire. He sent several of his poems to the Frenchman, who always replied, returning the verses with polite comments, each time encouraging Fekete to send him new verses. True, Fekete always added 100 bottles of Tokaj wine to a package of his verses.[8]

Fekete and Sztáray were archetypal enlightened aristocrats. But the majority of the Hungarian aristocracy living in Vienna accepted the Enlightenment after their own fashion. In 1790 it was stylish for a Hungarian aristocrat to be a Voltairean. Even during Maria Theresa's reign, it was almost a sport to acquire those French books forbidden by the censorship. Count István Csáky owned 5,000 French books; Sztáray had about the same number; out of 15,000 pieces in the Héderváry Library, 6,000 were French works reflecting the Enlightenment. It must be noted, though, that the aristocracy was attracted not by the social and altruistic aspects of the Enlightenment but by its anticlericalism. It gave the aristocrats an excuse for competing politically with the first estate.

During the last quarter of the eighteenth century, the gentry gradually regained its former position of dominance. In the time

[7] Szerb, p. 201.   [8] *Ibid.*, p. 203.

of Verbőczi, the dominance of the *bene possessionati* had been exclusively political. The new factor in the lesser nobility's second ascendancy was that its dominance was cultural as well as political. For almost a century, until the Revolution of 1848, the importance of the *bene possessionati* lay in this dual influence. Rousseau was widely read in the original in Hungary, so that his ideas had a direct impact on the minds of the Hungarian gentry.[9] The intellectual life of Vienna, the door to Western culture, helped channel Rousseau's ideas into Hungary. Professor Karl Anton Martini, the pioneer of later Austrian civil legislation[10] and teacher of so many young Hungarian gentry, played the most important part in spreading Western enlightened ideas to Hungary. But there were also several original Hungarian interpretations of Rousseau.[11]

The third group of Hungarian society which had its own interpretation of the Enlightenment different from, and far more radical than, those of the aristocracy and the lesser nobility comprised the burghers and the *honoratiori*. Professor György Alajos Belnay referred to the Social Contract in his leaflet demanding equal civic rights for each and every member of society:[12]

These rights, the basic tenets of all civic constitutions, may eventually be neither ignored nor violated. This has been shown by France's example, which has made the aristocracy of every nation tremble. France's example shows what human rights truly are. . . . The cloak with which the monstrous feudal system has shrouded the truth has been destroyed, and it [the truth] has been fully revealed.[13]

[9] In the mid-eighteenth century Montesquieu's *Esprit des Lois* was translated into Latin and sold in Hungary. In 1792 the Latin translation of *Du Contrat Social* was presented to the *Consilium locumtenentiale* for permission to be printed, but permission was not granted, despite the fact that several members of the *Consilium* (Counts Antal Haller and Ferenc Barkóczy and Baron József Podmaniczky) supported the request. Ferenc Szentmárjay had almost completed the Hungarian translation of the work before his arrest; the manuscript was among the papers of the Martinovics trial. *Vertrauliche Akten*, Secr. 11/A (No. 51), quoted in Eckhardt, p. 41.

[10] Kann, p. 134.

[11] One of the most prominent Hungarian interpreters of Rousseau was Pál Rosos, whose main work was *De interna rerum publicorum securitate* (Pest, 1777).

[12] Belnay, *Reflexiones cunctorum Hungariae civium non nobilum* (Pest, 1790). See also Hóman and Szekfü, V, 64, 65.

[13] In *Reflexiones cunctorum Hungariae civium non nobilum*, quoted in Eckhardt, p. 47. See also Benda, ed., I, xxxiii. Belnay turned to the delegates of the diet of 1790–91 to promote his ideas. Hóman and Szekfü, V, 64, 65.

The time was near, according to Belnay, when the suppressed people would challenge the privileges of the ruling classes. They would examine all existing privileges and, as happened in France, would abolish them. Men's original standards of equality would be restored. The people, all being equal, would not tolerate intermediaries between them and the king, who would rule in accordance with the publicly stated principles of the Social Contract. It would be better if the nobility were to renounce its privileges now before it was too late. It must bow to the interests of the people by restoring all those rights which nature gave to each man. These rights must not be denied anyone either by law or through custom.

All the early ideas of Martinovics[14] were based on the Social Contract and the Declaration of the Rights of Men and Citizens. The members of his conspiracy, long before it was formally organized, shared the beliefs of Rousseau. Szentmarjay showed his translation of *Du Contrat Social* to his friends.[15] Hajnóczy doubted that any state in which conditions existed as they did in Hungary could claim to have a constitution at all.[16] In 1790 it was Martinovics, above all, who based his convictions most fully on the principles of the Social Contract. In his first major work, *Oratio ad Proceres*,[17] translated and edited in Hungarian by Laczkovics, Martinovics demanded abolition of all class privileges, including the political privileges of the clergy. The aristocrats were the enemy of humanity, Martinovics asserted. It was they who prevented the people from bursting out of darkness into light by concealing from them the principles of the Social Contract which were so simple and so clear.

How grievously are the laws of humanity and liberty denied by those who consider it dangerous for the community to be led from the darkness of ignorance into the light . . . and to be allowed to know the simple truths of the [Social] Contract, which weld and harmonize the society of the citizenry.[18]

[14] Silagi, pp. 65–86; Benda, I, xv, 7–35, 349–57, 735–61.
[15] *Vertrauliche Akten*, Secr. 11/A (No. 51), as quoted in Eckhardt, p. 41.
[16] Hajnóczy, *De diversis subsidiis*, as quoted in Eckhardt, p. 48. The arguments for the taxation of the nobles in Chapter VII of *De diversis subsidiis* are reprinted in Benda, I, 600–12.
[17] Full text in Benda, I, 117–49.
[18] Quoted in Eckhardt, p. 51.

THE EARLY HUNGARIAN PRESS

Until about 1780, the book was the dominant printed form in Hungary. From the reign of Emperor Joseph II on, however, newspapers began to come into their own. The most important literary works were first printed in magazines, and only then appeared in book form. Newspapers and periodicals were the vehicles for lively literary activity and exerted considerable political influence.[19] It might be questioned how far Hungarian public opinion was informed about the ideas and events of the French Revolution, but, in fact, the reading, thinking, vocal sectors of Hungarian society were aware in detail in 1790 of what was happening in the West.[20]

This information was disseminated primarily by newspapers which, with the permission of Joseph II and the authorities, discussed the events of the Revolution. Pál Őz, one of the defendants at the Martinovics trial, argued in his defense that he, his companions, and everybody else in Hungary had been following the Revolution with interest for years. Countless revolutionary publications were in circulation and widely read, he asserted. Up to 1790, the arguments against the ideas of the French Revolution were very few and very weak in Hungary. No law or decree curbed the free exchange of opinion, and people did not hesitate to air their views freely.[21]

The Hungarian press in 1790 already had a long tradition. German-, Latin-, and Hungarian-language newsletters have survived from the sixteenth and seventeenth centuries, dealing mostly with the Turkish War. In April, 1705, Rákóczi's general, Antal Eszterházy, issued the *Mercurius Hungaricus*. Prince Ferenc Rákóczi II ordered the paper to be published regularly under the title *Mercurius Veridicus ex Hungaria*.[22] But after the Treaty of Szatmár, in the absence of a rich bourgeoisie, no stratum of Hungarian society was interested in promoting a regular newspaper. It is worth noting, however, that Maria Theresa's *Ratio Educationis* of 1777 prescribed the reading of news-

---

[19] Szerb, p. 229.
[20] Eckhardt, p. 100. On the general situation of the press in all the Habsburg lands, see Silagi, pp. 27–31.
[21] See the comments of Pál Őz on his indictment, in Benda, II, 725 ff.
[22] Dezsényi and Nemes, I, 15, 16.

papers by pupils twice a week.[23] Exclusively for teachers and students, Latin-language papers, such as *Ephemerides Vindobonenses,* were printed between 1776 and 1779 and between 1790 and 1793. The *Pressburger Zeitung,* served by a fine group of writers and scientists of the Enlightenment, appeared on July 16, 1764. It was the first newspaper in Hungary to be printed regularly for any appreciable length of time. In 1848 it became a daily, and from 1880 onwards it was printed twice a day. It went out of existence only in 1929, after 165 years of circulation.[24]

The *Magyar Hirmondó* [Hungarian Courier], the first Hungarian-language newspaper, began publication on January 1, 1780, and appeared continuously for nine years. The *Hirmondó* was a biweekly, and its subscribers rapidly increased from the initial 320 to 500.[25] When it went out of circulation there was no break in the continuity of Hungarian newspaper publication, however, for its traditions were taken over and expanded by a series of other newspapers and magazines.

The *bene possessionati,* who had previously shown little enthusiasm for the development of culture, now took a lively interest in the press. One reason for this was the additional income they were receiving from the boom grain markets engendered by Maria Theresa's wars. They became increasingly aware of their country's backwardness and the need for change. The editor of the *Magyar Hirmondó,* Mátyás Rát, writing about the editorial policy of that paper, underlined the need to know other peoples and compare them with one's own. He stated:

There does not exist a nation in Europe which would not read in daily, weekly, or monthly papers in its own language, either for instruction or just for entertainment, about changes in its native country, about the

---

[23] *Ibid.,* p. 19.   [24] *Ibid.,* p. 21.

[25] The known professions of the majority of the subscribers in Hungary were as follows: landowners, aristocrats, and *bene possessionati,* 133 (32 of them women); county officials, 28; priests and teachers, 18; lawyers, 18; landowners' agents, 18; military officers, 12; postal clerks, 12; burghers, 9; tutors and students, 8; state officials, 7; town officials, 5; college principals, 4; physicians, 3. The subscribers came from 103 different localities. Of the 275 subscribers whose professions are known, about 145 were definitely aristocrats or *bene possessionati,* and the remaining 130 were either lesser nobility or intellectuals risen from nonprivileged classes. The high proportion of nonlandowners is noteworthy. *Ibid.,* p. 23.

hardships of the world, about clever men's funny or useful inventions, about scholars' labors, and about a whole range of other matters of note.

Rát warned the *Magyar Hirmondó*'s readers that Hungary's lack of similar reading habits was proof of its backwardness. "We live isolated like a grub in a nut—and this is harmful and shameful," he declared.[26]

The *Hirmondó* tried to stimulate the public's interest in reading and accustom it to forming opinions on contemporary problems. All this was carried out in Hungarian, a particularly difficult task in the absence of a refined literary language. The selection and use of the exact words to express a particular fact or thought was a real pioneering feat.

The *Hirmondó* passed, in September, 1784, into the hands of Sándor Szacsvay, who may be considered the first Hungarian political newspaperman. He was a poor Székely (Sekler) who had previously been Rát's assistant. Under his able leadership, the number of subscribers rose to 449, despite the heavy mailing costs (out of an annual subscription of 10 florins, 4 florins went to postal expenses). Szacsvay abandoned Rát's didactic style. As a true political writer, he went in for a simple style, vivid reporting, and an abundance of good humor.[27]

Szacsvay, after quitting the *Hirmondó*, moved to Vienna, where he was able to begin publishing the *Magyar Kurir* [Hungarian Messenger] on December 2, 1786. Thus, for two decades, Vienna became the center of the Hungarian-language press.[28] The well-edited *Magyar Kurir* became a serious competitor of the *Hirmondó*, which had a series of new editors in quick succession. None of them was a match for Szacsvay. The number of subscribers dropped off fast and the last issue of the *Magyar Hirmondó* saw the light on October 8, 1788. Another reason for the newspaper's decline was the transfer of the state capital and government offices from Pozsony to Buda: with them went a large proportion of the newspaper's subscribers. The printing of a new paper in the new capital under the title *Magyar Merkurius* began under the editorship of István Török, a minister of the Reformed Church of Vác. The title was changed to the *Magyar*

[26] *Ibid.*, p. 22.
[27] *Ibid.*, p. 24. The first Slovak newspaper, *Presspurske Nowiny*, appeared on July 1, 1783.
[28] Dezsényi and Nemes, p. 25.

Merkur on January 3, 1789. The paper did not, however, gain enough readership, and publication was discontinued on December 30, 1789. From then until 1806 no Hungarian-language newspaper was published in the state capital.

The story of the *Magyar Kurir* of Vienna was the complete opposite.[29] Szacsvay was a friend of Grossinger, one of the cabinet secretaries of Emperor Joseph II. He was also close to leading members of the Hungarian literary and intellectual revival, which centered around the Hungarian Noble Bodyguard. His proximity to sources of news from the West enabled Szacsvay to edit an interesting and well-informed newspaper. His enterprise prospered, and he enlisted 370 subscribers. Another reason for Szacsvay's success was his devotion to the principles of the Enlightenment so current in the Imperial capital at that time.

The *Kurir* became a leader in the offensive against the Roman Catholic Church.[30] On May 24, 1787, a Capuchin monk preaching in Vienna denounced Szacsvay because he "scolded the Pope and stirred up hatred against Catholicism." Szacsvay was undeterred by such incidents and issued two leaflets attacking the clergy. The first was *Izé purgatóriumba való utazása* [Jigger Travels in Purgatory]; the second, *Zakkariásnak a pápa titkos iródeákjának Rómába költ levelei* [Letters Written in Rome by Zaccharias, the Pope's Confidential Secretary]. He also expressed his ideas forcefully in the *Magyar Kurir*.

The early Hungarian press followed the lead of the *Moniteur* of Paris in offering its readers vivid accounts of the French Revolution, and Sándor Szacsvay's *Magyar Kurir* was ahead in this field. The editor knew exactly what his readers wanted:

The whole of Europe is now listening to France, which over the last three years has become the scene of world events. [*Kurir*, April 8, 1791.] We know that our readers wish above all to know what is going on in Paris. What is the king of France doing? What is Petoin, the Mayor of Paris, doing? . . . La Fayette? . . . and the rest? [*Kurir*, April, 1792.][31]

The *Magyar Kurir* constantly quoted from the *Bétsi Udvari Deárium* (*Wiener Diarium*), the official court bulletin; its other sources were

[29] Joseph II commissioned the *Magyar Kurir* in 1786. Grossing to Francis II, December 29, 1792. *Kaiser Franz Akten*, Fasc. 154, K. 1, No. 23, Haus-, Hof- und Staatsarchiv, Vienna.

[30] Szerb, p. 229.   [31] Eckhardt, p. 102.

newspapers from Hanau, Cologne, and Frankfurt, and *Amy du Roy,* the French émigrés' newspaper.

The *Kurir,* which had taken an interest in French affairs from the first, published on May 27, 1789, an extensive account of the sessions of the Estates-General, which had been meeting in Paris since May 9:

> Since America became a free society after shaking the English yoke off her neck, all nations are yearning for the same golden liberties. The French, too, are being touched by the philosophy of Washington. . . . So that this outwardly civilized nation may show that it has intellectual enlightenment as well, several of its counties have given their deputies instructions which will amaze the stupid world when they have all become known. . . .
>
> Civil divorce, marriage for the clergy, abolition of the lottery, a new criminal code, abolition of the [Catholic] hierarchy's dependence on Rome, and several other matters relating to the nation's liberty are in the offing.[32]

On August 22, the *Kurir* published the draft of the Declaration of the Rights of Men and Citizens, remarkably so as this publication came four days before the declaration was actually promulgated. The same issue also contained the draft of the new French constitution. Since Hungarians have always enjoyed political humor, Szacsvay gave space to jokes about the French Revolution. One that appeared in this August 22 issue related:

> In the village of Montrus, not far from Paris, a peasant was looking at the green crops. He noticed that fine crops were growing in a place that had been badly damaged during the last year's games, and shouted, "What a great blessing! Anyone can see that God is not an aristocrat!" [33]

On February 1, 1791, the *Magyar Kurir* reported that the French clergy, except for a few fanatics, had taken the oath for the clergy on the civil constitution. It commented that some priests wanted to wear the martyr's crown by refusing to swear the oath but would instead simply be held in general contempt.

Szacsvay, a thoroughly political man, devoted the *Magyar Kurir* fully to political events. The county intelligentsia, ministers, village notaries, and their kind read the *Kurir* in growing numbers. Despite the displeasure of some of Joseph II's authorities, Szacsvay freely expressed his views on the Enlightenment. But this came to an end after the death of Leopold II. Early in 1793 Szacsvay retired to Kolozsvár, where he died in seclusion in 1815.[34]

---

[32] *Ibid.,* p. 106.   [33] *Ibid.,* pp. 106, 107.   [34] Dezsényi and Nemes, p. 27.

On July 7, 1789, Demeter Görög and Sámuel Kerekes began publication of another Hungarian newspaper, the *Hadi és Más Nevezetes Történetek* [Military and Other Noteworthy Stories]. It started as a vehicle for informing the public about the Turkish-Austrian-Russian War which had broken out in 1788. Very soon, however, its editors broadened its scope. The title of the paper was changed to the *Magyar Hiradó* [Hungarian News] on January 3, 1792. The editors, unlike Szacsvay, did not sympathize with the French Revolution, but sided instead with the swelling tide of feudal revolt. The *Magyar Hiradó's* main merit lay in its enthusiastic support for the Hungarian language and literature. On March 29, 1803, the paper was discontinued, not for lack of popularity (it had 1,300 subscribers), but because the owners had other obligations which prevented them from publishing it.

The early press in Hungary was born as an outlet for progressive and enlightened ideas. Subscribers grew from a few hundred to more than a thousand, showing the support these ideas had among the reading public. A number of subscribers were owners of coffeehouses and reading rooms (*Lesekabinette*), where many nonsubscribers could read the newspapers. Local intellectuals in the country read the newspapers to the villagers.[35]

HUNGARIAN PERIODICALS

The predecessors of modern weeklies and magazines were originally published as appendixes to newspapers. In 1786, in his capacity as superintendent of schools in northern Hungary, Ferenc Kazinczy visited Kassa, where he met Dávid Baróti-Szabó, with whom he had been in correspondence for ten years, and János Bacsányi. These three founded the Kassai Magyar Társaság (Hungarian Society of Kassa) and its quarterly magazine, *Magyar Múzeum*,[36] the most important literary endeavor of the Hungarian Enlightenment. Kazinczy quickly resigned because Bacsányi arbitrarily altered the text of an introduction Kazinczy wrote for the first issue. There was also a deeper

---

[35] A secret agent wrote in August, 1797, from Kisvárda: "When the newspapers arrive twice each week, five or six, sometimes ten or twelve persons gather. They read the papers with much shouting and discussion, speak in antireligious tones, and make it plain that they consider themselves enlightened. They also invite peasants to join them and encourage their feelings of disenchantment with their fate." *Ibid.*, p. 30.

[36] Szerb, p. 230.

reason for their disagreement. Kazinczy wanted to make the periodical exclusively a vehicle for the revival of the Hungarian language and literature. Bacsányi, on the other hand, wanted it to have both literary and political aims of a radical nature.[37]

Bacsányi wrote critically in the *Magyar Múzeum* that not a single magnate was willing to put up a few hundred florins for the magazine, whereas they were all happy to spend 40,000 or 50,000 florins on the beautification of their *banderia* (paramilitary units). The first issue of the *Magyar Múzeum* came out in 1790 and was circulated in the diet; the second, and last, issue appeared the same year. Four of its contributors, including both Kazinczy and Bacsányi, were members of the Martinovics conspiracy. Kazinczy, after he quit the *Múzeum*, started his own magizine, *Orpheus*, eight issues of which came out between 1790 and 1791.[38]

József Kármán and Gáspár Pajor anonymously edited the magazine *Uránia*. It aimed to reach a female readership interested in literature and was at pains to select proper material and present it in attractive form. Its editors wanted also to establish Pest as a literary center and published only original works, no translations.[39] The third and last issue appeared in April, 1795. The editors decided a minimum of 289 subscribers was needed to make the magazine viable; they had 138 for the second issue and 142 for the third.

Between 1790 and 1800 many small publications were launched, only to fade away almost at once. István Sándor brought out *Sokféle* [About Everything] first in Győr, and later in Vienna, between 1791 and 1801. It especially commemorated Bastille Day and campaigned strenuously

---

[37] Bacsányi was greatly influenced by the ideas of the French Revolution. Following is a translation by Matthew Mead of his poem "On the Changes in France" (1789), the first poem written in Hungarian in praise of the Revolution.

> Nations still trapped within the snare of servitude!
> Peoples who groan in pain, by iron bonds subdued,
> Who have not shaken off the collar of the slave,
> The yoke that drags you down into a wretched grave!
>
> You also sacred Lords who, consecrated kill
> —Since earth cries out for blood—the subjects of your will,
> To Paris turn your eyes, let France elucidate,
> For Lord and shackled slave, a future and a fate!

Reprinted, with permission, from *Anthology of Hungarian Verse*, ed. Paul Tábori (forthcoming).

[38] Dezsényi and Nemes, p. 35.   [39] Szerb, pp. 230, 250–51.

against superstition. Abbot János Molnár printed *Magyar Könyvház* [Hungarian Library] between 1783 and 1803, at first in Pozsony, later in Pest.

The golden age of the Hungarian periodical lasted from 1780 to the mid-1790s. From 1780 to 1790 a new periodical began publication almost every year, yet between 1794 and 1803 not a single new one was born. Newspapers reached their apogee in the years 1790–92. At this time, eighteen newspapers[40] appeared regularly in Hungary, half of them in the Hungarian language. The nadir was reached in 1805, when only one Hungarian, one Latin, and three German newspapers were published in Hungary.[41]

PAMPHLETS

"A shower of small booklets has suddenly inundated Pest and Buda," wrote the unknown author of one such booklet in 1790.[42] Pamphleteering reached its climax in 1790, and although it continued to be of importance right through the final decade of the century, it never again matched that one year. During the reign of Emperor Joseph II, innumerable leaflets had joined the chorus of criticism in the newspapers against the "crimes" of the aristocracy and clergy. Between 1790 and 1791 about 500 political pamphlets were printed, and from 1792 through 1795 a further 100 saw the light of day.

The most famous of all was Martinovics' *Oratio ad proceres et nobiles regni Hungariae,*[43] of which Szacsvay wrote in the *Magyar Kurir,* "This tiny pamphlet is so popular now that within thrice twenty-four hours of its publication more than 5,000 copies have been sold." [44]

In impressive numbers, pamphlets appeared, dealing with a whole gamut of political and social subjects. Written in Hungarian, Latin, and German, they were, almost without exception, anonymous.

[40] Including the Hungarian newspapers printed in Vienna.
[41] Dezsényi and Nemes, p. 34.
[42] *Meghamisitott mértéke az emberi polgárságban találkozható valóságos első-ségnek* [The Falsified Standards of Real Values to Be Found in the Human Citizenship] (1790), p. 32, quoted in Concha, p. 367. "Publications were cheap." Wangermann, p. 7.
[43] The full text is in Benda, I, 105–49.
[44] Dezsényi and Nemes, p. 30. Another memorandum of Martinovics dated October, 1791, suggested the transfer of feudal properties to the "industrious" classes. Benda, I, 453–68 (Doc. 31e).

A major group of pamphlets demanded a return to feudalism and complete reinstatement of the feudal constitution set aside by Emperor Joseph II. The authors of these pamphlets sometimes went much further than just demanding a return to the old constitution. This constitution had not, in fact, been formally abrogated; rather, it had been shattered by the enlightened despots. Charles III had begun the process. Maria Theresa had followed suit with more vigor. And Joseph II had shot the final, most damaging and dangerous holes in the feudal constitution. The authors of these pamphlets suggested that the *bene possessionati* seize the opportunity offered by the crisis in the Habsburg Empire in 1790 and set up a royal republic of the Polish type in Hungary.

The most interesting pamphlet of this group, entitled *Pia desideria cordis Hungarici Patriae Felicitatem et Securitatem aeternam exoptantis,* was barely fourteen pages long. Reactionary though it was, it was highly intelligent and was well organized. If Martinovics' pamphlet was socially the most important of 1790, this little anonymous publication had the most political influence on the diet, which had just been convoked, and on the plans of Péter Balogh.[45] It was most concise and must have been read by the greater number of those who advocated a return to feudalism. It turned with genuine wrath against the absolute monarchical form of government.

Written with sincerity and in a spirit of strong prenationalism, the pamphlet outlined a plan to prevent once and for all the return of Habsburg absolutist rule. Its goal was to restrict royal power and extend and protect the privileges of the estates. The author believed it essential that the country should have a written constitution, to be promulgated as part of the *Corpus Juris,* in order to forestall any future usurpation of governmental powers. If the king was to remain permanently outside the country, which had been the case since the Habsburgs had mounted the Hungarian throne, he was to appoint a royal *locum tenens* who should be the heir to the throne.

The most important reform suggested by the *Pia desideria* was for the legislative branch of government to have complete control over the executive. It proposed that in the future the Palatine, the Primate, the Lord Chief Justice, the Lord Chief Treasurer, and the Chief Justice

[45] See Chapter XIII on the feudal revolt.

should be elected by the diet, and the County High Sheriffs by the county assemblies.

The *Pia desideria* proposed establishment of a State Council (Senate) to control the executive power on behalf of the estates. This body was to be composed of two sections, after the pattern of the diet. The lords' section was to have eight members. The lower chamber, "the Council of the Hungarian Nation," was to consist of eight noblemen and eight representatives of the burghers, presided over by the Lord High Treasurer or the Chief Justice. In between sessions of the diet, the Senate should have the right to pass legislation. This institution, in practice, would introduce a permanent diet, not only to legislate, but to keep the executive permanently under the supervision of the legislative. The Senate would have the right to impeach those members of the executive who violated the laws of the land. The pamphlet also proposed setting up similiar bodies at county level to make the county assemblies into permanent organizations to exercise control over local administration.

All the proposals contained in the *Pia desideria* were incorporated into the draft constitution prepared during the early phases of the diet by the Balogh party as the feudal revolt evolved.

A greater say for the estates in the affairs of the executive branch of government was also demanded in a pamphlet printed in Transylvania. It urged that the diet should have control of the budget and the allegiance of the Hungarian regiments of the standing army. This pamphlet showed how closely the nobility of Hungary was watching events in the West by stating, "The happiness of our fatherland shall be complete if we receive the same grace from His Majesty as he has voluntarily given to the people of the Netherlands." [46]

Some pamphlets, belonging more or less to this group, were written by politically minded Catholic prelates. For these church dignitaries, reestablishment of the old constitution meant reestablishment of the privileges and the dominant position of the Roman Catholic Church. They wanted to erase the partial secularization of the state by the last two enlightened despots.

[46] Concha, p. 369. Other pamphlets in a similar vein included *Diétai Prédikácziók* [Orations in the Diet] by Ferenc Hunyadi; *Egyenesszívű magyar, azért igaz hazafi* [An Open-minded Hungarian Is Still a True Patriot] (Pozsony, 1790); *A jó magyarokhoz* [To the Good Hungarians] (Pest, 1790); and *Hazafiak Tüköre* [Mirror of Patriots] (Szeben, 1790). The last three were anonymous.

The most intelligently written pamphlet of this kind was the work of an anonymous conservative Catholic intellectual, *Hungaria graviter aegra ab successore coronae et statibus atque ordinibus regni in comitiis anni 1790. congregatis curam postulans. Auctore Angelo pacis 1790.* The author argued for reestablishment of the dominance of the Catholic Church in Hungary above all else. He proposed that education again be subjected to the bishops, in order to eliminate the "bad effects of shameless" teachers and of books, which were banned by the Church but permitted to be used by the state. The author hoped to see the expulsion from Hungary of professors of foreign origin, whom he accused of inciting students against the old constitution. Several German professors, believers in the Enlightenment, were teaching at the University of Pest at this time.

Opposition pamphlets appeared, of course, almost at once. *Hungarus pro lege, ex lege, pro rege et patria* (1790), supported the rights and prerogatives of the king. It denied that sovereignty lay with the nation, but backed the divine right of the king, on condition that he reign with due respect for the law of the land.[47]

A second main group of pamphlets appearing in 1790 was involved in the spirited struggle being waged between the different Christian churches. Had these pamphlets merely been concerned with disputes between differing cults, they would be of little interest now. But they were much more than that, for many of them represented outstanding enlightened political literature. Those joining the Protestant cause tried to safeguard the policies of toleration of Joseph II and, if possible, to expand them into full political emancipation for the Protestants. Opposing pamphlets argued in defense of the privileged position of the Roman Catholic Church, claiming that the Catholic Church was the only state church and that all Protestant denominations were foreign to Hungarian civilization, imported primarily from Germany.

A representative Catholic pamphlet stated that the sole, true Christianity had been represented in Hungary since the time of King Saint Stephen by the Roman Church. The pamphlet, *Germaniae conclusiones in materia relig[iosa]* (1790), claimed that all non-Catholic denominations had been declared fallacious by law, but, alas, they were still tolerated. Leó Szeitz, in his *Igaz magyar*, asserted that Roman Catholicism was the only constitutional religion in Hungary and

[47] Concha, p. 368.

that a true Hungarian could only be a Catholic. These pamphlets attacked the treaties of Vienna, Nickolsburg, and Linz on the grounds that they gave foreign powers the right to interfere in the internal affairs of Hungary. A pamphlet by Dániel Magyar denounced intervention as wrong, even if it was limited to protecting the contractual and constitutional rights of Protestants.[48]

Numerous pamphlets argued the Protestant case, especially preservation of the Patent of Toleration and eventual full political emancipation of the Protestants. These pamphlets predictably defended the constitutionality and validity of the treaties of Vienna, Nickolsburg, and Linz. They assailed measures which violated these treaties, such as punishment of Catholic apostates as criminals, Catholic churchmen's censorship of Protestant writings, and the ecclesiastical taxes Protestants had to pay to the Catholic clergy. Abolition of discrimination was demanded in such pamphlets as Sámuel Nagy's *Brevis et sincera deductio status Relig[ionis] evang[elici]* of 1790. The Catholics countered this immediately with *Vindiciae Cleri Hung[arici] contra suplicem lib[ertatem]. S. Nagy* (1790).[49]

Protestant views were summarized in a short work called *Igaz katholikus Magyar, a ki Magyar Dánielnek rövid megjegyzéseire az ország törvényeiből megfelel* [He Is a True Hungarian Catholic Who Answers the Short Comments of Dániel Magyar Referring to the Hungarian Laws] (1790). It decried the contention that a true Hungarian could only be a Catholic.

It is stupidity to give privileges to anyone in Hungary on the basis of his religious affiliation. . . . The constitutional people of Hungary are neither the Roman Catholics nor the Orthodox Catholics, but the Hungarian nobility.[50]

Several of the Catholic polemicists were enlightened intellectuals in their own way, but in their religious disputes they went only so far as to recognize the rights of the Protestants as defined in the treaties of

---

[48] *Igaz hazafi Magyar Dániel. Igen rövid megjegyzések, melyek ezen fels. magyar Haza ide Budára 1790. Eszt. összegyülek. tek. Státusai és Rendeinek . . . bemutattatnak . . .* [Very Short Comments to Be Presented to the Estates of the Majestic Fatherland, to Be Convoked Here in Buda, in 1790].

[49] Further important pamphlets in this debate, representing the Protestant views, were *Succinta deductio jur. et gravam. evang. auctore privato reri dico.* (1790), and Ferenc Szemere, *De juribus evangelici in Hungaria.*

[50] Quoted in Concha, p. 375.

Vienna, Nickolsburg, and Linz and no further.[51] Some of the enlightened Catholics supported the spirit of tolerance introduced by Emperor Joseph II.[52]

Another group of pamphlets touched on religion but was in favor of neither the Catholic nor the Protestant cause. These pamphleteers were interested only in the problem of freedom of conscience in the Protestant-Catholic clash and in securing the right of freedom of conscience and religion in a really enlightened spirit. Their writings tended to favor the idea of a secularized state. Two very interesting pamphlets belong to this group: Ádám Csébi Pogány's *Tentamen trium propositionum* (Pest, 1790), and the anonymous *Az erőszakos téritőknek a szent vallással való káros visszaélésekről* [About the Harmful Violation of Sacred Religion by Those Who Convert Others by Application of Force] (1790).

The first of these two asserted that even the people could not empower the king to administer their religious affairs, but only their lay concerns. Both pamphlets were deeply rational in argument. The second attacked bigotry by exposing the fallacy of the use of force in capturing men's minds.

To besiege a fortress by meditation or to besiege a man's mind by force are stupidities. There exists no sane, concentrated meditation before which a fortress will fall, even if a thousand Ciceros were to talk. There does not exist such might as could conquer a mind, even if all the potentates of the world were to join forces.[53]

Observationes super legis religionariae paragrapho 13. (1790) contended that a man had to be free to follow his own conscience. If freedom of conscience were suppressed, man could only follow his instincts and revert to barbarism. The pamphlet upheld freedom of opinion as a strong foundation for the freedom of the whole people.

Another remarkable pamphlet was the *Declaratio*, forty pages long, written by an enlightened Catholic, supposedly the historian György Pray.[54] It condemned the civil persecution of Catholic apostates who

---

[51] One of the clearest expositions of this is in *Ad amicum augustanae confessionis amici catholici de viennesi et lincensi pacific. epistolae tres.* (1790).

[52] "Anti-clerical pamphlets had been in fashion since the relaxation of the censorship in 1781." Wangermann, p. 7.

[53] Quoted in Concha, p. 369.

[54] *Declaratio sincera christiana et patriotica civis hungarici catholici ad questionem an sic dicta apostasia inter delicta civilia sit referenda* (1790).

embraced Protestantism. It asserted that the basis of the state must be secular and, therefore, it must not, and should not, prosecute its citizens for religious matters. The sole purpose of the state was to promote the commonweal. Nothing, it said, could be further from the state's duty than persecution of the citizen and suppression of his freedom of conscience. *Declaratio* averred that freedom of conscience was a basic human right.

Maria Theresa and Joseph II had already taken effective steps toward a limited kind of secular state, Maria Theresa perhaps unwittingly, Joseph II intentionally. They issued a number of patents regulating and limiting Church authority and indirectly taxing ecclesiastical foundations and Church property. Several pamphlets now urged expansion of this policy. They not only attacked the privileges and tax exemption of some ecclesiastical properties, but by these arguments they indirectly criticized the tax-exempt status of the property of the nobility.[55] The interdependence of the struggle against religious bigotry and Catholic dominance and that for social reform was slowly emerging.

The pamphlet *Jus Republicae* urged more intensive state control of Church foundations and periodic examination of them, so that those which could no longer serve the public interest if left in the hands of the Church could be nationalized.[56] One pamphlet, *Gravamina*, went so far as to demand complete confiscation of all Church properties, as well as the abolition of all lay offices and lay titles held by the clergy. It suggested legal enforcement of purely spiritual activities upon the clergy.[57]

Another pamphlet, *Egy nagynevezetü*,[58] recalled the abolition of the ecclesiastical order in France with the words: "The people began a new life, they needed brand new institutions; the dilapidated remains of the old [order] could no longer serve any end." The pamphlet attacked the privileges of both the clergy and the nobility and condemned existing political discrimination against Protestants.

Finally, one pamphlet, *Minek a pap az országgyülésen?* [What Are the Priests For at the Diet?] (1791), advocated complete secularization

---

[55] Concha, p. 384.   [56] *Jus republicae in bona ecclesiasticorum* (1791).
[57] *Gravamina cleri pastoralis.*
[58] *Egy nagynevezetü külsőországi embernek gondolatai a szerzeteseknek Franciaországban lett eltöröltetése alkalmatosságával. Cosmopolisban* [The Thoughts of a Very Prominent Man of a Foreign Land on the Occasion of the Abolition of Ecclesiastical Orders in France. In Cosmopolis].

of the state. It expressed the hope that under Emperor Leopold II the citizens might be looked upon as Hungarians, and not primarily as Catholics or Protestants. This was the theme of *Harminczkét okok* [Thirty-two Reasons], which also took to task the Archbishop of Kalocsa because of his insistence on discrimination against Protestants when what was needed was national unity. Other pamphlets criticized the part played by the prelates in various branches of government, and looked to a secular state.

A number of pamphlets appeared seeking the emancipation of women. Hungarian women first moved outside the home, apart from social work, in the field of literature. *Etwas für Ungarn von einer Patriotin* (Vienna, 1790) was one of several pamphlets that urged election of women delegates to the diet. Hungarian women, a fourteen-page booklet said, wanted to be "worthy of the most respected English ladies." [59] It argued that Hungarian noblewomen should enjoy the same privileges as noblemen. The liberties of menfolk depended on women, both as mothers and as wives, for women exerted the greatest influence on male children as they grew up. If women were to be properly educated, they would use their learning to foster the liberties and the well-being of the nation.[60]

Another pamphlet bemoaned the "subjugation of woman." It claimed there was no reason for women to be excluded from political life. If a queen could wear a crown, why should other women not be permitted to hold all and any offices in the land? "Let us fear not that women could not keep secrets and would gossip about the proceedings of debates; the welfare of the state should not be kept secret from the public, after all," the gallant partisan of female emancipation argued with tongue in cheek.[61]

Of course, the idea of female emancipation did not take long to elicit opposition.[62] One opposing pamphlet commented that female

[59] *A magyar anyáknak az országgyűlésre egybegyűlt ország nagyjai s a magyar atyák elejébe terjesztett alázatos kérések* [The Humble Requests of the Hungarian Mothers to the Magnates Assembled in the Diet and to the Hungarian Fathers] (1790).

[60] Quoted in Concha, pp. 384 and 385.

[61] *Magyar asszonyoknak prokátora a Budán összegyűlt rendekhez* [The Councilor of the Hungarian Women before the Estates Assembled in Buda] (1790).

[62] *Férfiak felelete az Asszonyokhoz. Arra a javallásra, hogy jó volna az Asszonyokat is a közönséges Gyülekezetekbe bebocsátani* [The Men's Answer to Women Regarding the Suggestions about the Advisability to Permit Women to Join Public Meetings] (1790).

emancipation was impractical because women "become denationalized and degenerate." Their demand for emancipation could be allowed only if they were to recognize the primacy of men, were to suckle their own children (instead of employing wet nurses), were not to abandon national dress, were to learn the Hungarian language, and, if admitted to meetings, were not to speak at all. It is tempting to quote from this pamphlet at length to show how funny even enlightened polemicists could be and the amazing variety and colorful complexity of the topics they argued.

The pamphleteers of the Enlightenment also argued hard for the emancipation of Jews.[63] A pamphlet by János Nagyváthy, written in a Masonic spirit, expressed deep regret that the Jews were still suppressed and urged that they be emancipated. It appealed to the magnanimity and humanitarianism of the nobility, and noted that the Jews brought considerable profit to the nation and to the nobility itself. The pamphlet, highly progressive, stated: "Since suppression [still] exists [in Hungary], it means that the Hungarian nation is not yet a free nation." It added:

If we dare to found our faith upon the Jewish Bible, and if we dare, and even like, to sing Jewish Psalms in our churches, we have no reason to exclude the Jewish people from society on grounds of their [different] customs, nor to collect from them taxes for toleration of their very existence. And why [is this done]? Just because they exist. Oh, Europe! When you behave like this, are you not acting against yourself? [64]

A final group of pamphlets dealt with the problems of the serfs. A good many were written in the spirit of the Enlightenment and sought reform of the serfs' social and political status.

Since the leading writers of enlightened literature, including pamphlets, were the *bene possessionati*, it is logical and natural that emancipation of the serfs was their least concern. Yet Fekete, Sztáray, Csáky, Forgách, and other intellectuals showed some stirrings of conscience, and several of them felt the need for closer contact with the lowest rank of society, the simple, common folk. This harking back to the bottom of the social scale may also, however, be viewed as merely a kind

---

[63] János Nagyváthy, *A Tizenkilenczedik században élt Igaz Magyar hazafinak örömórái. A nagyszivüségnél, MDCCCC* [The Hours of Happiness of a True Hungarian Patriot Who Lived in the Nineteenth Century. In Magnanimity, 1900]. (The year is naturally fictitious.)

[64] Quoted in Concha, p. 387.

of sentimental, pre-Romantic trend. The most outstanding of these writers was the cavalry general, Baron Lőrinc Orczy, who, but for his reformist views, would have appeared to be an archtype of the contemporary Hungarian aristocrat by his birth, wealth, and habits. General Orczy, like so many British generals, took to the pen at the end of a long and distinguished military career. He eulogized the simplicity of old ways. But his love for the quiet life of yore, instead of being conservative and reactionary, was progressive. His praise for peasant life and simplicity is like Rousseau in Hungarian guise. Orczy, in a pre-Romantic way, recognized the ills of his society. Referring to the newly built hall of a county assembly, he wrote:

I am fully aware that the whitewash which decorates the walls of such a structure is often applied with the tears of the peasants and the poor, and sometimes even blood is mixed with their tears. Therefore, when I look at this noble edifice from this angle, it represents for me a mournful, rather than a cheerful, prospect.[65]

Sámuel Décsy, another aristocrat, foresaw the rejuvenation of the Hungarian nation only on condition that the prejudices of a feudal society be set aside. He upbraided his fellow aristocrats because, like the Spaniards, they deemed trade to be unbecoming to the dignity of noblemen and held to other equally haughty and empty beliefs. He stripped the cover of hypocrisy from the landlords' patriotic persuasions.

Not true loyalty to our national language, but our fear of losing our privileges as noblemen, aroused our enthusiasm. As soon as we can put them [i.e., our privileges] on a secure footing, we shall throw the Hungarian costumes off our bodies and dress again in foreign fashions, we shall follow and look up to foreign customs and despise those which are our own.[66]

Léo Szeitz, reactionary apologist for the Roman Catholic Church and the feudal system in general, was one of the mordant opponents of reform of serfdom. He conceded that the serfs' condition was a *status poenalis,* the penal servitude to which criminals were condemned. He argued that many serfs might be happy to be alive as serfs, for they could very well have earned death penalties instead of merely serfdom. "There is therefore no reason for such an outcry that the serfs' lot, as assured by law, is not very good, for the peasantry has deserved its conditions many times over. After all, if the circumstances of the

[65] Szerb, p. 206.   [66] *Ibid.,* p. 227.

serfs are so bad in Hungary, why do so many Germans migrate to Hungary to become serfs?" [67]

János Nagyváthy, in his already quoted pamphlet, *A tizenkilencedik században élt,* championed the true equality of men. "Equality is the law of nature, which is the foundation of society. Men may not violate this natural law without due punishment." All men were created equal. Only fraud and malice had introduced titles, subjection, and other kinds of inequality. The enslavement of a part of society was a direct violation of the divine creation of equal men. "The creator, through identical birth and death, made all his creatures identical. He did not make of one a slave, of another a lord." A final outstanding feature of this excellent pamphlet was its emphasis on the importance of public education. Higher education, Nagyváthy said, was the channel for singling out talent and bringing it to fruition, regardless of its birth or origin.[68]

[67] Concha, p. 391.   [68] *Ibid.,* p. 392.

Part IV

THE DYNAMICS OF 1790

Chapter XIII

THE FEUDAL REVOLT AGAINST
ENLIGHTENED DESPOTISM

OWING TO the persuasion of Prince Kaunitz, among other causes, Joseph
II issued his famous decree of January 28, 1790, ordering the return
of the Hungarian crown from Vienna to Hungary as well as the abolition of all his reforms with the exception of three.[1] Then, on February
20, 1790, he died. In his will he expressed the wish to be buried at the
feet of his parents.[2] His body had not yet been confined in the *Kapuzi-
ner Kirche* when the Hungarian estates, with overwhelming joy, greeted
the return of the crown of St. Stephen to the ancient city of Buda.[3]
The news of Joseph's death reached the city exactly as a *Te Deum* was
being celebrated by the Prince-Primate of Hungary, Archbishop Count
József Cardinal Batthyány. On receiving the news, the Primate consulted *Országbiró* Count Károly Zichy, and they jointly decided to
keep the news secret for the time being lest the joyful nobles commit
"indecencies" on hearing the news.[4]

[1] Marczali, *Országgyűlés*, I, 1. The three exceptions were the Patent of Toleration, the regulation of the serf problem, and the settlement of the problems of
ministers and lower clergy. The partial restoration of feudalism by Emperor
Joseph II is discussed in Wangermann, pp. 50 ff. The complex causes of this "retreat from Enlightened Despotism" are given *ibid.*, pp. 25 ff. and pp. 54 ff. The concessions given to the estates were necessary to the continuation of Habsburg rule.
Link, pp. 149–51.
[2] Meszlényi, p. 34.
[3] Marczali, *Magyarország története III. Károlytól*, in Szilágyi, ed., VIII, 467–68.
[4] "The nobles and the burghers are frantic with joy, and if the news about
the death spreads, the occurrence of indecencies is to be feared." Letter of
Prince-Primate Cardinal Batthyány to Chancellor Count Pálffy, dated Buda,
February 22, 1790. Archives of the Royal Hungarian Chancellery No. 74, 1790.
Quoted in Marczali, *Országgyűlés*, I, 4.

Thus, although the highest officials of the country were already aware of the death of the Emperor, the festivities, the joy, and the celebration of victory over the enlightened despotism of Joseph II continued unabated. The happy noblemen rapturously feted the end of almost three decades of extraconstitutional rule of their land. Yet beneath these outward signs of joy and festivity, a deeper, more significant political current may be found: the determination of the estates of Hungary to bring their partial victory to a decisive finish, even if it meant breaking off relations with the Habsburg Empire.[5] At the time of Joseph's death they were united in this decision.

Thus began the feudal revolt[6] of the Hungarian estates. The effect of this strange phenomenon, combined with the repercussions of the French Revolution, the revolt in the Austrian Netherlands,[7] the mounting Prussian pressure on Austria, and, finally, the unfortunate Turkish-Austrian-Russian War, brought about the near collapse of the Habsburg Empire. The feudal revolt was, in general terms, an effort to reestablish the autonomous rule of Hungary, by force if necessary. Equally important, the estates demanded the reestablishment of former feudal privileges which had been frustrated to some extent, but not completely destroyed, by the last three Habsburg kings. In this, the removal of the foreign, centralizing, Germanizing[8] governmental system of Joseph II was the necessary prerequisite.

The feudal revolt, for a number of reasons, might well be considered as a kind of protonationalist movement which spread beyond the social borders of the privileged classes.[9] For example, some common soldiers deserted their units and went home; others joined the Polish army to fight against the Habsburgs. In addition to this demonstration

[5] Mód, p. 143. An account of the emergence of Hungarian resistance against the regime of Joseph II may be found in Silagi, pp. 55–58. For the possibility of disintegration of the Habsburg Empire, see Wangermann, p. 52.

[6] The feudal revolt contained four connected events: the activities of the diet; the *banderium* movement; the protonationalist stir in the Hungarian regiments of the Habsburg standing army; and the diplomatic adventure of the *bene possessionati* with the Prussian court.

[7] In November, 1789, Joseph II had to abandon his plan to send German troops from Bohemia to put down the rebellion in the Netherlands because of peasant unrest in Bohemia herself. Wangermann, p. 34.

[8] Kann, p. 141.

[9] In order not to push the peasants into the arms of the dynasty, the diet announced: "The rights of men are not unknown to us, and we shall not prevent the serfs from receiving all that sublime sentiments suggest that we give without causing damage to ourselves." Marczali, *Országgyűlés*, I, 11.

of patriotic sentiment on the part of serf recruits, a specific social phenomenon also pushed the feudal revolt toward a kind of proto-nationalism. The ratio of the lesser nobility in Hungary was extremely high, a large segment of society being made up of these masses. If one considers that other objective elements of modern nationalism were present as well (e.g., common descent, language, territory, political entity, customs, traditions, etc.), the patriotic movement may indeed be viewed as protonationalistic.[10] A living, active, corporate will motivated the assertion that a Hungarian nation-state was the only legitimate form of political organization of the lands of the crown of St. Stephen. It is also true, as Hans Kohn said, that, aside from the Poles, the "Hungarians preserved with their medieval aristocratic structure, their conscious nationhood." [11] Hence the existence of a protonationalism was, in the 1790s, a force which had specific roots in Hungarian society.

The feudal revolt showed signs of mass psychology, a phenomenon rarely found in movements of Western feudal classes, which were smaller in number and more exclusive than was the Hungarian lesser nobility. Mass psychology was present in the demonstrative fad of wearing Hungarian dress and speaking the Hungarian language exclusively; whoever did not comply was denounced. This frenzy was eventually accompanied by signs of Germanophobia which culminated in the molestation of those wearing German dress or speaking German, a common practice under Emperor Joseph II. "Long live Hungarian liberty" sounded around the country,[12] in society, in the streets, and in mass meetings held by the county nobility. On several occasions, these gatherings reached the frenzied pitch of mob meetings.

The most ferocious outbreak of mass psychology, however, was apparent in the onslaught against all preparations for a national geodetic survey that had been ordered by Joseph II to pave the way for the taxation of the lands belonging to the nobles. All indications of the preparations and all means for the survey were destroyed. Carts drawn by oxen transported the documents of the survey to the capital cities of the counties where they were then burned; the royal commissars who were in charge were expelled from the counties. Toward

[10] Wangermann, pp. 34–35, calls this movement "Magyar nationalism." In contrast with that view, the term "protonationalism" is used to indicate the lack of many components of modern nationalism in Hungarian society in 1790.
[11] Kohn, p. 534.   [12] Mód, p. 143.

very few reforms of enlightened despotism did the estates show such a burning hatred and so many signs of mass psychology as were present in their feelings about the national geodetic survey.[13]

Another indication of mass psychology was the open attack in county assemblies and other meetings by the impassioned lesser nobility upon those who were officials of the Josephine regime. Their noisy behavior intimidated and terrorized their opponents: the *bene possessionati* were getting the upper hand and becoming dominant.[14]

Joseph II's policy met with growing opposition early in his reign. Yet it was not until the state was sufficiently weakened by the Turkish War that the resistance blossomed into an active feudal revolt. The three ruling classes—the prelates, the aristocrats, and the lesser nobility—only partially pursued common goals, yet the common fear of absolute rule united their forces temporarily. It was the ecclesiastics who suffered the most from the Josephine reforms. Naturally they were resentful and were ready to join with those who led the revolt against enlightened despotism. In so far as the two lay estates were concerned, although their interests were far from identical, the atmosphere during the last years of Joseph's rule favored their cooperation.

As was previously mentioned, the ban on Protestants which kept them from taking jobs in the state and county administrations divided the ranks of the lesser nobility along religious lines, or, in other words, into Protestant and Catholic groups.[15] It is important to note that such a division could have paralyzed the lesser nobility if it had not been for the Patent of Toleration of Joseph II which opened the door to all state and county offices for Protestants. Consequently, the number of Protestants holding powerful offices of all kinds steadily grew. Indeed, Joseph even went so far as to bestow upon some Protestant gentry the rank of an aristocrat (e.g., Prónay and Vay).[16] These regulations of the Emperor helped to bridge the gulf between Protestants and Catholics and eased the tension between the lesser nobility and the aristocrats. The Protestants who occupied key offices were, for

---

[13] The *Consilium locumtenentiale* ordered the cancellation of the national survey on February 19, 1790. Marczali, *Országgyűlés,* I, 45. See also Marczali, *Magyarország története III. Károlytól,* in Szilágyi, VIII, 469.

[14] Mályusz, ed., *Sándor Lipót,* p. 7. See also Wangermann, pp. 72–73.

[15] Mályusz, *Sándor Lipót,* p. 3. [16] *Ibid.,* p. 4.

the most part, very well educated, many of them having studied in the West.[17]

The Emperor's decree of January 28, 1790, reestablished the conditions prevailing in 1780. It naturally left the lesser nobility dissatisfied, for it meant domination by the aristocrats. Once again there was a possibility that the aristocrats would capture the key positions in the state, as they had done during the reign of Maria Theresa. The lesser nobles were far too conscious of their own power to sit idly by in the face of such a threat. They began systematically to secure powerful positions for themselves, the *bene possessionati* leading the struggle. The poorer strata of the lesser nobility, still not conscious of their political significance, followed the lead of the *bene possessionati*.[18] As the feudal revolt became more intense, the prelates and the aristocrats opposed it and closed ranks with the dynasty.

THE FIRST PHASE OF THE FEUDAL REVOLT: THE DIET OF 1790–1791

The main field of struggle between Habsburg enlightened despotism and the Hungarian estates was the diet. It was here that the feudal revolt blossomed, then declined, and was finally defeated by a court coup. The diet convened on June 6, 1790, in Buda, the first time it had met in that ancient capital since the era of János Zápolyai.[19] The *bene possessionati* decided on the Lower Chamber as safe ground for the feudal revolt, and they were determined to launch a massive election campaign to ensure themselves a majority in agreement with them—in other words, partisans of a feudal revolt.

As always, delegates to the diet were chosen by county assemblies. In principle, all noblemen, aristocrats, and lesser nobility could attend these meetings. Resolutions were arrived at by a system of roll call voting. The aristocrats, who constituted a negligible minority and could thus be sure that they would be voted down, did not

[17] Elemér Mályusz states that Protestantism at that time had a definite role in transmitting Western civilization to Hungary. *Ibid.* During sixteen years of this era, seven hundred Protestant students studied in the West. Révész, *Magyarországi protestántizmus*, p. 57.

[18] Mályusz, *Sándor Lipót*, p. 8.

[19] János Zápolya was the rival king (1526–40) of Ferdinand I (1526–64), the first Habsburg on the Hungarian throne.

attend the county assembly meetings; nor, in some places, did the *bocskoros nemesek,* for their opinions were, practically without exception, overruled by wealthy nobles and their numerous supporters. Although the *bocskoros nemesek* in other parts of the country turned the county assemblies into mass meetings, it was the *bene possessionati* who, for the most part, dominated the assemblies. Hence the election of the delegates of their choice was merely a question of organization. First, a program was needed to rally partisans of a feudal revolt. One was elaborated by Justice Péter Balogh of Ócsa, a member of the *Septemviratus.* Copies of the program were distributed, and the organizational work was done by a network of Freemasons.[20]

One must consider that, at the time, Freemasonry was in its heyday in Hungary. Lodges maintained close contact with each other; the centers of Masonic life were the cities of Vienna, Pozsony, Buda, and Pest; aristocrats, *bene possessionati,* burghers, and *honoratiori,* outstanding scholars, physicians, and professors could be counted among lodge members. The spirit of the more progressive elements of the estates dominated the activities of the lodges. These elements went so far as to acknowledge the necessity of strengthening liberty in Hungary, although most of the enlightened nobles truly believed that liberty was due only to those born into the privileged classes.

Generally, the Hungarian brand of Freemasonry observed the formalities of the movement in the West, but the essence of the Hungarian spirit was protonationalistic rather than cosmopolitan.[21] The *bene possessionati* gradually gained the upper hand in the leadership of the lodges. Although the supreme master of all the Hungarian lodges was Count Károly Pálffy, the Royal Chancellor of Hungary, it was a well-known fact that the mastermind behind him was Sándor Pászthory, the most gifted man in the Royal Chancellery and one of the *bene possessionati.*[22] For this reason, the gentry felt that they could safely use the Freemasons to promote the goals of the feudal revolt.

The program written by Péter Balogh in accordance with the tastes of the *bene possessionati* was intended to influence public opinion and ensure the victory of the *bene possessionati* in the forthcoming

---

[20] For a general account of the status of the Hungarian Freemasons inside the Freemasonry of the Habsburg lands, see Silagi, pp. 31 ff.

[21] Mályusz, *Sándor Lipót,* pp. 9–10.   [22] *Ibid.,* p. 9, n. 3.

election. Circular letters[23] detailing the program were distributed to the lodges with instructions for its propagation during the campaign. The letters urged the Masons to use their influence in getting their fellow Masons elected as deputies to the diet. On the whole, the effort was surprisingly successful. A majority of the deputies were equipped with instructions similar in tone to, and reflecting the concepts of, the Balogh program. Furthermore, debates during the initial meetings of the diet were pregnant with the same spirit.[24] Yet despite their active participation, it would be an oversimplification to say that the feudal revolt of 1790 was brought about by the Freemasons alone. Without them the revolt might well have been more poorly organized and less widespread, but the protonationalist spirit of the lesser nobility and their opposition to enlightened despotism would nevertheless have come to the surface.

In the counties which were administered by officials belonging to the Freemasons, endorsement of the Balogh program was an easy matter. This was the case in Pest County where the deputy high sheriffs, Laczkovics and Szily, both Masons, were elected deputies to the diet. The third deputy of Pest County, Ferenc Darvas, an official on the *Consilium locumtenentiale,* was also a Mason. The story was much the same in other counties, and it is known that twenty-seven deputies of the 1790–91 diet were definitely Masons.[25] Even in counties where there were no lodges, the instructions issued to the deputies were drafted along the lines of the Balogh program.

It was in Pest County that the custom of sending circular letters to other counties was first originated. These letters informed the counties of Pest's stand on major issues and of the instructions given to its deputies. Because Pest was the largest of the counties and enjoyed the greatest prestige, its views greatly influenced the leaders of smaller counties. Somogy County, for example, followed the instructions of Pest to the letter, although, interestingly enough, there were no Masons in the platform committee of the county's assembly. A lively correspondence, aiming at the adoption of the Balogh program and encouraging a firm stand in the struggle for its principles, sprang up among the different county assemblies. Ideas were also spread by word of mouth. Several partisans of the program visited

[23] *Ibid.,* p. 10, n. 2.   [24] Hóman and Szekfü, V, 56.
[25] Mályusz, *Sándor Lipót,* p. 11.

the assemblies of neighboring counties and gave suggestions as to what could be done to ensure a successful campaign.

It is important to note that the correspondence in which viewpoints were exchanged by the individual county assemblies was an extremely effective medium for creating a uniform opinion among the lesser nobility. Viennese circles were openly hostile to this custom, and the court tried to check it as soon as it regained control. King Leopold II, in letters written to his son, the Palatine, on August 16 and August 31, 1791, urged a ban on all such correspondence. His wish was finally carried out in a resolution of the Court Conference dated December 3, 1791, and, again, in a resolution of the Crown Council of June 21, 1792.[26]

In view of the overwhelming power of the *bene possessionati,* the victory of the feudal revolt in the counties seems to have been assured. What is more, the election of the leaders of the movement as deputies to the diet gave them a solid foundation for victory. The most important leaders of the feudal revolt were Péter Balogh, deputy of Nógrád County; Baron József Podmaniczky and Ignácz Almássy, deputies of Heves County; József Vay, deputy of Borsod County; Imre Beöthy, deputy of Bihar County; Ferenc Darvas, deputy of Pest County; and Ignácz Bezerédi, deputy of Tolna County. All of these men were members of either the *Consilium locumtenentiale* or the *Septemviratus,* and while Almássy and Bezerédi were Catholics, the others were Protestants or Freemasons or both. They were prepared to keep the court from breaking their ranks by granting offices and/or decorations, and all were agreed not to accept any favors from the court without the consent of the deputies of the diet.[27] For that they pledged themselves by taking an oath (see Appendix G).

THE IDEOLOGY OF THE FEUDAL REVOLT

The *bene possessionati* thus created a conscientious, strong, and well-organized party of their own within the framework of the diet. During June and July of 1790, the party, following the stipulations of the Balogh program, compiled a draft for constitutional amendments that was later included in a draft of a new royal oath, also elaborated by

[26] *Ibid.,* p. 11, n. 4.   [27] *Ibid.,* p. 13.

the Balogh party.[28] The main proposals for the constitution were as follows: (1) annual meetings of the diet should be held in Pest, and royal invitations for the convocation should not be necessary; (2) all taxes and subsidies should be voted by the diet; (3) the convocation of the diet might be postponed, if necessary, only by the diet itself, and then for no longer than three years; (4) the crown should have only a suspensive veto regarding drafted legislative acts, and if the draft were passed over the king's veto, it must be promulgated by him as a law of the land; (5) a newly created Senate should control all royal decrees, and if any were found unconstitutional, they should be revoked; (6) the Royal Chancellery should be transferred from Vienna to Hungary, where it would be responsible to the diet; (7) the *főispánok* should be appointed by the king from four candidates nominated by each county; (8) all national officeholders should be appointed by the king from four candidates presented by the Senate; (9) Hungary should have her own national army, independent of the Imperial *Kriegsrat,* controlled and commanded by a central military headquarters to be staffed by members of the *bene possessionati;* (10) the Palatine should head the military headquarters and receive his instructions from the king by way of the newly created Senate; (11) the *jus resistendi* should be reestablished.[29]

Those who drafted the proposals aimed for the greatest possible control over royal power. They intended that all powers should be transferred to the diet and the newly established Senate. In both institutions, all the power would thus have been in the hands of the *bene possessionati,* for it was to them that all the offices of the central government, as well as those of the *főispánok,* would go. As a matter of course, in their excitement over their anticipated victory, the *bene possessionati* went so far as to distribute among themselves the senatorial posts still to be created.[30] The pamphlet *Pia Desideria* might well have been in the hands of many of the deputies.

The self-conscious efforts of the *bene possessionati* were founded upon a completely imaginary conviction that they were reviving the traditional constitution of the land. They found precedents justifying all their demands in the *Corpus Juris,* but their assumptions in this regard were on several occasions totally incorrect. Most notably, they misinterpreted some old stipulations which had been promulgated in

[28] *Ibid.*   [29] *Ibid.,* pp. 13–14.   [30] *Ibid.,* p. 14.

different times, under different circumstances, and which answered needs utterly opposed to those existing in 1790. An interesting psychological phenomenon is that the rank and file of the lesser nobility endlessly quoted former laws, thereby trying to convince themselves of the rightness of their actions. The highly educated leaders based their self-righteous convictions upon their intimate knowledge of enlightened ideas, a knowledge which also gave them much self-assurance.

Curiously enough, the leaders of the feudal revolt did not find it the least bit odd that, in demanding freedom in all areas for themselves, they yielded not an inch to the serfs. To them the prerogatives of the aristocracy were incompatible with the concepts of equality; therefore it was these prerogatives which had to be done away with. The *bene possessionati* were naïvely happy with their one-sided concepts of equality.[31]

The principles to be included in the draft of the new royal oath were intended to abolish all the Josephine reforms, reestablishing the conditions created by Maria Theresa. Above all, the draft rendered void Emperor Joseph II's patent on the abolition of perpetual serfdom. In this, the intention to bind the serfs again to the soil is apparent.[32] In the words of Gyula Szekfü, "Following the traditions of the Baroque era, the nobility stuck to the idea of patriarchal relations between lord and serf, an idea which was, of course, a clear-cut denial of enlightened ideas."[33]

The lesser nobility adhered to the ideas of József Vay,[34] who described the nobility as "nurses" of the serfs and as mediators between the king and the serfs, protecting the interests of the latter. The only thing necessary, they thought, was to convince the serfs of the lords' good intentions; and it was with this in mind that Vay suggested admitting village and community leaders to county assemblies as observers, where, in addition, they should be given the right to present the requests of those they represented. Thus they "themselves would be convinced of the paternal care of the nobility, and when returning home, they could lead the good people of their communities along the right road."[35] For Vay the people were still uneducated and in

---

[31] *Ibid.*, p. 15.   [32] *Ibid.*, p. 15, n. 1.   [33] Hóman and Szekfü, V, 62.
[34] József Vay was the theoretician of the *bene possessionati* in social matters, just as Péter Balogh was their theoretician in constitutional matters.
[35] Hóman and Szekfü, V, 62.

need of guidance: "The French pattern of events has clearly demonstrated that the people, imprisoned for a long time in a dark jail, cannot stand sharp rays if they reach their eyes too abruptly." [36]

The nobles were in fact willing to do something for the serfs, but at the expense of the Church. They suggested that the alodial lands of the Church be nationalized and the redemption payments be paid not to the Church but to the state, which would support new parishes from the fund.[37]

PARAMILITARY ASPECTS OF THE FEUDAL REVOLT: THE *BANDERIUM* MOVEMENT

The lesser nobility, led by the *bene possessionati*, were ready to attain their goals by any means necessary, including force of arms.[38] To this end, they set about persuading the Hungarian regiments of the standing army to shift their loyalty from the Habsburgs to the Hungarian diet. The gentry's initial success in this direction was remarkable, but for several reasons winning over the Hungarian units was not expected to be enough on its own to bring about the decisive military gains that the gentry aimed for. The Imperial Army was assumed to be too well organized to disintegrate, even if all the Hungarian regiments were detached from it.[39] The bulk of the troops—all the non-Hungarian units, that is—would remain faithful to the dynasty, and the gentry were wise enough to realize this fact. This was the reason behind the decision to organize the national *banderium* movement and to base plans on it, rather than rely exclusively on the possibility of Hungarian regiments deserting from the standing army.

It was neither unconstitutional nor an act of rebellion for the nobility to organize its own armed force, for the nobility enjoyed the interdependent prerogatives of tax exemption and the duty "to bear arms in defense of the country." [40] The *insurrectio* or noble levy as a practical means of national defense had become obsolete as early as the sixteenth- and seventeenth-century Ottoman wars. During the

---

[36] *Ibid.*, p. 63. [37] *Ibid.* [38] Mályusz, *Sándor Lipót*, p. 17.

[39] The Hungarian units of the Habsburg standing army accounted for a substantial number of men. They consisted of 12 regiments of foot in royal Hungary and 2 in Transylvania, 12 regiments of horse, 19 frontier guard regiments—in all, 45 regiments plus a river flotilla at Titel on the River Tisza. Hóman and Szekfü, V, 199.

[40] Verbőczi, Part 1, Article 9, Sec. 5.

nearly two centuries that these dragged on, the general *insurrectio* was never once called out. Yet the nobility stubbornly insisted on the continuation of the system in order to justify its own tax-exempt status. After the Hungarian standing army was set up in 1715, even this flimsy pretext vanished, since any last need for the *insurrectio* for national defense had once and for all been outdated. It is true that Maria Theresa called out the *insurrectio* in an emergency during the War of the Austrian Succession, but it was to little avail. And during the French Revolutionary and Napoleonic Wars the *insurrectio* was summoned four more times at moments of dire peril: in 1797, 1800, 1805, and 1809.[41] In the first three instances the nobility saw no action at all. On the fourth occasion at the battle of Győr the easternmost flank of Napoleon's column routed the Hungarian nobility.[42] The *insurrectio* was never again used before its abolition in 1848. The *banderium* of 1790 was nothing more than a specific form of the *insurrectio,* given a different name primarily because it was organized by the gentry-dominated county administrations and not called forth by the king, and also because it was mobilized not for the defense of the country but ostensibly for another, more peaceful reason.

The nucleus of the national *banderia* was formed by units of the county *banderia,* which were originally organized to escort St. Stephen's crown from Vienna to Buda, there to stand permanent guard over it in turns. As soon as the counties began selecting their detachments for the national *banderia,* however, it became known that they were to be organized on exactly the same lines as the fighting units of the standing army.[43] This would scarcely have been warranted if their only task were to guard the Holy Crown, so it rapidly became clear that the intention behind the national *banderium* movement was something less than purely pious.

Lőrinc Orczy, commander in chief of the national *banderia,* assumed the rank of colonel and collected about him an able staff. Cavalry General Barco, commandant of the Imperial forces (*Generalkommando*) in Buda, became alarmed at the growing strength and

[41] Hóman and Szekfü, V, 205–8.
[42] R. István Kiss, *Az utolsó nemesi felkelés századik évfordulója emlékére* [In Commemoration of the Centenary of the Last Noble Levy] (Budapest: Bankó Gyula, 1909), p. 10.
[43] Mályusz, *Sándor Lipót,* p. 19.

increasing cohesion of the national *banderia*. He reported what was happening to the *Hofkriegsrat* in Vienna and asked for instructions: What should he do? Were members of the *banderia* entitled to wear uniforms resembling those of the standing army? Had they the right to promote themselves to high rank? [44]

The *Hofkriegsrat* was also worried. It seemed to sniff a revolt somewhere behind the fuss over the *banderia* and its answer to General Barco demonstrated both the leadership's uncertainty and its alarm.[45] The court was still acting very defensively toward the feudal revolt in Hungary, more especially as the most pressing danger of the moment, the threat from Prussia, had not yet been overcome. The court still had not decided to deal sternly with the Hungarians. The *Hofkriegsrat*'s message to General Barco said in part:

The problems existing today must not be made worse by introducing harsh measures. With such groups, however, as take the concessions made to them as an excuse to let loose their ill will and obstruct public order, you will deal firmly, seriously, and cautiously; if necessary, with force.[46]

After such instructions, General Barco must have been more confused than before. He was no doubt aware that, whether the treatment he meted out was harsh or gentle, he would be held responsible for whatever went wrong—a scapegoat, if one was needed. As for the court, its alarm was due to the fact that it had no way of curbing the growing strength of the *banderia*.

The general intention of the gentry, meanwhile, was to keep the *banderia* at a high level of training and preparedness. Young noblemen were to be enlisted so that they would be ready to take command of rebel units in case of a general national uprising. "Your Majesty, it is no secret that the *banderia* were intended to serve as cadet-training schools," wrote the loyal Cardinal Count József Batthyány, Primate of Hungary, in a letter to Leopold II after the main threat of the *banderium* movement had receded in late 1790.[47]

In their eagerness to open the active phase of the feudal revolt,

[44] Marczali, *Országgyűlés,* I, 66.

[45] Wandruszka, II, 252. There was uncertainty in Vienna because the Emperor's decision was needed on all important issues and there was no Emperor present. Joseph II was dead, and the new Emperor, Leopold II, was in Florence. He did not arrive in Vienna until March 12, 1790. See also Marczali, *Magyarország története III. Károlytól,* in Szilágyi, VIII, 487.

[46] Marczali, *Országgyűlés,* I, 66.

[47] *Privatbibliothek* (microfilm copy), Fasc. 4, No. 3.

the gentry in Szabolcs County around the upper reaches of the River Tisza took the bull by the horns and proclaimed a general *insurrectio*.[48] Escorted by county officials, the unit commanders selected by the county assemblies to lead the *banderia* visited the villages assigned to them to assess the manpower they had available. They made an inventory of all weapons and able-bodied noblemen, and took oaths of loyalty. Much as had happened the year before in the Tennis Court at Versailles, in Hungary in 1790 people of all social classes took oaths of loyalty. To prevent the court from using the serfs against the lords, the *banderia* commanders took oaths even from the peasants. The nobles who had been registered were then called to arms in different districts on the pretext of mobilization exercises.[49]

The movement which began in Szabolcs County rapidly spread to neighboring counties: Szatmár, Zemplén, and Abaúj—all in northeast Hungary. Similar measures were also taken farther afield, even in some counties bordering on the hereditary Austrian provinces, such as Zala County in western Hungary.[50]

The gentry were not a numerically strong segment of the population and by themselves would not have been able to carry the feudal revolt to a successful conclusion. Allies were needed. Alliance with the serfs was out of the question, for one of the goals of the feudal revolt was to revive, at the serfs' expense, the estates' political and economic privileges that Joseph II had cut back. The only class of society that was reliable enough in the gentry's eyes and numerous enough to serve as a base for the feudal revolt was the lower, impoverished sector of the lesser nobility, the *bocskoros nemesek*.

The *bocskoros nemesek* were politically, socially, and economically in an intermediate position between the gentry and the serfs. Since nothing was more abhorrent to them than the thought that they might sink to the wretched status of serfs, their sentiments were naturally inclined toward the gentry, so when the latter proposed joint action, they accepted the offer enthusiastically. In Abaúj County, for example, the *főszolgabírák* and *szolgabírák* visited all the towns and villages to enlist the aid of the poor lesser nobles and to persuade

[48]Mérei and Spira, p. 24.
[49] *Staatsrat Archiv*, Nos. 1898 and 2046 (1790). See Mályusz, *Sándor Lipót*, p. 19, n. 3.
[50] *Staatsrat Archiv*, Nos. 2255, 3131, and 3321 (1790). See Mályusz, *Sándor Lipót*, p. 19, n. 4.

them to acquire arms. They were promised that in future they would be exempt from domestic taxes and free of periodic assessments for state taxes. This would make up for any expense incurred in obtaining arms. So the *bocskoros nemesek* began arming themselves and having uniforms tailored; some even sold their property to meet their expenses.[51] The gentry had found the allies they sought. The tide of the feudal revolt was rising fast, and with it the numbers, coordination, and martial spirit of the *banderia*.

MILITARY ASPECTS OF THE FEUDAL REVOLT

When Emperor Joseph II died, the Turkish-Austrian-Russian War was still going on. Most of the Hungarian regiments were concentrated in the south, in the zone of operations along the lower Danube. Without waiting for constitutional formalities to be completed, the *Hofkriegsrat* arranged for the Hungarian units of the army to take the oath of loyalty to the new king, Leopold II, even before he was crowned. Such alacrity was fairly normal in time of war. Nevertheless, it did not deter the Hungarian gentry from trying to enlist the support of these units against the king to whom they had so shortly before sworn allegiance.

At the same time several counties made representations to the Hungarian regiments, asking them to back the objectives of the feudal revolt. Zala and Zemplén counties suggested inviting delegates from the regiments to the forthcoming diet. The leaders of the feudal revolt wanted the new royal oath to be taken by Leopold II to stipulate that the Hungarian units of the standing army were subordinate to the diet. This, plus several other proposals, was made known to the rank and file by the Hungarian officers and was received very sympathetically. A few regiments even entered into a lively correspondence with the county assemblies.[52]

The Hungarian officers who corresponded with the assemblies were not typical Habsburg officers whose supreme loyalty lay solely with the dynasty. Hungarian officers devoted to the Habsburg cause were a later phenomenon, a product of the late nineteenth and early twentieth centuries. In the 1790s, the Hungarians who held commissions

---

[51] *Vertrauliche Akten*, Fasc. 55, No. B.95. Mályusz, *Sándor Lipót*, p. 20, n. 1.
[52] Hóman and Szekfü, V, 68.

in the Imperial Army were members of the nobility, particularly of the *bene possessionati,* and their outlook and patriotic identity was the same as that of their peers in the county assemblies and the lower house of the diet.

The Hungarian officers were especially responsive to the approaches of the county assemblies because they nursed grievances not only against the Habsburg *Hofkriegsrat* but also against their non-Hungarian comrades in arms. They felt that they were bypassed for promotion and assignments in favor of non-Hungarian officers. They also complained of many other lesser injuries. It was hardly surprising, then, that they responded promptly and affirmatively to appeals from relatives and friends to help uphold the ancient Hungarian constitution.[53]

Captain Ferenc Fekete, First Lieutenant Hódossy, and Second Lieutenant Rákóczi—all officers in the Zeschwitz Cuirassier Regiment—addressed a pledge to the diet. They were, they said, ready to obey the orders of the diet and "to shed their blood for the fatherland to promote the welfare of the nation and to protect its ancient privileges." [54]

Four points constantly recurred in the proposals, petitions, and appeals drafted by different Hungarian regiments. They sought to have Hungarians appointed as commissioned, warrant, and noncommissioned officers in the Hungarian regiments and to oust non-Hungarians from those ranks in these regiments. They wanted to increase the efficiency of the service by introducing Hungarian as the official language of command. They called for establishment of a Hungarian Supreme Command and War Council, subordinate to the diet. They proposed that in time of war the Hungarian units should be merged into a single Hungarian corps.[55] In addition, it was proposed that even in peacetime six Hungarian cavalry regiments—Splényi, Károlyi, Pálffy, Gyulay, Erdődy, and Tuscany—should be unified into one separate Hungarian cavalry corps. It was suggested that only members of the Hungarian nobility should be commissioned, but that

---

[53] Captain Laczkovics and Lieutenant Szily, for example, both officers in the Graeven regiment, were the brothers of the *alispánok* of Pest County. Mályusz, *Sándor Lipót,* p. 17.

[54] The copy of the captured appeal is in *Privatbibliothek* [of Leopold II] (microfilm copy), Fasc. 4, No. 8.

[55] Mérei and Spira, p. 24.

meritorious soldiers should also be rewarded with titles, land grants, and commissions.

The behavior of the Hungarian regiments did indeed weaken the morale and discipline of the Imperial Army. Leopold II himself regarded the Hungarian units as unreliable. He wrote to his sister Marie Christine on June 23, 1790: "Several Hungarian regiments are entertaining evil intentions." [56] On June 29 and again on June 30, 1790, he told her about the plans of the Hungarian officers and the deputies to the diet to make the Hungarian units independent of both the king and the *Hofkriegsrat*.[57] It looked by the early summer of 1790 as if the feudal revolt of the Hungarian gentry was really gaining momentum.

The feudal revolt was felt beyond the confines of the Hungarian privileged classes. Twenty-two foot soldiers of a Hungarian regiment garrisoned in Podolia, for instance, deserted from their unit and went home. They eluded pursuit, braved cold and hunger to cross the Carpathian Mountains, and reached Hungary. There they were arrested. Under questioning they expressed this surprising opinion:

Our decision was due exclusively to our love for our native land. We decided that, if in any event we had to bear arms, we would rather do so and shed our blood to defend our beloved homeland than foreign provinces.[58]

Four hundred soldiers of the Gyulay regiment stationed in Galicia deserted to join the ranks of the Polish army in the hope of fighting against the Habsburgs.

One of the factors contributing to these incidents was the strong influence that the opinions of commissioned noblemen had on the Hungarian rank and file, particularly in those regiments that had a majority of Hungarian officers. The men of the standing army were trained to follow their officers through thick and thin, without hesitation or complaint. Such discipline and *esprit de corps* made it easy for Hungarian officers to lead their men wherever they wished, even against the dynasty. This ability posed a serious threat to the Habsburgs in 1790. In the early summer of that year Hungary buzzed and pullulated like a hive of bees about to swarm. Rebellion seethed everywhere.

[56] Mályusz, *Sándor Lipót*, p. 18.   [57] *Ibid.*
[58] Marczali, *Országgyűlés*, II, 110.

In mid-August the alarming news reached the capital of Buda that the emissaries of King Leopold II and King Frederick William III had concluded the Reichenbach Convention. This agreement, which forestalled an armed clash between Prussia and the Habsburgs, dashed the only hope of victory of the leaders of the Hungarian feudal revolt. On August 15, 1790, the Hungarian gentry learned that eleven regiments of the Imperial Army were en route to Hungary from the Prussian border. The impressive power of such a column turned the tide: there was no longer any real possibility of the gentry defeating the Habsburgs, even by force of arms. With this turn of events, the feudal revolt and its concomitant *banderium* movement gradually faded into oblivion. Their fate was sealed on November 18, 1790, by Leopold II, who issued a strongly worded order to Count Károly Pálffy, the Royal Chancellor of Hungary, banning the *banderia*.[59] The order was completely effective.

The protonationalist unrest in the Hungarian regiments was crushed by stern disciplinary measures, including the cashiering of several Hungarian officers. Reichenbach doomed those first glimmerings of nationalism in the army as thoroughly as it did the *banderia*.

A DIPLOMATIC ADVENTURE AND CLANDESTINE NEGOTIATIONS

The third major event related to the feudal revolt was the diplomatic adventure of the *bene possessionati* with the Prussian court.[60] This project, bizarre though it was, was not entirely outside the realm of reality. The whole affair was based on the complex—and for the Habsburgs, extremely dangerous—international situation existing in early 1790.

It is true that in 1789 the Russo-Austrian alliance had resulted in important consequences: the Danubian principalities and Serbia had been conquered, and the Austrian army was ready to move into Bulgaria; panic reigned in Constantinople; and the combined Russian-Austrian victories were causing apprehension in European capitals (e.g., in Berlin, where Turkish partition was still opposed). Partition would have considerably strengthened both Russia and Austria without compensating Prussia. Thus in 1788 Prussia had joined Britain

[59] Mályusz, *Sándor Lipót*, p. 268, n. 7.
[60] It was started in July, 1788. Wangermann, p. 10.

and Holland in a Triple Alliance aimed at keeping France out of the Austrian Netherlands and at checking Russia and Austria in the Balkans.[61]

This was the situation when Emperor Joseph II died on February 20, 1790. His successor, Leopold II, was determined from the start to make foreign and domestic peace, to hold Habsburg territories intact by yielding readily to unimportant demands and only reluctantly to the important ones. He set out to pacify a state which seemed about to disintegrate.

Despite Leopold's pacific aims, it was not easy for Catherine of Russia to give up her "Greek Project," so long hoped for and now within her reach. But the pacific intentions of Leopold, the steadfast support given to Turkey by Prussia, Britain, and Holland, and, last but not least, Prussia's intrigues in both Poland and Hungary—these were ominous events for Russia and Austria. Both had to take into account the Prussian maneuvers. The conquest of the Danubian principalities and Belgrade prompted Prussia to conclude an alliance with the Porte on January 31, 1790.[62]

The Prussian court was involved in a three-cornered fraud. Just after Prussia concluded an alliance with the Ottoman Empire, she tried, through her chief minister, to promote a scheme, the price of which was to be paid exclusively by her new ally, Turkey. Furthermore, both countries were involved in diplomatic negotiations with the Poles with an alliance in mind; but this did not prevent the Prussian court from soon becoming a partner in the second partitioning of Poland. Moreover, the intensive exchange between the Prussian court and the representatives of the Hungarian estates was, as far as the former was concerned and most probably from the start, nothing but another fraud. In the final outcome, Prussia got what she wanted. After all, in diplomacy nothing is more successful than success, and the dignity of success usually wipes out the taint of fraudulent means. Both these historical lessons came true in the case of Prussian diplomacy.

The project of Count von Hertzberg, the Prussian chief minister,

[61] Crane Brinton, A Decade of Revolution: 1789–1799 (New York: Harper and Brothers, 1934), p. 79.

[62] Michael T. Florinsky, Russia: A History and an Interpretation (New York: The Macmillan Company, 1959), I, 533. On the relationship between the Prussian-Austrian antagonism and the internal situation of the Habsburg lands, see Wangermann, p. 52.

was, in R. H. Lord's words, a piece of diplomatic folly of monstrous impracticality.[63] Hertzberg proposed that the Ottoman Empire cede Bessarabia and Ochakov to Russia and the Danubian principalities to Austria, and, in return, secure for herself a European guarantee respecting the remainder of the Ottoman territories. Austria, as compensation for her gains, would cede Galicia to Poland, and Poland would cede the towns of Danzig and Toruń to Prussia. "Prussia would thus have something for nothing, and only Turkey, her ally, would be the loser." [64] Understandably, the Poles refused to accept the project. England and Holland both declined to back up their ally and, instead, urged a peace based on the *status quo ante bellum.*

When Prussia signed the Polish-Prussian Alliance Treaty on March 29, 1790, all references to the Hertzberg project naturally had to be omitted. This alliance provided that, in case of aggression against one of the contracting parties, the other would come to its assistance.[65] "Any attempt by Russia or Austria to revive their rights as guarantors in Poland would be acknowledged by Prussia as a *casus foederis.*" [66] The security of Poland thus seemed to be assured, but this was an unhappy delusion. For Prussia, the alliance was transitory, a tactical move which she was willing to use as long as her antagonism with Catherine II lasted; she was ready to renounce that alliance as soon as she could entertain hopes of extending her territory, even to the detriment of Poland. The Reichenbach Convention, concluded between Austria and Prussia on July 27, 1790, practically destroyed the entire meaning of the alliance, just as it took the wind out of the sails of the Hungarian feudal revolt. Finally, in 1792, when Russia invaded Poland, thereby creating a *casus foederis,* Prussia flatly refused to come to Poland's aid.[67] It is in the context of this general international framework that the diplomatic adventure of the Hungarian estates must be considered.

The Hungarian malcontents had already contacted the Prussian court during the reign of Emperor Joseph II. Unfortunately there are

[63] R. H. Lord, *The Second Partition of Poland* (Cambridge: At the University Press, 1915), p. 77.

[64] Brinton, p. 80.

[65] Oscar Halecki, *A History of Poland* (New York: Roy Publishers, 1961), p. 204.

[66] *The Cambridge History of Poland: 1697–1935* (Cambridge: At the University Press, 1951), p. 145.

[67] Halecki, p. 205.

no documents available which reveal the scope or dates of their plan, or the participants involved in it. It is known, however, that Joseph suspected Péter Balogh as being the brains and organizer behind the operation, and he therefore had him removed from his high position as a member of the *Septemviratus*.[68] As for the others involved, it is probable that András Semsey, Pál Beck, and Baron Ferenc Vécsey, councilors of the Hungarian Royal Chancellery, were among those who maintained contact with Berlin.[69] But, to be sure, they were only contacts in the operation, not the leaders.[70] King Leopold II, in trying to expose this operation, listed among its members the following personalities: Baron László Orczy, József Vay, Péter Balogh, Count Mihály Sztáray, Count Miklós Forgács, Baron József Podmaniczky, four of the Festetics cousins, and three of the Batthyány brothers. Vay, Balogh, and Podmaniczky were, in his opinion, the main organizers.[71]

After the opening of the diet, a new delegation visited Berlin. This delegation went so far as to suggest that the Hungarian crown be offered to Charles Augustus, the Grand Duke of Weimar. An interesting aspect of this whole bizarre project is that Goethe was personally involved in it.[72]

The Hungarians did not believe that their clandestine negotiations against their sovereign constituted treason. They wanted a foreign guarantor for the Hungarian constitution and especially for the new royal oath which they intended to enact. As was already mentioned, a guarantee of the Hungarian constitution by a foreign power was not a new idea. It had, in fact, been done in the past. The particular precedent which the Hungarian estates in 1790 had in mind was the guarantee of the Hungarian constitution in 1606 by the estates of Austria and Bohemia. At the time, the estates of Silesia were part of the Bohemian estates, but at the end of the War of the Austrian Succession, Silesia was ceded to Prussia. In the logic of the Hungarian statesmen, they thus had the right to turn to the sovereign of Silesia,

[68] *Staatsrat Archiv*, No. 239 (1794). See Mályusz, *Sándor Lipót*, p. 5, n. 2.
[69] Gragger, pp. 107–18.   [70] Mályusz, *Sándor Lipót*, p. 5, n. 2.
[71] Leopold II's letter to his son, Archduke Leopold, describing the character of the Hungarian leaders. The original was written in Leopold's own hand. Although it does not bear a date, everything indicates that it was written toward the end of 1791. *Privatbibliothek*, Fasc. 4, No. 28. Document No. 45 in Mályusz, *Sándor Lipót*, pp. 433–47.
[72] Hóman and Szekfü, V, 72; Gragger, pp. 5–11.

whoever he might be, to acquire a repetition of the guarantee granted in 1606 by the Silesian estates.[73] In 1790 the sovereign of Silesia was the King of Prussia, and therefore it was to him that the Hungarians felt they had to turn. Strangely enough, the old statesman Kaunitz found merit in this line of thought and urged King Leopold II to arrive at a compromise with the Hungarian estates rather than with Prussia.[74] In this, he was perhaps led more by sentiment than by reason, for an anti-Prussian policy was indeed a matter of sentiment and tradition for him.

In the *Staatsrat* the problem was not very clear, and thus a final decision could not be reached at an early date. Two projects were in circulation: in the event of war with Prussia, an occurrence which still belonged to the realm of possibilities, Kaunitz's suggestion was to be realized, and the Hungarians were to be pacified with several concessions;[75] in the event of a compromise with Prussia, the recalcitrant Hungarian estates were to be treated harshly.[76]

King Leopold decided against Kaunitz's proposal. He wanted a compromise with the Prussians, which would then allow him to concentrate all available force against the Hungarian feudal revolt. He sent Baron Spielmann to open negotiations with the Prussian court.[77] England and Holland, hoping to break up the Russo-Austrian alliance, gladly supported this diplomatic move. The negotiations were conducted at the Prussian royal military headquarters in the Silesian city of Reichenbach. On July 27, 1790, the Convention was signed on a basis of *status quo ante bellum* not only in the Balkans but in the relations of Austria and Prussia regarding Poland as well. In other words, the Habsburgs were obliged to conclude a peace settlement with the Ottoman Empire without territorial aggrandizement, and the fancy project of von Hertzberg naturally had to be dropped.[78]

The Austrian-Turkish peace settlement was finally concluded in

---

[73] The Treaty of Vienna was signed on September 23, 1606, by the representatives of the Habsburgs on the one hand and the representatives of the Prince of Transylvania and the Hungarian estates on the other. The treaty was then guaranteed by the estates of Austria and the Kingdom of Bohemia, which included Silesia. Hóman and Szekfü, III, 385-87.

[74] *Ibid.*, V, 72.

[75] *Staatsrat Archiv*, Nos. 1228 and 1828 (1790). See Mályusz, *Sándor Lipót*, p. 24, n. 1.

[76] Mályusz, *Sándor Lipót*, p. 24.

[77] Marczali, *Magyarország története III. Károlytól*, in Szilágyi, VIII, 501-2.

[78] Hóman and Szekfü, V, 73.

Sistova in August, 1791. Here Leopold made an interesting concession to the Hungarian diet: a Hungarian representative, Count Ferenc Eszterházy, participated in the peace talks.[79] This was a small and insignificant development, a formality rather than a concession of substance, for Eszterházy was a confidant of Leopold and represented the interests of the Habsburgs, Hungarian though he was.

Leopold's truly important decision, reached immediately after the Reichenbach Convention, was to pour the troops previously stationed on the Silesian border into Hungary.[80] This move must be considered primarily as an indication of royal determination to check the estates —if necessary, by use of arms. It was also intended to protect the estates against a *Jacquerie*, which was not an impossibility during the hot summer of that year.[81] However, rumors were spread by Leopold's agents that Hertzberg had revealed the names of those who had participated in the conspiracy with the Prussian court and that they were to be punished. This was a psychological ploy used to frighten the rebellious Hungarian leaders into cooperating with, and being loyal to, the dynasty.[82]

The Reichenbach concord gave the fatal blow to the Hungarian feudal revolt, for the movement thus lost its only foreign supporter, the conservative Prussian court. The Prussians never truly intended to provide substantial support for the Habsburgs' rebellious subjects to a degree that would have helped them achieve full national independence. Rather they intended to use their obscure connection with the Hungarian rebels to put pressure on the Habsburgs. Hence it is clear that, after Reichenbach, the tide of the feudal revolt was bound to ebb.[83]

[79] *Ibid.*   [80] Palmer, I, 394.

[81] While Leopold for all intents and purposes gave up his plan to cooperate with the peasants against the gentry in Hungary, he still continued to play that game in Austria and Bohemia up to his death. See Wangermann, pp. 84, 85.

[82] Mályusz, *Sándor Lipót*, p. 5, n. 2. There were several cases involving a change of heart. The most interesting was that of Péter Balogh, one of the outstanding leaders of the feudal revolt, who became most loyal to the Habsburgs. His new loyalty was rewarded by an avalanche of Habsburg favors.

[83] Mérei and Spira, p. 29: "The Treaty of Reichenbach meant a great setback for the Hungarian independence movement."

Chapter XIV

THE COURT AND THE BURGHERS

IN ORDER TO eliminate the threats the Habsburg Empire was facing on all fronts, Leopold II seems to have decided to concentrate first on the danger in Hungary. He quickly prepared the Reichenbach compromise with the Prussian court and forthwith launched a major effort to gain allies inside Hungary against the political force behind the feudal revolt, the *bene possessionati*.

The elements he attempted to gain as allies represented a cross section of Hungarian society: the Serbs in the south,[1] the peasants, and the middle-stratum burghers (the German-speaking residents of the royal free towns and the mining cities). The secret police, organized by Joseph II, functioned as the link between the Emperor and the German burghers.[2] The secret police organization was headed by regional directorates in Pozsony, Buda, Pest, and Nagyszeben (Transylvania). In 1789, jurisdiction over the secret police agency had been transferred from the Hungarian government to the minister of police of the Habsburg lands, Count Johann Anton Pergen.[3]

The police directorates henceforth reported on all matters of substance directly to Count Pergen. Under his supervision, the activities of the agency were expanded by enlisting agents from all walks of life in Hungary in return for cash, promotion, or various favors.[4] The operation of the secret police within Hungary had been supervised by the chief of police in Pest, Franz Gotthardi. After the death of

[1] See Wangermann, p. 87; Hóman and Szekfü, V, 69–71. See also Molnár, I, 398–99.
[2] Silagi, pp. 95–100.
[3] Wangermann offers a good description of Pergen's character and his activities, pp. 37–45, 50–55. See also Silagi, pp. 100 ff. and Wandruszka, II, 337 ff.
[4] Mályusz, "Magyarországi polgárág," I, 238.

Joseph II, his job was abolished and sole control was given over to Count Pergen. Gotthardi, however, was retained by Leopold in a quasi-official capacity,[5] and it was he who introduced Leopold Alois Hoffmann, professor of German at the University of Pest, to the King. Hoffmann was the author of a plan to organize the burghers into a force to offset the power of the *bene possessionati*. Leopold embraced the plan and took Hoffmann on as his special adviser and aide to implement it.

Hoffmann was a colorful man.[6] He began his career at the University of Breslau where he distinguished himself as an author of poetry, plays, and essays, and as an editor of periodicals.[7] His early writings already bore the marks of the Enlightenment, a philosophy he later championed. He joined the Freemasons and led their most radical wing, the *illuminati*.[8] His colleagues in the movement helped him in his career, which eventually led to an appointment at the University of Pest. By this time Hoffmann's "body and soul had become the loyal servants of the state and of the dynasty," according to Elemér Mályusz.[9]

As early as 1789, Franz Gotthardi recommended that the court publish a strong attack on the nationalist propaganda of the Hungarian nobles, which at that time was making increasing references to the upheavals in France. And Gotthardi's recommendation for author was Professor Hoffmann. Although Gotthardi's plan was at first given official sanction, the Emperor eventually refused to sponsor publication of Hoffmann's pamphlet because he disagreed with some of its conclusions about the French Revolution.[10]

As the feudal revolt's threat to the Josephine state increased, Hoffmann again offered his services to the court in 1790. In June he was introduced to Leopold by Gotthardi and on July 4 he presented a memorandum on the burghers to the Emperor.[11]

[5] Gotthardi was appointed by Leopold II as chief of the secret information service. On his activities in Pest see Hóman and Szekfü, V, 90. For Gotthardi's own exposition of his activities see Benda, I, 633–38.

[6] On Hoffman see Wangermann, pp. 11 ff.; Wandruszka, II, 277; Silagi, p. 37; Kosáry, II, 325, 352; Marczali, *Országgyülés*, II, 167–68.

[7] One of them was *Wöchentliche Wahrheiten*. Wangermann, p. 11.

[8] See Silagi, pp. 37 ff. See also Hóman and Szekfü, V, 90.

[9] Mályusz, "Magyarországi polgárság," I, 242.   [10] Wangermann, p. 11.

[11] *Projekt des Pester Kaufmanns Natorp zur Etablirung bürgerlicher Compagnien und Truppen in allen hung. Stadten. Privatbibliothek*, Fasc. 11, No. 29 (microfilm copy). (Naturally, the name "Natorp" was fictitious.)

The radical measures in Hoffmann's memorandum included the following points:

Able-bodied men of the royal free towns were to be organized as guards at the disposal of the king without constitutional restrictions or interference from the nobles. The nucleus of the guards was to be the Civic Guard formed on Joseph II's orders in Pest and Buda at the time of the transfer of the standing army's units from the twin cities to the Turkish front.[12]

The *Generalkommando* was to supervise the reorganization of the hitherto powerless Civic Guard, used mostly for ceremonial purposes, into a useful military force.

Both in Pest and Buda 300-man units were to be formed immediately from among those of unquestioned loyalty to the Emperor, mostly German and Serbian burghers. Hungarians were not to be enlisted until a later date and even then should not exceed a quarter of the units' total strength.

The members of the guards were to wear the uniform of the standing army and have regular military training. Officers of the standing army should be present "coincidentally" during drills to give advice to the instructors.

The strength of the guards was to be increased gradually by enlistment of poorer burghers and even the lowest strata of townsmen. They should receive a salary to be supplied secretly by the *Generalkommando.*

The guards' officers would take a loyalty oath under the supervision of the *Generalkommando,* with which they would keep permanent but covert contact.

After guard units had been formed in Buda and Pest, units were to be organized in other royal free towns. The *Generalkommando* would carry out this task by means of representatives in these towns who had to persuade the local burghers to petition the Emperor for permission to organize guard units.

The Emperor would grant permission to organize the guards simply on receipt of such requests; by merely giving consent instead of initiating action he could not be accused by the Hungarian nobles of masterminding the movement.[13]

[12] Mályusz, "Magyarországi polgárság," I, 242. On armed societies of the burghers see Oszetzky, pp. 23–24.

[13] Mályusz, "Magyarországi polgárság," I, 242.

Once organized, the guards would be at the disposal of the Emperor, for use, if necessary, as bodyguards at the forthcoming coronation.

All these actions could increase the burghers' loyalty to the crown, since they would feel that their new role of protecting the Emperor would bring them some sort of equality with the Hungarian nobles. In case of a rift between the nobles and the burghers, the guards could serve to protect the burghers; they could also be used in case of a peasant revolt.

The main purpose of Hoffmann's plan was to counterbalance the *banderium* movement of the Hungarian lesser nobility. Leopold welcomed it and supported Hoffmann, but he withheld final endorsement, mostly because he feared both an armed showdown with the Hungarian nobles and changes in the tide of opinion among the burghers themselves, who, according to some reports, "were behaving too much like Hungarians" under the influence of the feudal revolt.[14]

Hoffmann and his plan are important as evidence of the court's concern over the burghers and their role in a society seething near the climax of the feudal revolt.

From the time of Joseph's death until midsummer, 1790, the burghers seemed generally willing to cooperate with the nobles. With the opening of the diet, however, the burghers began to realize that a feudal revolt aimed at establishing a Polish-type royal republic dominated by the nobility in Hungary was scarcely in their interest. Even such meager opportunity for commoners to hold the higher offices of state as had been provided by Joseph was now in jeopardy, and this was the only chance for the sons of burghers to raise their social status. The town representatives at the diet, it has been noted, were members of the lesser nobility and hence gave the burghers no support. A major clash of interests was shaping up between the burghers and the nobility. The burghers, however, were slow to foresee the coming confrontation and their movement for self-defense was not to gain momentum for some time to come.

This, then, was the psychological setting for the beginning of Hoffmann's efforts to mobilize the burghers. He left Vienna in August, 1790, with Leopold's commission to rally the burghers against the nobles. First, he contacted his old friends in Pest, enlisting the aid of

---

[14] *Privatbibliothek*, Fasc. 11, No. 13, June 28, July 3, July 15, 1790 (microfilm copy). For the behavior of burghers in other Habsburg lands see Wangermann, pp. 77 ff.

such local burghers as the watchmaker Mahl and the merchants Liedemann and Leszár. Liedemann, at the same time, was working as an informer for Gotthardi.

Hoffmann's first reports to Leopold said that even the most informed burghers were unaware of their opportunity to eliminate or lessen the domination of the nobles.[15] Before Hoffmann's arrival, the burghers of Pest and Buda were completely quiescent. Gradually, Hoffmann made them aware of the threat from the nobility, of the need to organize in order to protect themselves. He finally persuaded them to send a list of their grievances to the King in an appeal. Hoffmann had such an appeal already drafted by the time he arrived in Pest. Professor Mályusz suggests that the purpose of the appeal was not so much to further the interests of the burghers as to annoy the diet.[16] This theory is borne out by the manner in which the appeal was forgotten once the diet and the crown had reached a compromise.[17]

The appeal itself was dated August 8, 1790, and it expressed the view that the burghers of Pest could "not be idle bystanders" during the debates of the diet. While the nobility, the Catholic prelates, and even the Protestants fought there for their interests, nobody was raising any argument for the burghers. The appeal said this was happening despite the fact that the burghers were "the tax-paying foundations of the state." It protested against a draft resolution presented on the floor of the diet to exclude commoners from high state offices and army commissions, and complained that those who were supposed to represent the burghers in the diet had voiced no opposition to it.

The reason for this silence was that, since the town magistrates, several of them nobles themselves, selected representatives to the diet from among their own ranks, the burghers themselves had, in fact, no true representatives. This, then, was why they now appealed directly to the King for permission for the burghers of the royal free towns and all other cities to send their own representatives to the diet so that the burghers, too, could be heard.[18]

[15] *Privatbibliothek*, Fasc. 15, No. 6, August 21, 1790 (microfilm copy).

[16] Mályusz, "Magyarországi polgárság," I, 246.

[17] In contrast to the apathy of the burghers in Hungary, their Austrian counterparts were eminently active in a struggle for their political and social advancement. See Wangermann, pp. 77, 78.

[18] Hungarian Court Chancellery, 14, 455 (1790). Quoted in Mályusz, "Magyarországi polgárság," I, 247.

The appeal was taken to Vienna by Hoffmann himself. He was received by the King, who sent a message of reassurance through him to the burghers, pledging his good-will.[19] No reference was made to the fact that Hoffmann's mission and the idea for the appeal stemmed from the King himself.

Of course, an appeal by a single city, even of Pest's significance, could not possibly have brought results or exerted considerable pressure on the nobility with its nationwide identity of interest. Hoffmann now began a two-pronged campaign. He persuaded several of his trusted friends in Pest to urge their acquaintances in other royal free towns and major peasant towns to send similar appeals to the King, and he started writing pamphlets to encourage the burghers to launch a national movement in defense of their interests.

To ensure consistent emphasis on his main points, Hoffmann had copies of Pest's appeal printed in Vienna, leaving only the name of the town blank; these he sent to all the royal free towns and major peasant towns in early September. He advised his supporters and those he made contact with through his friends in Pest to fill in the blank with the name of their town, sign the appeal, and mail it to the court. Some of the burghers followed his advice, but others in towns such as Ujvidék, Pozsony, and Arad took the extra effort to copy out the printed appeal and mailed to Vienna their own transcription of it.[20] But over-all, Hoffmann had a rather difficult time with the majority of the middle-stratum burghers, who lacked political experience and were too timid to act without a great deal of persuasion.[21] In spite of Hoffmann's every effort, only ten towns in addition to Pest sent appeals to Vienna.

Hoffmann's pamphleteering began with the publication of *Babel*,[22] in which he compared the activity of the Hungarian diet with the building of the tower of Babel. He suggested that the same amount of confusion reigned in both cases; he accused the nobles of demagoguery

[19] *Privatbibliothek*, Fasc. 15, No. 6, Hoffmann, August 21, 1790 (microfilm copy).

[20] Mályusz, "Magyarországi polgárság," I, 248.

[21] Gotthardi report on the delegation of Temesvár, September 9, 10, October 22. *Privatbibliothek*, Fasc. 13 and 15, 1790 (microfilm copy). On Gotthardi see Wangermann, pp. 10–11.

[22] *Babel: Fragmente über die jetzigen politischen Angelegenheiten in Ungarn* (Gedrückt im römischen Reiche, 1790). See also Wangermann, p. 86. On the philosophical roots of *Babel* see Eckhardt, pp. 29–42; also Kosáry, II, 325.

and of wanting to suppress all other classes by making the burghers their servants and the serfs their slaves. While *Babel* did not elaborate a specific program for those deprived of political rights, it indicated that, like their counterparts in France, they might demand representation. *Babel* had a limited circulation, and evidently most of the burghers who had a chance to read it did not quite understand it. Actually, it did not make clear the exact nature of the burghers' grievances or the possible course of action open to them, and thus failed to achieve its objective of mobilizing the middle section of the burghers.

The sessions of the diet were much more successful than *Babel* in clarifying things to the burghers. The draft for the exclusion of commoners from high state offices and army commissions in particular exercised them and led at least the younger burghers to take action. They drew up and sent to the diet a protest against the injustice of the draft.[23]

Hoffmann was greatly encouraged by this unexpected and spontaneous move on the part of the burgher youth. He tried to ride the wave of indignation, hoping to harness its energy for his own hitherto unsuccessful campaign. He succeeded in persuading several mining cities and the town of Vác, for example, to send new appeals to the King, yet even this new impetus was insufficient to start a nationwide movement by the burghers to defend their rights.

The indefatigable Hoffmann still refused to give up. In September he published his second pamphlet, *Ninive*.[24] In it he followed Leopold's instructions for writing a sequel to *Babel*. The draft of *Ninive* was submitted to Leopold, who approved of it so much that he directed the censors to allow its immediate publication.[25] Hundreds of copies were sent free to various towns.[26] The reason for Leopold's support was *Ninive*'s timing.[27] The compromise between the court and the estates came on September 21, 1790. In early September Leopold still needed all the support he could get, including pressure by the burghers on the nobility.

[23] György Szaller's manuscript, *Privatbibliothek*, Fasc. 30, No. 2, pp. 25–35. Prof. Gabelhofer's report, August 22, 1790, *Privatbibliothek*, Fasc. 11, No. 4 (microfilm copies).

[24] *Ninive: Fortgesetze Fragmente über die dermaligen politischen Angelegenheiten in Ungarn* (Auch im römischen Reiche gedrückt, 1790).

[25] Mályusz, "Magyarországi polgárság," I, 253, n. 46.   [26] *Ibid.*, p. 252.

[27] See Wangermann, pp. 84 ff.; Kosáry, II, 325.

The goal of *Ninive* was to induce the German burghers to bring this pressure to bear. *Ninive* was a vast improvement over *Babel*. It analyzed the burghers' circumstances, ridiculed the Hungarian estates' stupidity and shortsightedness in their new draft on the subject of the royal oath, and even blamed the nobility for the Empire's temporary failures in the Turkish War. Making a pitch for the German burghers and readers in the whole Empire, *Ninive* scoffed at the Hungarian language, customs, and dress and the budding new nationalism that glorified all these. It diagnosed the burghers' condition in Hungary and suggested cures. It asserted that serfs and burghers alone bore the burden of paying taxes, while the nobles enjoyed the fruits of others' labor, holding in contempt those whose labor they exploited. *Ninive* claimed the burghers were becoming the slaves of the nobles; it decried the lack of justice for the burghers in the nobility-dominated courts of the land; it complained about lack of security for the individual burgher and his property. Hoffmann's pamphlet then struck a monitory note by reminding the nobles of the events in France. It threatened a general recall of all burgher representatives from the diet and the sending of new representatives not only from the royal free towns but from groups of burghers everywhere. These new men would truly speak for the burgher and his interests.[28]

A radical innovation suggested in *Ninive* was to grant representation to peasant towns (*mezővárosok*). Hoffmann assured his readers that this could be attained even without a legal basis for it in the *Corpus Juris*. He claimed the behavior of the diet warranted such a revolutionary move since the nobles disregarded the interests of the burghers completely. *Ninive* made a strong point of the nobles' draft for the new royal oath, saying that the nobles forfeited their own rights by attempting to deny the King his constitutional prerogatives. The nobility, Hoffmann asserted, was foolish to tear down all the constitutional structure of the rights of the King, for this line could well be followed by the burghers against the nobles. Not content simply to arouse the readers of *Ninive*, Hoffmann now took action on some of his pamphlet's suggestions.

With the endorsement of Leopold, Hoffmann sent out letters containing a proposed burghers' oath[29]—clearly demonstrating the effect

[28] Mályusz, "Magyarországi polgárság," I, 253.
[29] *Ibid.*, p. 254. On the oaths of Hungarian burghers see Oszetzky, pp. 33–36.

of the Tennis Court Oath on the minds of both Hoffmann and those
he appealed to. It was the *bene possessionati* who had all the nobles
take an oath to safeguard the privileges of the estates, and who also
made the serfs take an oath of loyalty to their lords. Now, with
Leopold's blessing, Hoffmann wanted the burghers to take their own
loyalty oath, pledging their support of the King and of joint efforts
in their common interest. While Hoffmann urged the burghers to
defend their interests, his real intention appears to have been to convince the nobles that their own position would be imperiled if they
continued to challenge the monarch's privileges.

The most radical of Hoffmann's published writings, *Plan und
Zweck*, for example, began: "Plan und Zweck des bekannten Unterneh-
mers, Mein Herr!"[30] In this and in two similar pamphlets he emphasized that the burghers now had an opportunity to give new laws
to the land on their own, to gain rights such as the burghers had
won in the West. He exhorted them to align themselves with the
King in an alliance superior in strength to that of the nobility. Envisioning the breaking of the nobility's power monopoly, Hoffmann
suggested that this alliance would enable the King to declare the
present diet illegal and convoke a new diet with equal representation
for nobles and burghers. Hoffmann suggested in *Plan und Zweck*[31]
a number of demands the burghers should make, promising implicitly
that the King would support them in their efforts. These included
(1) easing the burden of present taxpayers by extending taxation to
the nobility; (2) preventing the nobility from becoming city magistrates or holding any positions which the burghers should occupy;
(3) ending the total subordination of towns to county governments
and securing a measure of self-government for the towns themselves;
(4) safeguarding the person and property of the burgher and arresting
violators of his safety, even if they were noblemen; (5) securing the
personal property of burghers by establishing credit courts to try
noblemen delinquent in their debts to burghers instead of leaving
jurisdiction with the county courts dominated by the nobles themselves; (6) allowing the burghers to fill higher church, state, and
army offices instead of only the lower ranks.

[30] Attached to Hoffmann's reports of September 14 and October 11, 1790,
Privatbibliothek, Fasc. 15, No. 6 (microfilm copy).
[31] A digest of *Plan und Zweck* is in Silagi, pp. 95–100.

Hoffmann admitted that the prelacy and nobility were certain to resist these demands, but he contended that, if the burghers persisted and stood united, their strength would, especially with the King's support, be greater than that of the nobles and prelates combined. Hoffmann's propositions would have held true in a country with a numerically and economically strong, united burgher class—a factor almost entirely missing in Hungary. Were Hoffmann and Leopold aware of this? Were they trying only to deceive the burghers in an attempt to gain their full support or, perhaps, were they deceiving themselves, too?

Both of them were sufficiently knowledgeable to realize the weakness of the burghers in Hungary, the fact that, even if united, their forces were inferior to those of the nobles. And yet Hoffmann, with the King's full encouragement, kept writing and preaching doctrines that to both of these informed men must have appeared nonsense. No indication of the reasons for this can be found in Hoffmann's writings. One can approach this obvious contradiction between facts and propaganda only speculatively. The most likely theory is that Hoffmann believed in the need for exaggeration in order to arouse the politically immature burghers. Moreover, *Babel, Ninive,* and *Plan und Zweck* were aimed primarily at the nobility, in the hope of scaring them into a more submissive attitude toward the King's demands.

Plan und Zweck adumbrates an improbable dream world. It told the nobility that they must ultimately yield or they would find themselves opposed not only by the burghers but also by the serfs, who would likewise demand separate representation in the diet. It even raised the possibility of a new constitution which would abolish old privileges, giving equality to all the other, hitherto oppressed, classes. Hoffmann again and again told the burghers that their demands could be realized in the near future if only they would unite and act in defense of their interests. The instrument of the first instance, he told them, should be the burghers' oath which would pledge them both to the King and to their own interests. He warned the burghers against listening to the promises of the nobility and pressed them to move steadily but cautiously in spreading the ideas of *Babel* and *Ninive* among all their fellows.[32]

---

[32] Mályusz, "Magyarországi polgárság," I, 254–55.

While Hoffmann worked ceaselessly in September organizing the burghers, and while some of his associates, such as Szalkay, were spreading the word among the serfs in the countryside,[33] Count Zichy and Ürményi were negotiating in Vienna on behalf of the nobles for a compromise with Leopold II. On September 21, 1790, the agreement between court and estates was concluded, reinstating some of the ancient privileges of the estates, who, in exchange, conceded to Leopold the royal privileges secured formerly by Charles III and Maria Theresa. The agreement opened the way to the coronation of Leopold as King of Hungary as well as the election of his son, Alexander Leopold, as the first Habsburg Palatine of Hungary.[34] These agreements fulfilled the hopes of Leopold, who thus had no more need for the pressure which the burghers and serfs could be expected to exercise on the estates. Yet he did not cancel his instructions to Hoffmann. Mályusz suggests that the reason for this was that, immediately upon reaching the agreement with the estates, Leopold left for Frankfurt to be crowned Emperor of the Holy Roman Empire and thus he simply had no time to communicate with Hoffmann.[35] However, it is also conceivable that he did not deem it urgent to lift the pressure on the nobles, still using this as a weapon in his dealings with them.

There is little doubt that the sole moving force behind the burgher movement was Leopold II. The burghers themselves were passive and inexperienced in political movements; their maximum effort seemed to be the signing of forms provided by Hoffmann. But, significantly, the nobility realized the potential danger they would encounter in face of an active, organized burgher movement, and moved swiftly to abate this threat so masterfully instigated and sanctioned by the King. The gentry responded to a menace, the origin of which was unknown to them, unsuspecting as they were of the King's part, and countered the least activity suspected among the burghers with immediate actions of their own.

In September, for example, when the nobles learned about the appeal of the burghers of Pest to the King, they launched a widespread

[33] Details of the court's efforts to gain the cooperation of the peasants are described in Chapter XV. On Szalkay see Wandruszka, II, 282–86.

[34] The office of the Palatine of Hungary from that time on was always filled by a Habsburg archduke until 1848.

[35] Mályusz, "Magyarországi polgárság," I, 258.

investigation by the magistrates of Pest, headed by the *biró*, János Boráros, to find the authors of the appeal which "scandalously expressed contempt for the nobility, putting the whole fourth estate to shame."[36] The town magistrates ordered the Captain of the Town to confiscate all copies of the appeal; the man suspected of being its author was subjected to long and thorough investigation; an inquiry was opened into all the persons who signed it. These measures frightened the burghers, ensuring that they carefully avoided all those connected with the organization of the movement. Three signers of the document, János Temesváry, Miklós and János Stankovics, testified that they had signed only because their German was insufficient to understand the text; now that they had a Hungarian translation, they had solemnly withdrawn their signatures.[37]

The counteroffensive of the nobility was all the more successful since so very few were aware of the King's involvement in the movement; the King's secret role was not realized even by high government officials, who thus made no effort to protect the burghers from the wrath of the gentry. This was clearly shown by the case of *Babel*, which was confiscated seven days after its publication on August 23 on the orders of Van Swieten, who banned further distribution of the pamphlet.[38] While the gentry used their connections with the *illuminati* in Vienna to have the ban issued, Leopold's hands were tied because his own officials were unaware of his involvement. Leopold finally ordered his son, the crown prince Francis, to cancel Van Swieten's ban.[39] To confuse the situation further, Van Swieten, in the dark like most others, took an active part in writing and editing a pamphlet denouncing *Babel*,[40] and then ordered the censor Szekeres to let this pamphlet be published at once to counteract *Babel*'s influence.[41]

The *Staatsrat*'s two most influential senior members, Prince Kaunitz and Count Hatzfeld, also objected to the idea of playing with such

[36] The report of secret agent Strohmayer, September 22, 1790, *Privatbibliothek*, Fasc. 11, No. 3, as well as the reports of Hoffmann dated September 17 and 19, 1790, *ibid.* (microfilm copies).

[37] Strohmayer's report of September 22 and Hoffmann's reports of September 17 and 19, *ibid.* (microfilm copies).

[38] Hoffmann's report of August 24, 1790, *ibid.* (microfilm copy).

[39] Mályusz, "Magyarországi polgárság," I, 260.

[40] *Beurtheiligung der Fragmente über die jetzigen politischen Angelegenheiten in Ungarn, Babel genannt* (Deutschland, 1790), in Ballagi, pp. 393 ff.

[41] Mályusz, "Magyarországi polgárság," I, 261.

a potentially dangerous force as a burgher class united in opposition against the nobility. Kaunitz and Hatzfeld thus supported the efforts of the Hungarian gentry to suppress a movement aimed at arousing the burghers and serfs.[42] Meanwhile, Leopold forwarded the burghers' appeals—which he himself had secretly fostered—and the spontaneous protest drafted by the burgher youth to the Hungarian Royal Court Chancellery for advice. The most talented of the councilors, Sándor Pászthory, prepared a report for the King. Although Pászthory was a *bene possessionatus* who cooperated loyally with the leaders of the feudal revolt, his intellect and character prevented him from being an extremist. In response to the appeals which the King had forwarded, he advised that laws be drafted to define the opportunities for commoners to hold administrative office and suggested that lower offices be made available to them in the *Kammer* system, in the salt, mining, and postal administrations, in the Chancellery itself, and in the *Consilium locumtenentiale*. He further counseled that those commoners who served in these offices with distinction should be ennobled and then allowed to advance even to the highest offices.[43]

The majority in the *Staatsrat* might have gone along with Pászthory's draft, but the general atmosphere of apprehension dissuaded them from doing so. The draft suggested revising the regulations for filling financial posts, appointment to which was an established royal prerogative requiring no reference to the diet or any other Hungarian authority. Submission to the diet of new legislation on these offices would implicitly have acknowledged that the diet had some authority over posts in the *Kammer*—an authority which never belonged to it. The officers of the *Staatsrat*, as well as Leopold, opposed this, and the entire draft was subsequently dropped. Leopold issued a royal proclamation which declared that there was no need for new legislation on the holding of offices of state by commoners, but, at the same time, he instructed the Chancellery to make assurances to the burghers and serfs that the court had their interests in mind. Both the Chancellery and the *Consilium locumtenentiale* were instructed by the King to open all offices to qualified commoners. In the same document containing these instructions, the King pledged that he

[42] *Ibid.*

[43] Hungarian Royal Court Chancellery, 12,230 and 13,926 (1790), quoted *ibid.*, pp. 261, 262.

would safeguard the interests of the burghers and serfs with the utmost diligence (*auf das kräftigste*).[44]

In the growing spirit of compromise with the estates, Leopold changed his mind again, and on November 7, 1790, he modified his order so that commoners were to be employed only in positions below that of secretary in both the Chancellery and the *Consilium*, but he left open to them any post in the *Kammer* system and in all other departments directly under royal jurisdiction.[45] The *Staatsrat*, generally speaking, was conservative and opposed the demands of the burghers and the serfs; the majority were afraid of changes they regarded as revolutionary and resisted all reforms as harbingers of a coming revolution. Leopold, again in a spirit of compromise as the day of his Hungarian coronation in Pozsony approached, decided on November 5 that all documents, including the burghers' appeal and the serf leaflets from Szepes County, should be transferred to the Chancellery, where they were to be considered when the matter of reform of the diet came up on the agenda.[46] This meant that Leopold in effect was setting aside the burgher and peasant movements. Both movements had brought about the results which he wanted and thus were expendable. Eventually, Leopold decided to make no demands at all on the nobles concerning the grievances of the burghers and the serfs.[47]

The burgher movement, no longer necessary to Leopold, now completely collapsed. And yet it did not disappear without a trace. Just like the defeated peasant movements of the eighteenth century, the artificially inspired burgher movement left its mark before expiring for good. Some of the politically conscious members of the middle stratum now realized that they had to work together in order to emancipate themselves from the oppression of the gentry in general, and from the domination of the county and town magistracies by the *bene possessionati* in particular. These awakened burghers witnessed with alarm their fellows' relapse into the stagnation and indolence

[44] *Staatsrat Archiv*, No. 3191 (1790). See Mályusz, "Magyarországi polgárság," I, 263.

[45] Mályusz, ed., *Sándor Lipót*, p. 252, and *Staatsrat Archiv*, No. 3519 (1790), in Mályusz, "Magyarországi polgárság," I, 263.

[46] *Staatsrat Archiv*, No. 3344 (1790). Mályusz, "Magyarországi polgárság," I, 265.

[47] Mályusz, *Sándor Lipót*, pp. 242 ff.

from which they had never really been aroused. Many of the burghers felt, if not knew, that a compromise between the King and the nobility was inevitable and spelled an end to their aspirations. Hoffmann blamed the apathy engendered by this conviction for the fact that many towns did not even bother to send to Vienna the appeal which he had had printed and which merely required signing.[48]

The King's disregard of all burghers' demands caused widespread resentment against him among the burghers. The Burghers' Guard disintegrated and the growing discontent was expressed in harsh terms even in public. The well-organized secret police reported all this to the court, where Leopold received the news with resentment, unable to comprehend the burghers' behavior. He retaliated by refusing to receive Hoffmann and by exerting all his influence to prevent the burghers from attempting to revive their movement in preparation for the planned diet of 1792.[49]

The *publico-politicus* committee of the diet drafted a reform plan for future representation of the burghers,[50] envisioning a system of three representatives from each county and one from each town. Of course, even under this system the diet would still have been dominated by the nobles, since each representative was to have one vote. Even so, the burghers' vote would have increased from one to about fifty and, considering the increasing liberalism of the lesser nobility, the position of the burghers would have been greatly strengthened under this scheme. Indeed, an alliance of the town representatives with liberal noblemen was the pattern in the French National Assembly of 1789, and the same political coalition could have set in motion the Hungarian reform era decades before its actual beginning. But, in the pattern of events, this progressive draft, too, was shelved and forgotten.

Left to themselves, a few of the burghers now tried to build a permanent organization for the furtherance of their interests and the gradual acquisition of political power.[51] The plan originated with Sámuel Liedemann,[52] a wealthy burgher of Pest. He thought of setting

---

[48] Hoffmann's reports of October 26 and November 12, 1790. See Mályusz, "Magyarországi polgárság," I, 258.

[49] The confiscated manuscripts of Ferenc Verseghy, *Vertrauliche Akten*, Fasc. 51, A, No. 13, p. 280. See Benda, I, 890 ff., and Oszetzky, pp. 59, 68.

[50] For the work of the various diet committees see Hóman and Szekfü, V, 77–87.

[51] Mályusz, *Sándor Lipót*, p. 275.   [52] Kosáry, II, 352.

up an organization similar in structure and method to the Freemasons. Liedemann intended to establish five grades, with public participation in the lower three and secret membership in the upper two. The two upper grades were to outline strategy, make policy, and provide leadership. Promotion from grade to grade was to be based on merit and service. Liedemann's plan divided Hungary into five lodges, with a supreme grade at the head of each and headquarters in Pozsony, Pest, Temesvár, Kassa, and Besztercebánya. Ironically, Liedemann wanted to name the organization the "Leopold Order" in an expression of loyalty to the King.

Liedemann's complete plan was presented to Leopold II by Gotthardi on March 9, 1791.[53] Its fate was no different from that of all the other projects concerning the burghers: the King, following his usual treatment for such plans in 1790, shelved it after a brief consideration. Yet it is worthy of note as evidence of a wide-ranging political consciousness already inchoately astir at this period as well as an indication that an aware burgher class with a political philosophy of its own was just beginning to come into being. The major obstacle to realization of the Liedemann plan was that it depended entirely on sponsorship by Leopold, to say nothing of its inclusion of a request for a 5,000-florin grant from the court. Typically, Gotthardi, the eternal conspirator, suggested to the King that the throne should advance a loan of 10,000 florins to Liedemann at 4 percent interest. Liedemann could then set himself up as a merchant of considerable capital whose business would be able to sustain the cost of organizing the "Leopold Order" as well as paying back the King's interest. Leopold shelved both the Liedemann plan and Gotthardi's suggestion. Gotthardi made a note of the affair, mentioning the King's approval in principle, and his decision to shelve the plan temporarily because the time for it had not yet arrived ("zu dessen Errichtung noch nicht Zeit wäre").[54] It should also be noted that, had the plan been put into effect, it may have aborted, for there was still no really self-conscious burgher class sufficiently developed as a whole to give the organization a viable nucleus from which to grow. Leopold's rejection, moreover, did not seem final. "Noch nicht Zeit wäre" carries the implication that, had Leopold lived longer, he might have reconsidered his decision.

[53] *Privatbibliothek,* Fasc. 11, No. 13 (microfilm copy).
[54] *Ibid.,* Fasc. 14 (microfilm copy).

Chapter XV

PEASANT UNREST AND AGITATION

THE PEASANT AGITATION of 1790 comes almost midway in point of time between the war of Ferenc Rákóczi (1703–11) and the revolution of Lajos Kossuth (1848–49). In both these major upheavals large masses of peasants participated eagerly from the beginning, and supported them more or less enthusiastically throughout. Their main motivation for involvement was the hope that the outcome would result in major social reforms which would ease their plight. This mass participation by the peasantry gave both movements a truly national character.

True, the passing years in the case of Rákóczi and the passing months in the case of Kossuth saw growing disillusionment on the part of the peasants; their efforts lost momentum as they realized that they were not gaining the political and social benefits that they had hoped for. But this does not obscure the basic fact that twice in 160 years all social classes, including the peasants, participated in major national endeavors in full cooperation together.

Between 1711 and 1848, however, there occurred no such complete cooperation. The era was one of growing social tension as the peasants sporadically resorted to force in an effort to better their conditions. The violence of these peasant uprisings was greater than at any time since the Peasant War of Dózsa in 1514. The peasants' role in the events of 1790 must be viewed in the light of earlier peasant insurrections.

The first major peasant revolt of this period erupted in Békés County in 1735. It was a brief uprising, lasting two weeks, but significant because of its intensity and consequences. Its causes were

Map No. 3

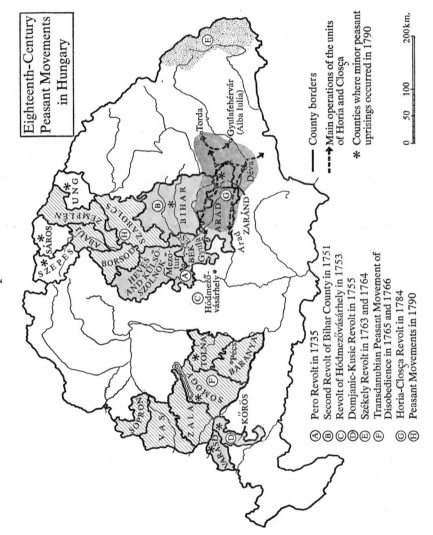

Eighteenth-Century
Peasant Movements
in Hungary

SZEPES

*SÁROS

ABAUJ *UNG

ZEMPLÉN

SZABOLCS

BORSOD (H)

HEVES
AND KÜLSŐ-
SZOLNOK

Mező-
túr

BÉKÉS (A)

BIHAR (B) *

Gyula

*Hódmező-
vásárhely (C)

SOPRON

VAS

ZALA

SOMOGY (F)

TOLNA *

BARANYA °Pécs

KŐRÖS

*TARACZ (D)

Arad

ARAD (G)

ZARÁND

Déva

*Torda

Gyulafehérvár
(Alba Iulia)

(E)

———— County borders

- - - -► Main operations of the units
of Horia and Closça

* Counties where minor peasant
uprisings occurred in 1790

0   50 100   200 km.

Ⓐ Pero Revolt in 1735
Ⓑ Second Revolt of Bihar County in 1751
Ⓒ Revolt of Hódmezővásárhely in 1753
Ⓓ Domjanic-Kusic Revolt in 1755
Ⓔ Székely Revolt in 1763 and 1764
Ⓕ Transdanubian Peasant Movement of
   Disobedience in 1765 and 1766
Ⓖ Horia-Closça Revolt in 1784
Ⓗ Peasant Movements in 1790

many and complex, but above all was the traditional cause of unrest: the misery of the peasants. The immediate causes in Békés County were the crushing duties imposed on the inhabitants of the Serbian Military Frontier Zone[1] and the flagrant exploitation of the local serfs by the tenants of the absentee landlord Harrucken, who had immense holdings in the county. Religious grievances also played a part. The Catholic Church, in the wake of the new Counter Reformation, militantly suppressed the local Protestant and Orthodox denominations to which most of the rebels belonged. The revolt spread through the counties of Arad, Zaránd, Heves, Külső-Szolnok, and Bihar. The rebellious frontiersmen were led by a Captain of the Guard, Pero Segedinać. All levels of the peasantry joined in the revolt, even members of the local *honoratiori*. The legend of the exiled Rákóczi was an important source of inspiration for the rebels, just as it had been many times before in smaller, local uprisings. Long after Rákóczi died in 1735, the peasants looked to his triumphant return to lead them to victory.[2]

One of the outstanding features of this uprising was the speed with which the peasants organized. They swiftly mobilized recruiting teams, formed military units, and found able commanders from among their own ranks. The rebels' main weakness was their lack of modern weapons in contrast to the fairly well-equipped standing army.

Within a matter of days, the rebels marshaled a well-organized force of 1,300 men. One column proceeded to lay siege to the city of Gyula while another advanced to capture the fortress at Arad. The standing army, along with an *insurrectio* of nobles, who mustered immediately, quickly countered and put down the rebellion before it could spread. Captain Segedinać and fourteen of his associates were executed in Buda.

[1] Map No. 1 shows the Military Frontier Zone running along the southernmost frontiers of the kingdom. The boundaries were different in 1735. The zone at that time still followed the western shores of the Tisza River from where it runs into the Danube to the confluence of the Tisza and the Maros. From there, it ran along the northern shore of the Maros River. Thus, the major portion of Arad and Zaránd counties still belonged to the Military Frontier Zone. The zone boundary was moved south to its final location only afterwards, in the period between 1743 and 1751.

[2] Mód, p. 115; also Tamás Esze and Ágnes Várkonyi, "A Rákóczi-hagyomány mozgósító szerepe a 18. században" [The Mobilizing Effect of the Rákóczi Tradition in the Eighteenth Century], in Spira, ed., pp. 117 ff.

The rebels sought only to free the peasantry from the harsh burdens of their urbarial obligations and the *portio;* they did not aim to alter the feudal social system. It was a peasant revolt par excellence, doomed to failure, as such revolts usually were, when confronted by the superior forces of the organized state.

In 1753, Hódmezővásárhely, a peasant town, was the scene of another significant peasant uprising, again the effect of absentee ownership. The local landlords let their holdings to Greek merchants, whose only concern was to squeeze as much as possible out of the serfs. They increased the urbarial obligations enormously. This revolt, too, was quelled by the overwhelming force of the standing army.

In 1755 an insurrection broke out in Croatia, centering on the counties of Kőrös and Varasd. Under the leadership of Franjo Domjanić and Mihajlo Kušić, 20,000 peasants rose up.[3] The Croatian nobles and churchmen fled to Zágráb, the Croatian capital. The rebels marched on Zágráb, devastating thirty castles and fortresses on their way. Within days the nobles were able to field an army which routed the rebels. The rebellion was followed by bloody reprisals against the peasantry.[4]

In 1763–64 the Székelys revolted, prompted by Maria Theresa's order to organize the Székely region into a Military Frontier Zone similar to those operating along the southern frontiers of Hungary. The unmerciful suppression of the Székelys by the Imperial Army resulted in a bloodbath. The most notorious massacre was the Disaster of Mádéfalva (*Mádéfalvi veszedelem*).[5] A large number of recalcitrant Székelys migrated to Moldavia rather than serve in Maria Theresa's military frontier units.

In 1765 and 1766 there was a widespread peasant disobedience campaign in several counties in the Transdanubian region.[6] As before, excessive urbarial duties and fees were the principal cause of unrest. In 1751 Maria Theresa had tried to persuade the diet to pass a military levy of 1,200,000 florins, to be paid in part by the estates. The diet balked. It voted instead an extraordinary war tax of 700,000 florins[7] but refused to pay any part of even this reduced sum. The

---

[3] Mód, p. 117.   [4] *Ibid.*   [5] Hóman and Szekfü, V, 124–25.
[6] Spira, pp. 308 ff.
[7] *Ibid.*, p. 299. See also Ferenc Eckhart, A *bécsi udvar gazdasági politikája Magyarországon Mária Terézia korában* (Budapest: Budavári Tudományos Társaság, 1922), p. 255.

whole onus thus fell on the serfs. The diet, however, passed the following pious resolution: "God bless and help the poor taxpayers with this new burden, so that they may be able to pay this new tax in addition to their old obligations. This is the object of all the prayers and hopes of the estates." [8] The serfs, who would have preferred fewer taxes to the most profuse prayers, launched a broad movement of protest in the Transdanubian region.

The peasants in 1765–66 refused to pay part of the urbarial fees or to perform the prescribed *robot*. They dismissed the village leaders appointed by the lords and elected representatives who enjoyed the confidence of the people. Delegations were sent to Vienna to explain the peasants' grievances. In some places peasants took over manorial lands, chasing off the bailiffs of their lords and sacking administrative offices. To encourage the revolt, word was spread that the Queen and her sons were supporting the peasants.

In Vas, Zala, and Somogy counties, groups of 200–300 peasants held meetings at which they solemnly took an oath to abstain henceforth from the *robot* and pledged eternal loyalty to their cause. In the Tolna County village of Ozora, a band of 200 men drove out the landlord's representatives. Pécs was invaded by 3,000 peasants in a move to free the prisoners there. In Sopron County in 1766, women surrounded the Eszterházy castle and demanded abolition of the tithe.

While the Transdanubian movement encompassed far more territory than the previous peasant revolts of the eighteenth century, it never turned into armed uprising. Unlike Rákóczi's war, which involved other social classes, these exclusively peasant movements failed to attain national proportions, and, lacking adequate leadership, appealing ideology, or sufficient organization to withstand the repressive forces of a semimodern state, were doomed to defeat. Yet the efforts of these years were not wholly without result. It was the protest movement in Transdanubia which led to the promulgation of the long-overdue urbarial regulations in 1767. [9] Moreover, the landlords were made aware for the first time that they would have to limit their exploitation of the serfs. To ensure that the landlords would still receive the maximum share of their serfs' labor, the estates began to oppose any further taxation of the serf by the state. [10] The increasingly

[8] Mód, p. 118.   [9] Spira, pp. 345 ff.   [10] Mód, p. 124.

bitter competition between Vienna and the Hungarian estates for a share of the serfs' production was therefore partly the cause and partly the result of the peasant movement.

The greatest and most ferocious peasant revolt of the eighteenth century occurred in Transylvania in 1784, under the leadership of Horia and Cloşca. The urbarial regulations of Maria Theresa had never been introduced in this region. The domination of the landlord over the peasant was therefore far stronger than in royal Hungary.[11] In most parts of Transylvania urbarial obligations had risen by between 400 and 1000 percent since the Szatmár Treaty of 1711. Many of the peasants, the Rumanians in particular, tried to escape exploitation by joining the Frontier Guards as whole-village units. Unlike the Székelys, for whom military duty on the frontier meant a loss of former liberties,[12] the Rumanian peasants gained security and a higher standard of living by joining the Guards. On enlistment they ceased rendering all dues and services to their lords. The lords, for their part, continued to demand *robot* and urbarial services from all their peasants, whether or not they claimed immunity as members of the Guards. The serfs considered such demands illegal, and finally active resistance broke out. Within a few days serfs all along the Maros River valley had put to death the inhabitants of 232 noble houses in 80 different places and in many instances had pillaged the landholdings of the nobility as well. About 30,000 Rumanian, Saxon, and Hungarian peasants rallied to the call of Horia and Cloşca. Imperial forces were brought in to suppress the revolt, and executions and general bloodshed ensued. However, just as the Transdanubian unrest resulted in issuance of the urbarial regulations, so the Horia-Cloşca revolt, however bloody, succeeded in some measure by causing Emperor Joseph II to decree the abolition of serfdom.[13] In truth, this reform was more symbolic than real, for the urbarial obligations of the serfs continued undiminished. Moreover, the expenses of a growing modern state were increasing sharply and were climaxed by the costs of the Turkish War.[14] Once again the serfs had to bear the financial burden, and they found themselves in a more difficult

[11] Spira, p. 386.   [12] All the Székelys were free men.   [13] Spira, p. 454.
[14] All through the Habsburg lands even the peasants, who had benefited most from Joseph's reforms, were in a rebellious mood toward the end of his reign. Wangermann, p. 30.

position than ever before. This, then, was the situation at the beginning of the turbulent year of 1790.[15]

PEASANT LEAFLETS OF 1790

By 1790 the aristocrats and the gentry were enjoying a period of cultural progress and had already achieved a certain degree of intellectual sophistication. Among the peasantry, too, intellectual advances had begun. Pál Almássy, the Emperor Joseph's commissioner at Pest, noted that "the peasants possess not only natural talents but even a certain degree of culture and well-being." [16] A confidential report addressed to the court at Vienna stated that even the uneducated people were used to reading.[17] Priests, ministers, and village notaries read magazine and newspaper articles to the peasants. Peasant lads of this generation, like their fathers and grandfathers fighting the War of the Austrian Succession and the Seven Years' War, saw much of Western lands during their service in the Habsburg standing army. The serfs were thus able to compare their miserable living standards with those of the West, and began to give serious thought to their backward state. While they enjoyed improved conditions as a result of the reforms of Maria Theresa and Joseph II, and had come to consider the Emperor as their protector against the depredations of the lords, after the death of Joseph II they began to grow restive.[18]

The literature of the peasant movement in 1790 is very slim. Other events of the year and the gentry-oriented early Hungarian history of this era suppressed most of the facts related to the peasant unrest of 1790. Credit should be given, however, to contemporary historians in Hungary whose intensive research in the nation's archives has brought to light many documents and details of the 1790 peasant movements.

Peasant unrest began during this period in Zaránd County. Miklós Kovács, the *alszolgabíró* (district submagistrate) of the county, reported on April 9, 1790, that "rebellion is openly preached here, and Rumanian priests are leading the movement. The nobility has been

[15] On resistance by the peasants after the death of Joseph II see Adler, p. 20.

[16] Marczali, *Magyarország története III. Károlytól,* in Szilágyi, ed., VIII, 479.

[17] Rácz, p. 232, n. 73.

[18] The peasants were just awakening politically as a result of their recent improvement and social elevation. Wangermann, p. 32.

forced to begin arming."[19] At the same time the central government received news of similar occurrences in many other counties.

All these scattered disturbances merely reflected the peasants' fear that the enlightened reforms of the last two kings would be revoked.[20] The nobles, in turn, were alarmed that an uprising along the lines of the Horia-Cloşca revolt was in the making. However, both fears proved to be unfounded even at the very center of peasant unrest in the Upper Tisza region.[21]

The peasants' uneasiness is clearly shown in three documents which have survived: (1) a letter sent by the villagers of Taktakenéz to the headman and village council of Dob on March 14, 1790 (the Petition of Taktakenéz); (2) the minutes of a meeting of the peasants of Szabolcs County (the Szabolcs Project); and (3) the famous Peasants' Declaration, the most important of the three.[22]

THE PETITION OF TAKTAKENÉZ

On March 14, 1790, the villagers of Taktakenéz in Szabolcs County gathered for an extraordinary meeting. Normally, in the past, such meetings were held annually, and participation was compulsory. They were convoked and presided over by the village *biró*, who acted as the representative of the landlord, for by the eighteenth century village self-government by the peasants, a flourishing institution in earlier centuries, had virtually disappeared. At this special meeting on March 14, the serfs were joined by the *bocskoros nemesek*, whose conditions were particularly miserable in the Upper Tisza region. Lesser nobles working on serf holdings in the counties were not subject to urbarial fees or *robot* but paid only fees (*taksa*) to the lords. Here in the Upper Tisza region, however, contrary to law, these taxed nobles were compelled to perform all urbarial duties and pay fees just like the serfs. Thus, the only difference between the two groups was that the taxed nobles possessed the political rights of nobility.

The Taktakenéz affair is of particular interest not for any results it yielded but as an indication of the nature of the whole peasant move-

[19] Marczali, *Magyarország története III. Károlytól*, in Szilágyi, VIII, 480.
[20] Scattered unrest occurred throughout the Habsburg lands. Wangermann, p. 33.
[21] Marczali, *Magyarország története III. Károlytól*, in Szilágyi, VIII, 480.
[22] Texts of Nos. 1 and 3 may be found in Appendixes E and F.

ment of 1790. The petition approved at the village meeting is significant for the program it contained, the tactics outlined by the village
leaders, and the light it shed on the social and political relationship between the serfs and the *bocskoros nemesek* in this period.

The program laid down in the petition was of a radical character
rather than a revolutionary one. It did not strike at the foundations of
the feudal system, but merely called for elimination of the major grievances of the serfs and taxed nobles. It demanded total abolition of *robot*,
the most obnoxious of all serf obligations, and proposed that in future
the lords should receive only a tithe and one florin in cash annually.
The petition also demanded that the taxed nobles be relieved from
paying the *portio* and suggested that all these reforms be incorporated
into "the country's books of law." The petitioners insisted that the
harsh urbarial obligations of both serfs and taxed nobles were viola-
tions of the law of the "fatherland." (This was a widespread view of
significant importance similiar to that of the Russian serfs who believed
after the emancipation of 1861 that the lords had robbed them of land
belonging rightfully to them.) From these demands it is obvious that
the people of Taktakenéz were reformers who wanted to reaffirm and
strengthen the old laws of the land, rather than overthrow them.

The principal leader behind the protest, Gábor Kövér, a *bocskoros
nemes,* called for immediate and forceful action. "Let us destroy houses,
let us lay waste [the properties of the lord], and we shall be second
Horias," he declared. When his appeal for action fell on deaf ears, he
complained, "The Hungarians are foolish, subordinating themselves
to the lords now when they have an opportunity to take action and
raise their heads." [23]

In addition to Gábor Kövér, the leadership at the Taktakenéz meeting
consisted of Ferenc Vágó, the village *biró,* and István Jász Szabó,
another *bocskoros nemes.* They decided to present their petition to the
Szabolcs County assembly that was to be convoked on March 18 in
the town of Kálló. Providing the county assembly endorsed the
petition, they would then present it to the diet scheduled to meet in
Buda soon after. Thus, the leaders envisaged not merely a local protest
but one of national scope and significance. Here lies the importance
of the whole affair.

---

[23] The minutes of the county assembly of Szabolcs, quoted in Rácz, p. 215.

In a significant passage the Taktakenéz leaders warned the county assembly that the serfs and taxed nobles would obey only the king if their demands were not met: "We will, in loyalty to His Majesty our King, obey his orders alone." Indeed, in 1790, a real possibility existed for the Habsburgs to incite a *Jacquerie* against the estates, similar to the Polish peasant uprising of 1846. The Habsburg Empire was in much too volatile a state, however, to risk such a policy.

From the records of several county courts, it can be established that the petition was circulated widely and its existence was known even farther afield as the news traveled by word of mouth. At county fairs and in village inns people talked about it and, again locally, some peasants and *bocskoros nemesek* took to advocating its demands. Several village leaders did their best to make the project successful, among them the village headman of Tiszalök, Pál Kocsis.[24]

Yet the masses were impassive and the majority of their leaders shied away from the petition. The idea of a pressure group, based on the voice of an aroused peasantry, was stillborn. Soon the enthusiasm of its first advocates burned out and the entire project failed. There were several reasons for this. The village leadership, as already shown, was well subordinated to the lords. Village leaders were dependent on their masters and afraid to risk their special privileges and perquisites, such as exemption from paying urbarial duties. Furthermore, the project had no support from outside the peasantry. There might have been a chance of *bocskoros nemes* participation in a serf movement, with the possibility of the landless nobles providing the leadership; the meeting in Taktakenéz suggested such a possibility. The majority of the *bocskoros nemesek*, however, looked down on the serfs and were unwilling to mingle with them, much less to ally themselves with them. One of them, Péter Fazekas, declared, "It would be a shame to sully ourselves by [associating] with the peasants."[25]

But perhaps the most important reason for the failure of the Taktakenéz petition was the strategy of the *bene possessionati*. At a very early stage they realized the importance of the loyalty of the *bocskoros nemesek* and set about purchasing it with promises, dividing them from the serfs for whom the *bocskoros nemesek* were the only natural ally. The peasant movement at the time of the Taktakenéz petition

---

[24] Testimony of several witnesses. *Ibid.*, p. 217, n. 27.
[25] *Ibid.*, p. 218.

was already losing strength owing to the combination of all these factors.

THE SZABOLCS PROJECT

Chronologically, the second document to be circulated was an outline for a peasants' village meeting which bore the title: "Minutes of the Meeting of the Peasants of Szabolcs County." [26] The title was misleading because no such meeting took place; the project referred simply to the manner in which a village meeting should be held. Like the Petition of Taktakenéz, the Szabolcs Project was circulated both outside and inside its county of origin; it had no immediate results, but assumed significance because of its historical and sociological setting.

The style of the document, the legal knowledge of its authors, its intelligent organization, all suggest that the men who wrote it must have been other than simple peasants. Another point is the project's surprising sympathy for the large landowners with hundreds of serfs but sizzling hatred for the petty nobles who wrung the utmost from just two or three serfs. The project's impassioned attack on county administrators is more understandable when one realizes that the petty nobles formed the main body of the county administrators, who were objects of special hatred for the serfs. The project demanded strict limitation, if not outright abolition, of these county officials' administrative and judiciary authority.

The project suggests that as early as the end of March, 1790, just when Leopold II began to take up the reins of government, the peasants were becoming aware that the nobility was trying to undo the reforms of the last two enlightened despots.[27] Specifically, they were suspicious of the speed with which the nobility was altering county administrations back to their pre-Josephine form and reinstalling reactionary officials dismissed by Joseph II. The project emphatically rejected any return to a system of political patronage in the counties and planned to call peasants' meetings to discuss the problem. It was concerned with the "burden of the county being carried by the peas-

---

[26] The full text of the Szabolcs Project was first printed in Rácz, pp. 252–58. See also Marczali, *Magyarország története III. Károlytól*, in Szilágyi, VIII, 480–81.
   [27] Molnár, I, 398.

ant," the exorbitant salaries and expenses of county officials, and the high county budgets which the peasants had to finance.

The project listed a series of proposals to alleviate the peasants' lot:

1. A proposed criterion would recognize as lords only those who owned at least a quarter of a village and would exclude all others from power over the peasants. "True landlords," the project stated, "when seeing our just intentions, will endorse our plans and will agree with us."

2. Local administration should be improved.

3. County officials' judicial authority should be abrogated.

4. No new officials should be added to county governments.

5. Legal procedures should be streamlined. A limit should be set on the time that a serf could be imprisoned without trial.

6. Rules should be established for filling public offices. The peasants demanded the right to eliminate those candidates who had been dismissed during the reign of Joseph II, and those whom they believed to be incompetent, biased, or of bad character.

7. The local landlords should supervise the activities of village magistrates.

8. Magistrates should lose their authority over criminal prosecution.

9. All plans approved by the lords should be sent to the diet, as such reforms might be beneficial for the whole nation.

The Szabolcs Project was distributed in Szabolcs County as early as the end of March. The source of its first version is not known, but soon it spread throughout neighboring counties, just like the Petition of Taktakenéz. The first copy of the project to reach official hands was received by the village headman of Tokaj, Mihály Killer, on April 9, 1790. For some days he talked about it only to his most trusted associates and then he sent it to the head of the local *Kammer* at Tarcal in Szabolcs County. From there, the document was forwarded to the district *Kammer* director at Kassa, Baron Miklós Vécsey.

Vécsey informed the *Főispán* of Szabolcs County, Mihály Sztáray, as well as the acting president of the *Consilium locumtenentiale,* the Lord Chief Justice, Count Károly Zichy, who immediately informed the Royal Court Chancellery in Vienna. The quick presentation of the project to the highest governmental authorities clearly indicates how much significance the officials attached to this document. The district

Kammer of Kassa, in its report of April 14 to the Lord Chief Justice, commented that the "slowly spreading peasant movement is something against which effective remedies must be found." [28]

THE PEASANTS' DECLARATION [29]

The most important, widely distributed, and violent of the peasant leaflets was the Peasants' Declaration, a document that attacked the very foundations of feudal society. The Peasants' Declaration flatly rejected the idea of the lords' right to enforce urbarial services. It stated that peasants would no longer need to serve the lords but only to offer their services to the king. It boldly claimed rights for the peasants: "Do we not all . . . deserve in this country at least a tiny lot?"

Like the Szabolcs Project, the declaration found county administrations the main threat to the interest of the peasants. It bluntly told county administrators to quit their jobs and give up their titles. Going a step further, the declaration even turned on the household servants of the lords as puppets of the oppressors, enemies of their own people. It warned the servants to leave the lords' households within one week lest they "be tied to the stakes and burned like witches."

The declaration opposed the holding of any diet but it also enounced a democratic principle in case the diet were held; it demanded that any diet "should act in our [the peasants'] behalf." The declaration affirmed the peasants' loyalty to the crown, to the despots of the Enlightenment, with the words, "We stand by all the regulations of our Emperor and King, Joseph II; we shall not let one jot of them be abolished, for all of them are as sacred, just, and beneficent as if God Himself had suggested them to him."

The principles of the declaration constituted a major, unprecedented attack on the social, political, and economic foundations of the feudal system.[30] Demands alone, however, do not make a revolution; the use of force is needed to alter an existing system. The declaration, however vehement in its threats, colorful in devising fantastic tortures for the peasants' enemies, and prolix in its advocacy of violence, never

[28] Rácz, p. 222.

[29] See Appendix F for full text of the declaration. See also Marczali, *Magyarország története III. Károlytól*, in Szilágyi, VIII, 480–83.

[30] The necessity of a legislative with true representatives of all social classes was also emphasized by such highly placed personalities as Sonnenfels. Wangermann, pp. 75–76.

actually called for the unconditional use of force. Almost every paragraph includes an "if," an out for the offenders, a way to avoid the application of its dire threats by doing this or that. Hanging by the feet, burning at the stake, flaying alive—all these threats were conditional. Indeed, the declaration did call on "every peasant who can stand up" to "take up arms immediately, sound the horn, raise the banner," but only "as soon as the slightest skirmish occurs." Even its call to battle is conditional on the peasants' being attacked first.

Professor Palmer felt its violence to be the crux of the declaration.[31] He even claimed to have detected the flavor of Mau Mau terror tactics in it. The primitive and wordy cruelty of the declaration implies no such thing: it has too many "if's" and "but's" to be classified as a document of terror, one that relishes violence for its own sake.

When considering the possible use of force, the declaration wisely took into account the probable behavior of the army under such circumstances. Its authors were aware that without army support their revolution would be doomed in advance, but they were optimistic, perhaps too much so: "What have we to fear from the soldiers? Nothing, for they are our sons." This premise, moreover, gave further grounds for the peasants' demands: "Is the Army not made up of our sons, who serve our King faithfully? Do we not sustain the King and his troops? Do we not all, therefore, deserve in this country at least a tiny lot?"

Setting out their claims to have rights of their own led the peasants of the declaration to deny all the privileges of the lords, whom they depicted as "cruel, lazy, good-for-nothing . . . who destroy the country and rob the King." At the same time, to the king were ascribed the attributes of a veritable saint, all-good, all-powerful. The declaration thus went a significant step further than all other peasant documents in inciting the peasants against the nobility while allying them with the crown.

The men who drafted the declaration were never discovered or convicted. One can only speculate about their background. The first logical assumption about their identity would be to suppose that they were simple peasants expressing their bitterness. Another supposition, based on the style and phraseology of the text, would be that the declaration was the work of either *honoratiori* or, less likely, of *bocs-*

[31] Palmer, I, 392–93.

koros nemesek. The latter speculation is grounded specifically on such things as the mention of the book of law as the source of the nobility's privileged position, which indicates considerably more knowledge than the average peasant of 1790 could be expected to possess. The indelicacies in the language of the declaration, in this case, could have been interpolated as a deliberate screen for the authors. A third theory would have it that the declaration was nothing but a trick played on the nobility by the court—something that actually happened later on in Hungary.[32] Certainly, the combination of excoriation of the nobility and unqualified praise for the monarch would support this possibility.

This writer would tend to the belief that the declaration was drafted by persons whose interests were similar to those of the peasants, afraid of the abolition of Josephine reforms. This would suggest authorship by *honoratiori* or, as a secondary possibility, by *bocskoros nemesek.*

The place where the declaration was drafted is also unknown. Most probably it was written in either Szabolcs or Zemplén County. The assembly of Szepes County suggested that the writers must have been *majoris ingenii impostor.*[33] In whichever county it originated, the declaration was disseminated in leaflet form mostly in the Upper Tisza region. The first official report about it was dated May 8 and was written by József Ragályi, the deputy high sheriff of Borsod County, who sent it to the *Consilium locumtenentiale.*[34] This report said the leaflets were distributed at the county fair in the town of Tarcal where the declaration was also read aloud to the peasants by persons unknown.

It was Zemplén County which, as early as June 21, appealed to the court for military aid in case of trouble, although the nobles' spies mingling with the peasants found no signs indicating the possibility of an uprising. The assembly of Abauj County announced a reward of 100 gold pieces for information leading to the arrest of the declaration's authors and immunity for any member of the group who would denounce the others. The *Consilium locumtenentiale* raised the reward to 200 gold pieces,[35] to no avail. Borsod County presented a copy of the declaration originating in Szabolcs County to the *Consilium* on May 8. Five days later Szabolcs County itself sent a copy with a letter from

[32] Rácz, p. 246, opposes this theory.   [33] *Ibid.,* p. 226.   [34] *Ibid.,* p. 228.
[35] *Ibid.,* p. 229.

High Sheriff Sztáray pointing out that the declaration's attack on the nobility could spell disaster for the dynasty; the letter also included an appeal for military help. The county assembly appealed to the clergy in the thoroughly feudal conviction that the Church must teach the peasants to obey and be loyal to their masters. The assembly showed less piety, however, in discussing the possibility of using military force to suppress any future peasant uprising.

In May reports came from Transylvania of a Rumanian priest reading the declaration to peasants at Maroskeresztur, a village near the town of Marosvásárhely. The assembly of Abauj discussed the declaration on May 17. Though in Szatmár County no copy of the document had yet been found, there also the county leadership discussed it and considered the need for preventive action. During the months of May and June, copies of the declaration spread around the country, with reports of them coming in from Zemplén, Szabolcs, Borsod, and Abauj counties and the city of Debrecen. The court in Vienna considered the problem serious enough to order military preparations for possible trouble. Officials in Szepes, Zaránd, Ung, and Sáros counties expressed fear of such a possibility. The "alarming news," as it was called, circulated as far as Croatia. The reaction of the nobility to it was summed up by an official of Szepes County who wrote: "The tongue cleaves and the pen trembles." [36]

Authorized by a secret court order, troops moved into the village of Tokaj on May 14. On the same day the High Sheriff of Borsod County was informed by the *Consilium locumtenentiale* that "if there is trouble, appeal to the military for help, for they have received instructions to offer assistance." All this was communicated to the Court Chancellery by the Lord Chief Justice. Leopold himself took action by ordering all cases of irregularities to be reported to the court immediately by special courier.[37]

Most counties directly affected introduced such special preventive measures as searching those traveling between villages; inaugurating a passport system for peasants to travel; requesting the clergy to pacify the peasants; sending nobles in disguise to spy on the peasants; arresting those suspected of incitement (among these were Gábor Kövér and István Jász Szabó, the writers of the Petition of Taktakenéz, both

---

[36] *Ibid.*, p. 231.   [37] *Ibid.*, p. 232.

bocskoros nemesek); imposing strict censorship; putting military units on alert; and speeding up formation of the *banderia*.

The general mobilization of the nobility in Szabolcs County on May 21 may be considered the climax of precautionary measures against the peasantry. In Zemplén County, as well as in Abauj, Bihar, and Szatmár, all the above measures were implemented, including the mobilization of the nobility.

Leopold II, in addition to the authorization for local action by the counties, ordered a number of specific measures himself, especially in the counties most affected by peasant unrest—Abauj, Borsod, Szabolcs, and Zemplén. His instructions called for the search for the authors of the declaration and any arrests to be undertaken with utmost caution, avoiding mass arrests if possible and detaining only those held on substantial charges; the use as spies only of loyal noblemen used to mingling with peasants and wearing their clothes; keeping meetings of the nobility about the peasant danger private and secret, maintaining regulations affecting taxpayers without change, treating peasants with restraint, and avoiding demands for illegal taxation.

Leopold also instructed the military not to help with the collection of taxes (*executio*), leaving it entirely up to the county police forces in order to avoid generating any peasant hostility toward the military or even the king.[38]

Leopold's orders show him at his best as a master of secret dealings, spying, and politics. The steps taken by the counties bore quick fruit. By mid-June, reports from the counties of peasant unrest began to drop off and soon no complaints at all were received by the authorities or the court.[39]

After the Upper Tisza movement had died down and the tide had turned in favor of the Habsburgs with the conclusion of the Reichenbach Convention, though still before the signing of the final compromise between the King and the diet, Leopold felt the need for a campaign of his own among the peasantry in order to exert pressure on the nobility. Parts of *Ninive*, which had Leopold's approval, dealt with the peasantry, but the main appeal of the pamphlet was aimed at the burghers, not the peasants. Also, it was written in German and

[38] Marczali, *Országgyűlés*, II, 162.

[39] In Austria, however, peasant unrest increased. Provincial governors there were authorized to declare an emergency, which made possible the taking of the peasants into the army without any formalities. Wangermann, p. 68.

only a very few peasants in Hungary read German. What *Ninive* did for the peasants was to describe their miserable conditions to the burghers and point to the possibility of a burgher-serf alliance in their common interest against the nobles. *Ninive* emphasized for its burgher readers that the nobles were trying to prevent the King from helping the serfs and that even in German states, where serfs were much better off than their counterparts in Hungary, there were still peasant revolts.[40]

At the time of *Ninive's* circulation a leaflet to the peasants was already in preparation. Although there is no evidence to support speculation that the court had a hand in the Upper Tisza peasant movement, there is plenty of documentary proof about the court's intention at this time to initiate a movement to arouse the peasantry. The plan was suggested by a councilor of state, József Izdenczy, who was the first member of the *Staatsrat* with a Hungarian background. The drafting of the leaflet to the peasants was assigned to *Ninive's* author, Professor Hoffmann, whose work was then translated into Hungarian and Slovak. By August the leaflet was in print, with a suggested oath for the peasants (similar in tone to the Hoffmann-created burghers' oath) attached. Leopold, however, changed his mind at the last minute and, although he permitted distribution of the pamphlets for the burghers, he forbade distribution of the peasants' leaflets. There are few existing documents regarding this entire secret operation, as most of the King's instructions were verbal. Yet, communications sent to Leopold do exist, indicating the nature and scope of the operation.

Hoffmann informed Leopold on August 21, 1790, that the manuscripts directed to the peasants and the burghers had reached him with Leopold's orders. Hoffmann promised to prepare final drafts at the greatest possible speed. On August 24, Hoffmann reported further that the printed pamphlets, together with their Hungarian translations, were ready for dispatch.[41]

Gotthardi's report to Leopold on September 7, 1790, clearly refers to the involvement of both King Leopold II and his son Archduke Alexander Leopold in the whole affair. Gotthardi indicated that both he and Hoffmann still expected further orders from the King. Gott-

[40] Mályusz, "Magyarországi polgárság," I, 258.
[41] *Privatbibliothek*, Fasc. 15, No. 6 (microfilm copy).

hardi reported in addition that more than 100 copies of the pamphlet already had been sent to the burghers. He also indicated that, regarding the peasants, he and Hoffmann still had not begun the campaign, since the Archduke communicated the King's orders in that respect.[42]

By mid-September distribution of the leaflets was begun, under complicated conditions.[43] Leopold now used for this the agents originally assigned to spy on the peasants for incitement against the nobles. The King's chief agent in this operation was András Szalkay, one of those ordered to mix with the serfs, wear their clothes, but remain inconspicuous.[44] Szalkay was suggested to Leopold for the double operation by Gotthardi as early as June 10.[45]

Leopold assigned Hoffmann to interview Szalkay to assess his suitability for the job. Hoffmann's report approved Szalkay for the assignment but said that he demanded a well-paid position after the operation, payment for all his expenses, a secret order to military authorities in case of danger, and sanctuary for his family in Vienna during his stay in Hungary.[46]

The leaflet, with the title of *Jó hir a parasztoknak* [Good Tidings for the Peasants] or *Bonum novum pro rusticis*, was distributed widely among peasants in the Great Hungarian Plain in early October. Szalkay completed the operation in a few days and returned to Vienna.[47] The court was so satisfied with the job he did that Leopold not only gave him a coveted position in the retinue of the new Palatine, Archduke Alexander Leopold, but also called the Palatine's attention to Szalkay's ability several times, stressing that he was a man well suited for carrying out secret missions.[48]

No copy of *Jó hir a parasztoknak* can be found except for a Slovak edition seized by the county administration of Szepes. As the texts of the Hungarian and Slovak leaflets are believed to have been identical or closely similar, this copy from Szepes is a good indication of what was in the leaflets written in Hungarian. The Slovak version urged the

[42] *Ibid.*, Fasc. 13 (microfilm copy).

[43] Mályusz, "Magyarországi polgárság," I, 256.

[44] János Illéssy, "András Szalkay élete," in *Irodalomtörténeti Közlemények* (Budapest, 1889), p. 142.

[45] Gotthardi's report, June 10, 1790, *Privatbibliothek*, Fasc. 13 (microfilm copy).

[46] Hoffmann's report, September 14, 1790, *ibid.*, Fasc. 13 (microfilm copy).

[47] Report of Gotthardi, dated October 18, *ibid.*, Fasc. 13 (microfilm copy).

[48] Mályusz, ed., *Sándor Lipót*, pp. 52 and 438.

peasants to seize the opportunity given them by Leopold, who, the leaflet said, like Joseph II, wanted to crush the noblemen and uphold the serfs. The leaflet added that Leopold was angry with the nobles because they had wanted to submit themselves to the Prussians and had asked for Prussian help against the King. The diet wanted to withhold recognition of Leopold, the leaflet stated, until he allowed the nobles a free hand to exploit the serfs. The peasantry should not be afraid of the military because it was made up of the sons of peasants and was supplied out of money given by the peasants. As the King was on the peasants' side, they could count on the army's being so too. The nobility, according to the leaflet, was weak, divided, a hateful minority. The peasants should revolt and put an end to their oppression by the nobles. Landlords and their representatives should be seized, their property confiscated, and, using the supplies thus gained, the serfs should launch a general war on the nobility. The Emperor, the leaflet assured the serfs, was on their side, and would support and help them against the nobles.[49]

AN EVALUATION OF
THE PEASANT MOVEMENTS OF 1790

The peasant movements of 1790 came as the culmination of the Hungarian peasant movements of the eighteenth century, or even of that 160-year period between the Rákóczi and Kossuth wars. The year 1790 was the peak of the eighteenth-century class struggle, in respect to the ideological content of the documents of the time. The demand for diminished urbarial obligations in the Petition of Taktakenéz, the attack on county administrations in the Szabolcs Project, and the call for fundamental changes in the social order in the Peasants' Declaration—all these, with variable clarity and emphasis, embodied legal, social, and political aims marking a true high point in the history of Hungarian peasant movements.

The events of 1790, however, also marked a curious downgrade in the

[49] Mályusz, "Magyarországi polgárság," I, 258. Interesting similarities and contrasts might be found between the Peasants' Declaration and a book published in Austria in 1790 entitled *Klagen der Unterthanen der österreichischen Monarchie wegen Aufhebung des neuen Steuersystems.* (A summary of this publication is in Link, pp. 152–55.) The most important contrast was not so much in content but in the fact that socially the peasants in Hungary were isolated while in Austria they found allies in particular among the burghers.

use of force. Less violence occurred in the movements of that year than in any of the other peasant disturbances of the century, ending what was virtually a tradition of violence of more than fifty years. Between the era of continual, although small-scale, violence and the revolution of 1848 only once after 1790 did the peasants resort to the use of force: in the "plague revolt" of 1831. The mild nature of the 1790 peasant movements is evident in documents that indicate no mass preparations to use force. One may even be inclined to believe that the nobility's exaggeration of the risk of peasant violence might have stemmed from their own guilty consciences. Another possibility, of course, is that for political reasons the counties issued scare reports on possible serf violence, in order to induce the court to yield to the estates in the face of the danger from the peasantry.[50]

The fact of peasant unrest in 1790 is indisputable, but there was no revolution in the making. Even the most violent of the documents, the Peasants' Declaration, was more evolutionary in concept than revolutionary. The use of force was mentioned only as an act of self-defense, as a last resort if all else failed. Every aspect of the peasant unrest of 1790 was a symptom of the crisis of that year, which erupted immediately upon the death of Joseph II, fed by the fear that the nobles might turn back the clock on the peasantry. The climax came in May through early July; by the end of July the tide was already on the ebb.

The military occupation of Hungary which started in mid-August was intended to serve as a warning to the recalcitrant nobles—but at the same time it also served as a shield for the estates in case of a peasant revolt. The dual purpose of the military's presence was understood by nobles and serfs alike. The subsequent compromise between the estates and the dynasty cleared up the situation, going far to meet the demands the estates had made of the court, and safeguarding the Habsburgs' constitutional prerogatives in Hungary. The compromise put an end to the peasant movements, which were not to be revived again for a very long time. The mere fact that an outside factor— the compromise between the estates and the court—could stop the peasant movements so short indicated the very weakness of the move-

---

[50] Some historians suggest as a possibility that the authors of the Szabolcs Project might have intended to pacify rather than to incite the peasants. Mérei and Spira, p. 31.

ments themselves. Yet in the long run they bore fruit. Among many other events, the peasant unrest of 1790 was an important cause of the social legislation the 1790–91 diet passed on the serf problem: the urbarial regulations of Maria Theresa, hitherto an extraconstitutional royal rescript, were incorporated into the laws of the land; the abolishment of perpetual serfdom was solemnly reendorsed, thereby reensuring the freedom of migration of the serfs; and a diet committee of very distinguished personalities was appointed to elaborate new reform projects.[51] In short, the peasant movements of 1790 were not in vain.

[51] Acsády, pp. 390–91. At the end of 1790 the rebellion of the peasants had been put down in most parts of the Habsburg lands. Wangermann, p. 69.

If the Hungarian movement is compared with the peasant movements of the rest of the Habsburg lands, it stands halfway between the more sophisticated and longer lasting Styrian movement and the practically inactive peasantry of Bohemia. Wangermann, pp. 78–82.

Chapter XVI

COUNTERCOUP AND COMPROMISE

WHEN THE TIDE turned in the latter part of August, 1790, the *volte-face* of the Prussian court and the concentration of Austrian troops in Hungary caused disappointment and alarm in the diet. "The leaders of the gentry ruminated with broken hearts for several days about the unwelcome turn of events there [Reichenbach] until they pulled themselves together again," wrote Mályusz.[1] From August, the main effort of the members of the diet was to save what they could of their earlier projects. They came to realize that they had to reconcile themselves to the acceptance of the hereditary system of the monarchy and drop the great prospect of an elective kingdom, but they tried to reestablish at least the old time-limit on royal power through constitutional provisions.[2] On the other hand, Leopold and his aides tried to exploit the changes in their favor to get maximum benefits from the new situation. The clash between these two conflicting efforts characterized the second stage in the diet, which had begun with the coronation of the King and the election of the Palatine in November. Between August and November a short period of transition occurred; during this time distinguished national leaders emerged and began to capture attention, most notably *Országbíró* Count Károly Zichy and *Személynök* József Ürményi, the presidents of the Upper and Lower Chambers, respectively. Until this period they had been compelled to yield to the majority opinion and they had drifted along with the current. But now, wrote Mályusz, "they were

[1] Mályusz, ed., *Sándor Lipót*, p. 25.
[2] An account of the designs of Leopold II and his actions is in Silagi, pp. 86–94. See also Wangermann, pp. 56–57.

both able to emancipate themselves from the overwhelming hypnosis of a single class interest and through their talents and learning they were able to rise to the heights of statesmanship to hold universal progress and the interests of the whole nation in view above all." [3]

As the prestige and influence of these two men began to dominate events, other leaders gradually sank into obscurity. Péter Balogh, the former heart and mind of the feudal revolt, was still delivering speeches but he was not the leader any more. The court now had little trouble turning him into one of its supporters. Leopold granted him an audience in the fall of 1790; Balogh felt deeply honored and acted as a loyal partisan of the court thereafter. He soon received an appointment to the office of *Főispán* and then to the *Staatsrat* in 1794.[4]

After the turn of events in August the diet began to think of compromise, of small constitutional changes inside the framework of hereditary monarchy rather than of breaking off from Habsburg rule or returning to an elective monarchy; it began to listen to Ürményi and Zichy rather than to Balogh. A logical consequence of this turn of events was the sending of a deputation to the court on September 5. At this time the demands of the diet were already radically toned down, but the court was not ready to accept them anyway.

The draft of a new coronation oath was still basically different from that of Maria Theresa, and some *antecoronalis* articles defining the method of dividing state power between the crown and the estates were also drafted. These two new projects did not intend to eliminate royal power but rather to curtail it, attempting to diminish it by a considerable measure; significantly, they contained assurances against the reintroduction of an absolutistic rule on the pattern of the Josephine reign. The gentry were convinced that these drafts were right and necessary, just as they had been convinced of the righteousness and necessity of their former, more radical demands.

Leopold's advisers opposed the drafting of any new form for the coronation oath. In their view, his coronation oath must follow the pattern of that of Maria Theresa or Charles III. Prince Kaunitz, the most influential of all the members of the *Staatsrat*, was of the same opinion:

[3] Mályusz, *Sándor Lipót*, p. 26. See also Wangermann, p. 88.
[4] Mályusz, *Sándor Lipót*, p. 27, n. 4.

The coronation oath is a bilateral contract between the king and his subjects. It binds both parties. Neither the king nor the estates may disregard it. Hungary is a continuity of rule. New capitulations permissible in an elective monarchy are never to be allowed in a hereditary kingdom. Hungary must be satisfied with the *Diploma Carolinum* [the oath of Charles III]. The king should make only minor alterations or additions to that document. The *Diploma Carolinum* must satisfy the Hungarian estates, as it reconfirms all the stipulations of the old Hungarian constitutions, including all the existing laws as well as the privileges of the estates. The draft presented by the estates differs fundamentally from the stipulations of the *Diploma Carolinum;* consequently it is unacceptable.[5]

Of the delegates, Zichy was the most active; he was received by the King the day before and the day after the whole delegation was granted audience. His efforts were futile, however. The King shared the opinion of his advisers and told Zichy flatly that no new form of the coronation oath was possible. This inflexible stand created a new deadlock. An early concord was out of the question. The court sent more troops into Hungary as the international situation became more advantageous for the Habsburgs. The tables were turned on the Hungarian estates now: the court was able to enforce its will by arms, while during the first stage in the diet it was the estates that had the power behind them in case of a showdown. The cause of the estates, now seemingly lost, was finally saved by Zichy and Ürményi.

The cardinal point the King's advisers insisted on was the inviolability of the old form of the coronation oath. At a proper time the two Hungarian lords accepted this condition and from then on the advisers ceased to worry about the wording of the oath. The King willingly accepted this solution, as well as the draft of a royal resolution presented by Zichy and Ürményi which stated: "The king shall permit and by a royal rescript assure that the stipulations of the royal diploma [coronation oath] as presented [by the diet delegation] are in concordance with the ancient laws of the realm and will be inserted into the texts of new laws to be promulgated after the coronation." [6] Thus the demands of the gentry would not be granted through a royal oath but would be realized by regular legislation, according to which the royal supervision of Hungarian administration was to be executed not by the Austrian councilors but exclusively by the Royal

[5] *Ibid.,* p. 33.   [6] *Ibid.,* p. 34.

Hungarian Chancellery. On September 20 and 21, 1790, on royal invitation at the Hungarian Chancellery, important negotiations took place. The participants were the highest of the Hungarian notables: Royal Court Chancellor Pálffy, Lord Chief Justice Zichy, Chief Justice Ürményi, Vice-Chancellors Teleki and Majláth, Councilors Nagy and Pászthory.

The group rewrote and moderated the original draft of the diet delegation, elaborating the exact methods by which the royal oath should be enacted and codified. This rewritten draft was then included in various parts of the royal proposals for the diet.[7] The King, at the persuasion of Primate Batthyány, signed this draft as the final royal proposal for the diet on September 21, 1790,[8] opening the door for the enactment of laws passed by the diet of 1790–91. Among these laws, the two most important were the promulgation of the principle that legislative power should again be shared by crown and diet and the reconfirmation of the independent status of the Kingdom of Hungary (Acts No. 12 and 10). These laws again restricted the royal power in a constitutional manner.

The main reason for the success of the deputation was its exclusion of the King's Austrian advisers from the last phase of negotiations. The final agreement between the King and the deputation was administered by the Royal Hungarian Chancellery and not by the *Staatsrat*. Thus the negotiations were transacted by Hungarians alone. Kaunitz and other advisers of the King repeatedly expressed their view that he went too far in these concessions and that they were dangerous.[9]

The royal rescript of September 21 signaled the King's readiness to make peace with the Hungarian estates. The enthusiastic reception of the rescript by the diet demonstrated on the other hand the pacific intentions and nature of the estates. They were very happy indeed to receive substantial concessions after the unsuccessful feudal revolt faded away. As soon as the ice was broken the date of the coro-

[7] No one else but the king possessed the right formally to initiate laws. The royal proposals were thus the only draft legislations.

[8] Mályusz, *Sándor Lipót*, p. 35.

[9] Kaunitz expressed his views on the meaning of the limited concessions given to the Hungarians in September, 1790, thus: "For the future one supreme law remains [valid]; all the rest, if and when they collide with it, must yield to it, and that *suprema lex* is the *salus universae republicae*." *Staatsrat Archiv*, No. 2434 (1790), in Mályusz, *Sándor Lipót*, p. 29.

nation was set. It was carried out on November 15, sealing the compromise between the dynasty and the estates. The bill was paid by the peasants.

The court flirted with the peasants in order to frighten the estates, and for a very short time the diet did likewise in order to separate the peasants from the King. Neither of these two flirtations was based on an intention to yield to the peasants considerable concessions altering the existing social structure. The "great fear"—the burning of the castles and archives of the French nobility—was already an event of the fearful, recent past. Neither the court nor the Hungarian estates failed to draw their own conclusions from it. The nobles were ready to check a possible peasant outbreak with their own *insurrectio* if need be. The eleven regiments poured into Hungary by the court between mid-July and mid-August were intended, at least partially, to checkmate the estates and discourage their high ambitions. On the other hand, they were also intended to guard the estates against a peasant uprising in case the peasants overestimated the meaning of the court's support and rose against their masters. The basic social concept of both parties was an important factor behind the September compromise of the crown and the diet. At the moment of their arrival at a compromise, no other force could or did challenge their settlement.

If, then, this political crisis was solved by means of a compromise —as actually happened—the famous *Ausgleich* of 1867 was not a unique event in the history of Hungarian-Habsburg relations. In fact, nothing was more characteristic of these relations than the sequence: tension—clash—compromise. The absolutist policies of King Rudolf (1576–1608) were brought to an end by the Vienna Peace Treaty of 1606, the first *Ausgleich* between the Habsburgs and the Hungarian estates. The absolute rule of King Leopold I (1657–1705) led to the Sopron Compromise of 1681. The same monarch's second period of absolute rule, which kindled the war of Ferenc Rákóczi, ended with the Szatmár Peace Treaty, yet another compromise. The period of extraconstitutional rule by Maria Theresa and Joseph II between the time of her last diet and his death (1765–90) was concluded by the 1790 accord. All these agreements had one feature in common—they were compromises in the proper sense of the word. By each of them the estates acknowledged the validity of the crown's rather broad prerogatives and the hereditary rights of the Habsburgs (except in the cases of the 1606 and 1681 compromises, for at those times the kingdom was still elective). The dynasty, for its part, recognized the privileges of the estates. The serfs were left virtually unprotected against the caprices of the lords and the prelates each time; in other words, it was the serfs who paid the cost of the repeated *Ausgleiche*.

To recapitulate: The compromise of 1790 speeded the decline of enlightened despotism, which came to a complete halt when the Hungarian Jacobins were executed in Buda on May 20, 1795.

Appendix A

THE CONSTITUTIONAL STRUCTURE
OF THE KINGDOM OF HUNGARY [1]

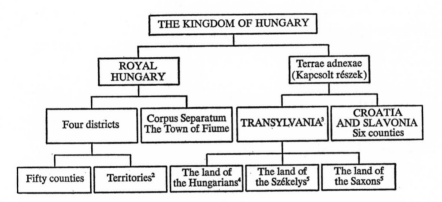

[1] See Map No. 1.
[2] The Jász and Kun districts and the Hajdu towns.
[3] Grand Principality (*Magnus Principatus*).
[4] Organized into counties.
[5] Organized into *Székek* (*Stühle* or districts).

Appendix B

THE POPULATION OF HUNGARY

Constitutional Components of the Kingdom	In 1720	In 1787
Kingdom of Hungary		
Royal Hungary	1,717,861 [a]	6,467,829
Transylvania		
(with the *Partes*)	864,737	1,440,986
Croatia and Slavonia		647,017
Total of the		
civilian population	2,582,598	8,491,806 [b]
Military Frontier Zones		700,000 [b]
Soldiers of the standing		
army		260,000 [b]
Grand total		9,451,806

[a] With Croatia and Slavonia.

[b] The final computation of the census of Emperor Joseph II and its rectifications. HNA: *Locumtenentiale* 2900 (1788), Conscr. No. 8. Thirring, p. 34. See *supra*, p. 20, n. 11.

Appendix C

THE DENOMINATIONS OF HUNGARY[a]

	Hungary	Croatia and Slavonia		Total
Catholics[b]	3,958,550	514,423		4,472,973
Non-Catholics				
Lutherans	619,626	185	619,811	
Calvinists	976,729	3,443	980,172	
Greek Orthodox	832,639	130,300	962,939	
Jews	80,783	111	80,894	
Total				2,643,816
Grand total	6,468,327	648,462		7,116,789 [c]

[a] The census of Emperor Joseph II and its rectifications. HNA: *Locumtenentiale* 2900 (1788), Conscr. No. 8.
[b] Roman Catholics and Greek Catholics (Uniats).
[c] The denominational division of Transylvania is not available.

Appendix D

THE SETTLEMENTS OF HUNGARY [a]

Constitutional Components of the Kingdom	Terri-tory (in square km)	Number of Towns		Villages and Peasant Towns	Inhabitants per square km	
		Royal Free Towns	Others		In Gen-eral	Except-ing the Towns
Royal Hungary and Croatia and Slavonia	227,346	52	16	11,456	31	30
Transylvania	60,703	9		2,615	24	23
Military Frontier Zones	33,552		13	1,739	21	21
Total	321,601	61	29	15,808	29	28

[a] The census of Emperor Joseph II and its rectifications. HNA: *Locum-tenentiale* 2900 (1788), Conscr. No. 8. Thirring, p. 18.

Appendix E

LETTER FROM
THE RESIDENTS OF TAKTAKENÉZ
TO THE VILLAGE HEADMAN
AND COUNCIL OF DOB[1]

ALL God's blessings on you, honorable and noble gentlemen of Dob, head-man, and the whole community!

We are forwarding our opinion for the attention of your excellencies and honors, who have been summoned to the town of Kálló on the eighteenth day of the current month of March for the county assembly, at which the agenda will deal with the restoration of the liberties of our dear fatherland and the easing of our numerous burdens. We note that among many griev-ances in the Hungarian fatherland a serious complaint is excessive *robot*, a violation of the old laws of the land with which the taxed nobles (*bocskoros nemesek*) and the *contribuens* [serfs] are alike encumbered. Further-more, those who have the privileges of the nobility [i.e., the landless nobles] are also being forced to pay *portio*.

We, the residents of Taktakenéz, consider it absolutely vital that this great national grievance (!)[2] be brought publicly to the attention of Their Excellencies, the honorable and noble estates, so that *robot* may be abolished along with all our other ghastly, bloodsucking afflictions, and the abolition confirmed in the country's books of law. Only a tithe and a fee (*taksa*) of one florin should be paid to the lords. If this wish of ours is fulfilled, we shall ally ourselves with Their Excellencies, the honorable estates, in defense of justice in accordance with the laws of our land: we pledge ourselves to stand by this to the last drop of our blood. If, however, Their Excellencies, the honorable estates, do not respond to this justified request of ours, we will, in loyalty to His Majesty our King, obey his orders alone [in future].

[1] Printed in Rácz, pp. 250–51.   [2] So punctuated in the original.

We wanted to communicate these wishes of ours to you honorable gentlemen of our neighboring village of Dob. If you endorse them in concert with us, and if you find them worthy of communication to other villages in this noble county, such as Dada, Lök, Szentmihály, and Bük, do not hesitate to do so. Moreover, you should make haste to reach the [forthcoming] assembly at least one day early so that this may be communicated to the others [delegates].

Submitting ourselves to your good will, we remain on this fourteenth day of March, 1790, at Taktakenéz, our benevolent masters' faithful servants,

The residents of Taktakenéz

Appendix F

THE PEASANTS' DECLARATION

(*A PARASZTOK DEKRÉTUMA*)[1]

OH, poor peasants, who from the first have witnessed so much anguish, listen to what we say! Let us take matters into our own hands, for we can see how the lords want to turn us into beasts of burden and make us wear their yoke six days out of seven.

They deem our blood no better than that of dogs and pigs, and so they torture us, beat us, and kill us at their whim; we are no more than property to them, just like swine; they treat us like swine, and they sell and slaughter us as they would their swine.

They want the King to grant them the explicit right to treat us this way, and they would even have the King take an oath not to interfere with them when they treat us so.

Should we don an animals's yoke? Are we swine? Do we deserve no more respect than swine? Is our blood not human? Is our blood to be shed by somebody for his amusement? Is the Army not made up of our sons, who serve our King faithfully? Do we not sustain the King and his troops? Do we not all, therefore, deserve in this country at least a tiny lot?

But they would have us sired by asses and born by sows, so that even the dogs would bark, "The peasant is a fool." Frogs would be more respected than we.

Come then, all peasants, take mercy on yourselves, raise your cudgels, pitchforks, and axes against the cruel, lazy, good-for-nothing lords, who destroy the country and rob the King, and let us cry with one voice and one heart:

First: We stand by all the regulations of our Emperor and King, Joseph

---

[1] Archives of the Archbishop of Eger. The declaration was presented by the administration of Szabolcs County on May 14, 1790, to the Archbishop of Eger, who was also the *örökös főispán* of the county. The full text of the declaration was published in Marczali, *Országgyűlés,* I, 230–34; cf. the text in Rácz, pp. 258–63.

II; we shall not let one jot of them be abolished, for all of them are as sacred, just, and beneficent as if God Himself had suggested them to him. And if anyone persecutes or maligns you for this, kill him at once, and if any peasant refuses to strike him even after he is dead, kill that peasant also, for he, too, deserves death;

Second: Within one week all the servants, valets, cooks, coachmen, farm-hands, guards, and other domestics shall leave the lords' manors, and rather than try to entice them back it would be better for the lords to dismiss them, lest the peasants living in the nearby villages flay the lords and all their families alive, and their remaining servants be tied to the stake and burned like witches; and if the village peasants will not do this, then they also must want to die, and they will not even have time to catch sight of us before we shall have set upon them and put them and their children to death;

Third: The county high sheriffs, deputy county high sheriffs, district mag-istrates, and other officials must quit office and give up their titles, or they will spell their own doom. *Hajduk*[2] [household guards], you sons of witches, go back to your homes, too, you are peasants yourselves and should stay with the peasants, lest we hang you by your feet with seven lords standing over you to skin you alive with pincers;

Fourth: No peasant shall go into the lords' service for fear of his life; and he shall kill anyone who tries to compel him to do so, and if he cannot overpower him alone, the other peasants shall help him; if not, we shall condemn to death every dung-hearted peasant we lay hands on. We shall render the lords no service for our lots, but, as in other countries, shall render our services and pay our taxes only to the King;

Fifth: We shall elect to be King dear Joseph's younger brother, His Maj-esty Peter Leopold II, whom our lawless lords have rebelled against because of the justness of Joseph II, whose father and mother and whole family the lords have cursed and vilified.

Long live His Majesty Peter Leopold II, King of Hungary; he is the King, not the man the lords want, so let them beware!

Sixth: All the peasants in the villages shall have a horn and a banner of black pigskin edged with red ribbon and bearing in the middle a piece of paper with the inscription: *"His Majesty Peter Leopold II is our King"* and the name of the village. And as soon as the slightest skirmish takes place or is reported anywhere in the country, every peasant who can stand up shall take up arms immediately, sound the horn, raise the banner, go into the fields, slaughter the cattle, broach the barrel, eat and drink, and slay all the lords in the land;

Seventh: What have we to fear from the soldiers? Nothing, for they are our sons. His Majesty Peter Leopold will not harm us, for we are not to blame; it is the lords' fault, for it is they who have sinned against him, even mortally. What do we have to fear from the lords? We should be ashamed even to think of that.

[2] Not to be confused with the *Hajduk* or free men of the Hajdu towns.

Let us stand as firm as a stone wall. Let us call on God's name for our aid; He will free us from this great misery of ours.

What is the difference between serfs and free peasants? It is that the serfs are tortured by the lords, and by the free peasants as well.

The diet, which is not needed because we already have our King, should act in our behalf, or else we shall hold a diet here, the like of which has never been seen, and to it will go only those who support the King.

There are two particularly important things:

First: By not permitting them [the lords] to hunt and torture and kill peasants in defiance of nature, our Joseph showed that our noble lords are not really saints (as their book of law pretends) and that jail is not reserved for peasants alone, because the lords also deserve it; and for this reason they have reviled him to the end.

Let us then honor him by raising a marble column in each of the fifty-two counties of the country for the well-earned glory of his memory. And in the meantime let the peasants in every village with all dispatch erect wooden posts at the village gates and fix to them papers with the following inscription: *"Post Erected in Honor of the Late Joseph II."* Otherwise, if the peasants in any village are so dung-hearted that they do not dare to do this, we shall have their bodies stacked high at the village gates in Joseph II's honor before they even realize what is happening.

Second: Another post should be set up beside the one to Joseph with the following inscription: *"His Majesty Peter Leopold, King of Hungary and Our Father."* Woe betide anybody who tries to cut these posts down. Dated Hungary, Anno 790 [*sic*].

Carry this manifesto to every village so that the poor, suffering, forsaken peasants shall know what to do and may act throughout the country with one heart. Let us not be afraid.

If you wish to know, this was written by more than eighty peasants.

Appendix G

NOBLEMEN'S OATH[1]

I, N.N., take my oath by the living, omnipotent God, creator of this world, and on this my faith I truly pledge myself and promise that throughout my life

I will uphold the free Hungarian nation,

Its original constitutional form of government,

The perpetuity of this noble nation's natural privilege to have complete authority to make its own laws,

The perpetual maintenance and inviolability of all the fundamental and basic laws and liberties of the land, and, finally, the King, who is to be crowned, having pledged his loyalty to the country, its laws, and its liberties;

I will make every effort to promote harmony among my compatriots, regardless of any other considerations;

I will diligently preserve public peace and security among the people within my purview and in my district during the session of this diet;

I will not fail to avert and redress to the best of my ability any evils and dangers in whatever form I may encounter them;

I will report them without delay to my county, town council, the appropriate prelature, and, if necessary, to the diet itself;

I will not accept or seek from the supreme authority for myself or my descendants at the expense of betraying the liberties of the noble Hungarian nation any kind of gifts, grants, offices, dignities, orders, or royal titles, whether they be effective during the sessions of the diet or fulfilled only after its adjournment;

---

[1] All the deputies to the diet of 1790–91 took this patriotic oath. Members of the Upper Chamber hesitated to do so, but when the Lower Chamber announced that it would deal with no one who had not taken the oath, the majority of the lords swore it, with the exception of the bishops. Szilágyi, ed., VIII, 492; full text in Rácz, p. 263.

I will not fail, furthermore, to report to my county, town council, and the appropriate prelature any such offer made to me by the supreme authority,

Except where it was proposed unanimously by, or with the consent of, the county, the diet, or those whom I represent;

So help me God.

Appendix H

PEASANTS' OATH[1]

I, N.N., take my oath by the living, omnipotent God, creator of this world, and on this my faith I truly pledge myself and promise that during the sessions of the forthcoming diet and throughout my life

I will be loyal unto death to the free Hungarian nation and its original privileges, liberties, and laws,

And to His Majesty the King to be crowned at the forthcoming diet under obligation to uphold the glorious Hungarian nation, the laws of the country, and the citizens of every standing and to ensure their protection;

I will make every effort to maintain harmony, Christian love, and civil peace among my compatriots and fellow citizens, whatever their standing, setting aside all other human considerations and evil advice: I will not permit to the best of my ability that they be disturbed;

I will not fail, furthermore, to report to the nearest official of the noble county any evil advice, secret attempts, or intentions to disturb internal civil peace if and when I should observe them: I will prevent them to the best of my ability;

I will report to the nearest official of the county without delay, as a true Christian and a true patriot, any attempt by any person or persons, in writing or by word of mouth, to incite me, or to my knowledge anybody else, to disturb the internal order of the country or of the county, or to induce me to do such ungodly things by the promise of gifts, at any time but particularly during the sessions of the forthcoming diet, at which the representatives of the county and the noble estates will be working with all their energies for the welfare, and to diminish the burdens, of the poor common people: I will present to him all evidence of these men, writings, promises, and delusions;

So help me God.

[1] Rácz, p. 264.

GLOSSARY

ABLEGATUS, deputy of the county to the diet. The *ablegati* were not members of parliament in the modern sense, but deputies of the counties bound by the instructions given by the county assemblies.

ALISPÁN, deputy county high sheriff, elected by the special assembly (see *Közgyűlés*) as head of a county administration. This was the position of highest prestige in the counties, though the prestige was due much more to the social position of the man and to his wealth than to the actual office. By law the position was open only to the local *bene possessionati*.

ALZSELLÉREK, see *Zsellérek*.

ANTECORONALIS ARTICLES, conditions to be accepted by a new king before coronation.

ÁRENDÁS or TAKSÁS serfs, tenant farmers whose obligations to the lord were determined by bilateral contracts and were much lighter than those of the rest of the serfs.

ARMALIS NOBLES, see *Bocskoros nemesek*.

ARRONDIROZÁS, the procedure through which the great landowners expropriated the small possessions of the lesser nobility which were squeezed between their own lands.

AUREA BULLA or ARANY BULLA, the charter issued by King Endre (Andreas) II in 1222 guaranteeing the basic freedoms and privileges of the Hungarian nobility.

BANDERIUM, a paramilitary unit consisting exclusively of young men of noble birth, organized to serve as guards of the Holy Crown, which was returned to Buda from Vienna before the death of Emperor Joseph II. The *banderia* were looked upon as units for training young noblemen in military leadership so that they could command fighting units if armed forces were ever needed against the dynasty or the serfs, or both. The *banderia* were a specific form of the *insurrectio*.

BENE POSSESSIONATI, see Gentry.

BENIGNA RESOLUTIO, see *Humillima repraesentatio*.

BIRÓ, village headman, elected by the village council from three candidates put up by the lord. While in office the *biró* was exempt from serf obligations.

BOCSKOROS NEMESEK, the poverty-stricken majority of the Hungarian lesser nobility. They were also called *taksás nemesek* (taxed nobles), referring to the fact that everywhere the county officials forced them to contribute to the county taxes and periodically the state also taxed them. The *bocskoros nemesek* were divided into several groups. The *armalis* nobles had no landed property but lived and worked on serf sections. *Curialis* nobles owned a plot not larger than a serf section which they cultivated themselves. *Profugus* nobles were those who had escaped from Turkish-occupied regions and lived as either *armalis* or *curialis* nobles. Despite the poverty the *bocskoros nemesek* lived in, their political rights were, in principle, equal to those of the higher strata of the nobility. The *bocskoros nemesek* were also known as *mocassin* nobles.

BRIEFADEL, a poverty-stricken noble who possessed only his patent of nobility.

CAMERA HUNGARICA, see Hungarian Court Chamber.

CAROLINA RESOLUTIO, a patent issued by King Charles III in 1731 restricting the religious liberties of non-Catholics and guaranteeing all the privileges of the Catholic Church.

CASSA DOMESTICA, domestic fund, the taxes paid by the serfs, and in part by the *bocskoros nemesek,* to cover the expenses of county administration, including those of deputies attending sessions of the diet. By 1790 the *Cassa Domestica* was higher than the war tax and had become a cause of bitter serf discontent.

CASUS NOCET DOMINO, the obligation of the lord not to extract extra labor from the serf to make up for any loss when bad weather prevented completion of work already begun.

COMMISSARIATUS PROVINCIALIS, or ORSZÁGOS BIZOTTSÁG (Provincial Commissariat), the civilian organ responsible for supplying the standing army in Hungary. The *Commissariatus* was subordinate to the *Consilium locumtenentiale,* which had final responsibility for army supply. The *Commissariatus* was responsible for a wide variety of tasks, such as recruitment, prosecution of army deserters, granting exemption from military service, etc. The practical discharge of these duties was undertaken by the ten district commissaries (*Commissarii districtuales*).

CONSILIUM REGIUM LOCUMTENENTIALE HUNGARICUM (*Helytartótanács*), the executive branch of government established by Acts 97–122 of the 1723 diet. Its members were appointed by the king from among aristocrats, prelates, and lesser nobility from all parts of the kingdom. In principle the *Consilium* was not subordinate to any court bureau, only to the king, yet it communicated with the king through the Hungarian Royal Court Chancellery. The *Consilium* had no authority over the Imperial troops stationed in Hungary nor any influence over diplomatic affairs. It was abolished in 1848, giving way to the first Hungarian parliamentary government.

CONTRIBUTIO, war tax, paid by the peasantry and burghers for the maintenance of the standing army.

COUNTY ASSEMBLY, see *Közgyűlés*.

COUNTY COURTS (*Sedria*), dealing with criminal offenses (*delictum publicum*) except treason. The county court was also the appeal court in serfs' civil suits.

CREDITIVA, the credentials of the deputies to the diet.

CURIA REGIS, the Supreme Court of Justice, consisting of two chambers: the *Judicum septemvirale* (*Hétszemélyes Tábla*) and the *Tabula regia* (the King's Bench).

CURIALIS NOBLES, see *Bocskoros nemesek*.

DECREE, a writ ordering the implementation of some specific measure.

DECRETALIS OATH, a form of oath all civil servants, state officials, and public functionaries were obliged to take before installation in office. The text of the oath included references to the Virgin Mary objectionable to non-Catholics, who found themselves therefore unable or unwilling to swear it and were, consequently, excluded from public office. Emperor Joseph II abolished use of this oath.

DEPERDITA, see *Regulamentum*.

DICA, a unit for assessment of the tax-paying capacity of individual serf families.

DICALIS CONSCRIPTIO, the registration of the tax-paying capacity of entire serf communities.

DICASTERIUM, governmental department or institution. In the semi-modern system of Habsburg government, each *dicasterium* was responsible to the king for a specific field of administration assigned exclusively to it. That put an end to the confusion of the feudal system of government, which lacked precise division of power and responsibility among the different central government organs.

DIET, or ORSZÁGGYŰLÉS, the bicameral legislative branch of government, consisting of the king and the representatives of the estates, who jointly created laws.

DIPLOMA CAROLINUM, the *antecoronalis* oath of King Charles III.

DOMESTIC TAX, a tax collected to cover the expenses of the county administration and that of the county deputies to the diet.

DOMUS ANNONARIA, storehouses built and maintained by the *Consilium locumtenentiale* to store food and fodder to supply army units stationed in nonagrarian areas or in areas temporarily unable to keep the military supplied.

EDUCILLATIO, the right of the serf communities to operate taverns.

ESKÜDTEK, jurors elected as administrative and judicial assistants to the village headman (*biró*).

EXEMPTUS or SZABADOSOK, peasants free from servile obligations.

EXPLANATIO LEOPOLDINA, a patent issued by King Leopold I in 1690, arbitrarily changing and restricting earlier Hungarian legislation which had guaranteed freedom of religion for the privileged classes. The *Explanatio* reestablished the dominance of the Catholic Church in Hungary.

FAIZÁS, see *Lignatio*.

FALCASTRUM, see *Kaszáló*.

FAMILIARES, see *Servitori*.

FELUJULÁS (revival), the intellectual revival in Hungary which began during the last quarter of the eighteenth century.

FŐISPÁN, county high sheriff, appointed by the king, whom he represented as the head of the county autonomy. Aristocrats were appointed to fill this post. Some aristocratic families and bishops possessing large landed estates in certain counties were appointed *Örökös Főispánok* (Perpetual County High Sheriffs). The Palatine was the *Örökös Főispán* of Pest County. In addition there were nine ecclesiastic and fourteen lay perpetual high sheriffs in Hungary (*Supremus et perpetuus comes*). The *Főispán* represented the county ex efficio in the Upper Chamber of the diet.

FŐJEGYZŐ, county notary, the head of the County Hall.

FŐSZOLGABIRÓ, district magistrate, head of the district administration; his aides were the *szolgabirák* (administrative aides) and the *jurasszorok* (judicial aides).

GENERALKOMMANDO, the highest military command of the Habsburg army. Its status was equivalent to a present-day army corps. The *Generalkommandos* were under the direct supervision of the *Hofkriegsrat*. In Hungary there were six *Generalkommandos*, one each for royal Hungary, Transylvania, Bánát, Slavonia, Croatia, and the Military Frontier Zones.

GENTRY, the upper stratum of the lesser nobility, comprising the *bene possessionati* and the *possessionati*. The *possessionati* owned land cultivated by a few serf families. The *bene possessionati* owned middle-sized estates (1,000–10,000 yokes), several villages, and a great number of serfs and were men of learning, a great many of whom had higher education.

GRAVAMINA, a list of grievances of the estates, of individual counties, or even of a single nobleman (*gravamina particularia*) presented to the diet. Most of the *gravamina* in the late eighteenth century were against the disorderly conduct of the largely foreign soldiers of the standing army in Hungary. Since there were countless grievances presented to each diet, the *sessio mixta* selected the most important grievances and only these were put on the agenda of both chambers (*gravamina praeferentialia*).

GYALOG ROBOT, servile labor performed without horses, such as sowing.

HAJDUK, see *Kúnok*.

HELYTARTÓTANÁCS, see *Consilium regium locumtenentiale hungaricum*.

HÉTSZEMÉLYES TÁBLA, see *Judicum septemvirale*.

HOFKRIEGSRAT, the central organ for all military matters in the Habsburg lands.

HOF- UND STAATSKANZLEI, the Court and State Chancellery, the body which managed the external affairs of the monarchy, as well as the affairs of the dynasty. Owing to the extraordinary prestige of the head of this office, the Chancellor, from 1753 to 1792 Prince von Kaunitz-Reitberg also had great influence over the internal affairs of the Habsburg lands, including Hungary.

HONORATIORI (intelligentsia), educated lawyers, engineers, physicians, etc., not of noble origin. In their outlook the *honoratiori* were much nearer to the gentry than to the *bocskoros nemesek*. During the reign of Emperor Joseph II several of them assumed responsible and influential positions in the state. In the feudal revolt of 1790 the lesser nobility tried with partial success to oust some of them from office.

HUMILLIMA REPRASENTATIO, "humble representation" to the king of a draft of a law passed by the diet. Whether the king accepted the version passed or rejected it, he gave his answer to the diet in a *benigna resolutio* or benevolent resolution. The *benigna resolutio* might promulgate the law as passed by the diet, quash it, or propose its amendment. In case of promulgation the law became part of the *Corpus Juris Hungarici*.

HUNGARIAN COURT CHAMBER (*Camera hungarica* or *Ungarische Kammer*), founded in 1528 by Ferdinand I, the first modern governmental institution in the kingdom. The original responsibility of the Chamber was administration of the *regaliae*, but it also handled the taxes voted by the diet. Constitutionally the Hungarian Chamber was independent of all Austrian authorities, but in practice it was supervised by them.

INDIGENAE, see *Nemesek*.

INQUILINI, see *Zsellérek*.

INSTRUCTIO, the county assemblies' instructions to the deputies to the diet. The instructions bound the deputies, and violation of them might cause the revocation of the credentials of the violators.

INSURRECTIO, see *Posse comitatus*.

IRTÁSDIJ, a small fee that the serf paid the lord in recognition of the lord's property rights over the *irtványföldek*.

IRTVÁNYFÖLDEK, cleared lands which were reclaimed from nature through the initiative and hard work of the serfs. The *irtványföldek* consisted of such former unproductive land as forests, swamps, or heaths.

JÁRÁS, component part of the county, a district.

JÁSZOK, see *Kúnok*.

JEGYZŐ, village notary, elected by the village council to carry out the clerical part of village administration under the supervision of the *biró*.

JUDICUM SEPTEMVIRALE or HÉTSZEMÉLYES TÁBLA, Supreme Court of Appeal, the appellate court of last resort, presided over by the

Palatine. The members of the court were the *Országbíró*, two Catholic archbishops, three titular bishops, six aristocrats, and nine members of the lesser nobility. The members were chosen so that all regions of the kingdom were represented in the court.

JUS GLADII, the right of certain lords to pass sentence on their serfs, including the death penalty, without the possibility of appeal.

JUS RESISTENDI, the prerogative of the nobles to offer resistance to the king if he should infringe the liberties and privileges guaranteed them by the *Aurea Bulla*. In 1687 the *Jus resistendi* was abolished, but the feudal revolt of 1790 tried, unsuccessfully, to reintroduce it.

KAMMER, see Hungarian Court Chamber.

KANCELLÁRIA, see *Magyar Királyi Udvari Kancellária.*

KASZÁLÓ or FALCASTRUM, a measurement of pasture. The area of the *kaszáló* depended on the fertility of the soil. One *kaszáló* was the area of pasture which at the first mowing of the year yielded a wagonload of hay. One serf section included a pasture measuring from 6 to 22 *kaszáló.*

KILENCED, a ninth of annual crops and breedings of the serfs' cattle to be given in lieu of servile dues to the lord.

KIRÁLYI TÁBLA, see *Tabula regia.*

KÖZGYŰLÉS, county assembly, a meeting in which all the nobles of the county were entitled to take part, convened and presided over by the *Főispán,* or in his absence by the *Alispán.* The regular assembly dealt with routine matters of administration. Special assemblies (*sedes restauratoria electoria*) were called to elect county officials.

KÚNOK. After the Tartar onslaught on Hungary, the *Kúnok* and the *Jászok,* oriental relatives of the Hungarians, were ennobled as a whole body. István Bocskay, Prince of Transylvania, ennobled and settled the *Hajdúk,* a host of martial individuals, partly cattlemen, partly marauders, who fought gallantly for the cause Bocskay represented. They were donated land and whole privileged districts were set aside for them.

LESEKABINETT, a reading room, often part of a coffeehouse, where all the current periodicals could be read. *Lesekabinette* enjoyed great popularity and were widespread in Hungary in 1790.

LESSER NOBILITY, comprising the gentry and the *bocskoros nemesek.*

LIGNATIO or FAIZÁS, the right of the serfs to gather wood in the lord's forest.

LITTERAE REGALES, letter of convocation of the diet announcing the reasons for convocation and containing the drafts of legislation suggested by the government.

MACELLUM, the right of the lord to maintain butcheries in serf communities and monopolize the meat market for himself.

MAGYAR KIRÁLYI UDVARI KANCELLÁRIA, Hungarian Royal Court Chancellery, in principle provided liaison between the king and the three branches of the Hungarian government. In practice, however, it was much more than that. In direct attendance upon the king at all times, it had immense influence over royal resolutions. On the king's behalf, the Chancellery supervised all the branches of government until its abolition in 1867.

MAKKOLTATÁS, or PANNAGE, right of the serfs to feed their pigs mast on the lord's forest land.

MARADVÁNYFÖLDEK, surplus lands. The urbarial regulations of Maria Theresa took into account the fertility of the land in different parts of Hungary when they defined the minimum and maximum sizes of holdings which the lords had to allot to the serfs. These holdings were supposed to enable the serfs to supply their families and to fulfill their obligations to lord, state, and church. If a serf possessed more than what was defined as the maximum size for a serf holding, the lord considered this excess to be *maradványföld* and arrogated the right to expropriate it—and frequently did so.

MEGYE, county.

MELIORATIO, a minimal investment in the cultivation of land. It involved no modernization and therefore contributed neither to the progress of agriculture nor to an increase of produce.

MEZŐVÁROSOK, the larger peasant towns on the Great Hungarian Plain. They were creations of the Ottoman era, when for greater security peasants moved into towns and gave up their isolated and insecure cottages. Though major settlements, the *mezővárosok* did not possess burghers' privileges but remained under the jurisdiction of the territorial lords. Many of the *mezővárosok*, however, redeemed themselves from certain serf obligations by cash payment, thereby enjoying a higher degree of self-government than the serf villages possessed.

MILITARY FRONTIER ZONES (see Map No. 1). Along the southern frontier of Hungary a broad zone was detached from the kingdom and administered directly from Vienna by the *Hofkriegsrat*. This zone was divided into regimental areas. All the male inhabitants of the zone were obliged to perform military service and were under military discipline at all times. In return they were granted land tenure. In Transylvania, Maria Theresa also organized military frontier guard units, but in that zone only the guardsmen themselves and military buildings, fortifications, and similar installations were under military jurisdiction, and only small adjacent areas were administered as military territories.

MOCASSIN NOBLES, see *Bocskoros nemesek*.

NÁDALÁS, the right of the serfs to cut reeds in the swamplands of the lord.

NATIVI, see *Nemesek*.

NEMESEK, the nobility, comprising all the aristocracy and the lesser nobility. The *nemesek* were categorized as *nativi*, Hungarian-born noblemen, or *indigenae*, naturalized nobles.

NE ONUS INHAEREAT FUNDO, the principle that neither the person nor the property of the noblemen should be taxed by the state.

NOBILE OFFICIUM, offices held without salary. In principle all the county offices were such. In practice, however, the officers of the county voted themselves very considerable salaries, even though they pretended to be holders of *nobile officium*.

NOBILE UNIUS SESSIONIS, noblemen possessing no more land than the size of one serf section.

ÖRÖKÖS FŐISPÁN, see *Főispán*.

ORSZÁGBÍRÓ, Lord Chief Justice, vice-president of the *Judicum septemvirale*. In the absence of the Palatine he presided over the House of Lords as well as over the *Consilium locumtenentiale*.

ORSZÁGGYŰLÉS, the bicameral diet of the Kingdom of Hungary.

ORSZÁGGYŰLÉSI IFJÚSÁG, Youth of the Diet, young aristrocrats and young *bene possessionati* who escorted the delegates to the diet and served as secretaries. They wrote minutes of district meetings and caucuses, served as page boys, messengers, etc. Their expenses were paid by the counties. The *országgyűlési ifjúság* consisted of students, junior lawyers, secretaries, junior county officials, and the like. The youth of the city where the diet was held (Buda in 1790) and these youth from the country represented the most progressive elements in the kingdom. They influenced public opinion and thereby affected the work of the diet, crowding the galleries to express their approval or disapproval of the proceedings.

ORSZÁGOS BIZOTTSÁG, see *Commissariatus provincialis*.

PALATINE, the highest officeholder of Hungary, a kind of viceroy. He was commander in chief of the Hungarian armed forces, but after establishment of the standing army in 1715 he had authority only over the *posse comitatus*. He was president of the House of Lords and the *sessio mixta* of the diet, president of the *Judicum septemvirale*, and president of the *Consilium regium locumtenentiale hungaricum*. The Palatine was elected by the diet from candidates proposed by the king. In 1790, Archduke Alexander Leopold, son of Leopold II, was elevated to the office, and thereafter all future Palatines were Habsburg archdukes until the office was discontinued in 1848.

PERSONALIS, see *Személynök*.

PIAE FUNDATIONES, Church foundations.

PLACETUM REGIUM, the right of the king to permit or prohibit promulgation of papal documents in Hungary.

PORTA, a general unit for the assessment of war taxes in the counties.

PORTIO, matériel of the standing army, divided into three categories. The *portio oralis* was the daily mess ration: one pound of meat and two pounds of bread per man. The *salganum* covered provisions other than foodstuffs: wood, light, salt, and a bed. The *portio equalis* provided for provender for each horse: six pounds of oats and eight pounds of hay a day and three units of straw a week.

POSSE COMITATUS, Muster of the Nobles, called also *insurrectio*, the obligation of the nobles to go to war if the land was in danger and the king called them to arms. This obligation was the foundation of the nobles' tax exemption. Since the establishment of the standing army in 1715, it had gradually lost all meaning. The last time the Muster of the Nobles was effectively used was by Maria Theresa during the Seven Years' War. The repeated calling to arms of the nobles during the Napoleonic Wars had no military effect. The *banderium* of 1790 was a form of *insurrectio* called by another name because it was called out not by the king but by the counties, and not for defense of the country but for other reasons.

POSSESSIONATI, see Gentry.

POSTULATA, the right of the individual chambers of the diet as well as of the individual legislators to present a "request" for certain legislation. Neither the delegates nor the diet as a whole possessed the right of legislative initiative; that privilege was reserved to the king alone.

PROFUGUS NOBLES, see *Bocskoros nemesek*.

RATIO EDUCATIONIS, Maria Theresa's patent for the reform of education in Hungary issued in 1777.

REGALIAE, those revenues which, following medieval tradition, were considered the personal income of the king and were not supervised by the diet. These revenues came from the output of mines, income from the salt monopoly, profits from minting coins, all tariff duties, and proceeds from the landed properties of the crown. The *regaliae* provided a very considerable source of income from Hungary for the Habsburgs. In 1780 they amounted to 5,755,988 florins, not counting income from mines—nearly as much as the total war taxes voted by the diet. Annual income from the gold, silver, and copper mines added another four to five million florins. Consequently, the taxes voted by the diet represented only one third of the king's total income collected from Hungary.

REGULAMENTUM, a royal patent issued in 1751 which set the prices for supplies rendered in kind to the army. These prices went unchanged, despite the immense increase in market prices over the years, and caused the serfs great losses. The difference between the value of the supplies and the prices credited to the serfs according to the *regulamentum* was called the *deperdita*.

REGULATIO, the right of a lord to exchange the whole or part of a serf's holding for another, neither smaller nor worse than the original. This right was abused by several lords in the eighteenth century to allot the serfs holdings of very poor quality, or even to expropriate their holdings outright.

RESCRIPT, an ordinance issued on the basis of, and in explanation of, existing laws.

ROBOT, physical work performed by the serfs and *zsellérek* for the lords and prelates. The robot could be performed by the serf alone (*gyalog robot*) or by using his draft animals also.

SALGANUM, see *Portio.*

SEDRIA, see County courts.

SEPTEMVIRATUS, see *Judicum septemvirale.*

SERVITORI or FAMILIARES, lesser nobles who voluntarily attached themselves to the households of aristocrats as retainers, either as administrators of the lords' estates or as officers of the lords' private armies.

SESSIO, Section or session (*jobbágytelek*), a measurement of serf holdings. The area of the *sessio* varied according to the fertility of the soil. One *sessio* was an area large enough to yield eight serfs enough produce to supply themselves and their families, and to fulfill their obligations to lord, state, and church.

SESSIO MIXTA, joint session of the two chambers of the diet, presided over by the Palatine. The *sessio mixta* was convoked as the inaugural diet session at which the royal law proposals were read. This session decided whether the royal proposals or the *gravamina* should be discussed first. All the working sessions were then held separately in the two chambers. A draft law was only considered passed if endorsed by both chambers. Differences were eliminated by exchange of messages between the two chambers. If this procedure did not yield results, the Palatine convoked a *sessio mixta* again to reach a compromise. If this joint session did not produce a compromise, the draft was shelved for the time being.

SESSIONES CIRCULARES, district meeting, unofficial session of the Lower Chamber, held in four groups, each including all the county representatives from one of the four diet districts of the kingdom (see Map No. 2).

SESSIONES REGNICOLARES, full sessions of the Lower Chamber of the diet.

STAATSRAT, organized by Maria Theresa as the supreme coordinating body for the political, economic, and educational affairs of the monarchy and practically all matters of state concern. The *Staatsrat* had no constitutional authority over Hungarian affairs, yet all the papers of the Hungarian governmental organs presented to the king were supervised by the *Staatsrat* before they reached the monarch. Without question, the king's final word was given under advice of the *Staatsrat.*

SUBINQUILINI, see *Zsellérek.*

SUBSIDIAE, extraordinary levies on the serfs for ransom of their lord if he were captured, for wedding presents, for first mass presents, and for major holy day presents.

SZABADOSOK EXEMPTI, free peasants who redeemed themselves from serf obligations by cash payment. Numerically they were a negligible part of the peasantry.

SZÉKELYEK, a branch of the Hungarian nation located in East Transylvania. All the *székelyek* were free men.

SZEMÉLYNÖK or PERSONALIS, Chief Justice, appointed by the king from among the *bene possessionati*. The *Személynök* presided over the Lower Chamber of the diet and the *Tabula regia.*

SZOLGABIRÓ, aide of the *főszolgabiró*, elected by the special assembly (see *Közgyűlés*).

TÁBLABIRÓ, county magistrate, primarily a part-time judge of the county court. *Táblabirák* were often assigned temporary duties by the county assemblies in various parts of the county. These missions might be political, judicial, administrative, punitive. More often than not they were simply excuses to give salaries to poverty-stricken landless nobles. Hence the peasants' complaints against the unwarrantable expense of a large number of county officers. Some nobles coveted the mere title of a *táblabiró* since a landless noble was considered a nonentity without real or titular position in the local government. In 1790 there were between 100 and 500 *táblabirák* in each county and from eight to ten thousand in the whole country.

TABULA REGIA, the King's Bench, the supreme court of the nobility dealing with all suits concerning land grants, ownership of land, treason, and criminal cases against nobles. In most of these cases it was the court of first instance. Criminal cases against the nobility, however, were appealed to this court from the district courts. The president of the court was the *Személynök;* its membership was similar to that of the *Judicum septemvirale.* The whole court sat in the Lower Chamber of the diet.

TAKSÁS NEMESEK, see *Bocskoros nemesek.*

TAKSÁS SERFS, see *Árendás* serfs.

TÁRNOKMESTER, Lord High Treasurer.

TELONIUM NAULUM, the right of the lord to collect customs duties and ferry duties.

URISZÉK, manorial courts, the lords' lower courts of justice with authority over the serfs. Several of them possessed the *jus gladii.*

VOTUM CURIATUM, the single vote all the representatives of the royal free towns could cast jointly in the diet. All the prelates sitting in the Lower Chamber also had only one joint vote.

ZSELLÉREK, or cotters, the lowest stratum of the peasantry, bound in their persons to the lord and possessing no land, or a lot smaller than one eighth of a serf section. The *zsellérek* were divided into *inquilini* (cotters) and *subinquilini alzsellérek* (sub-cotters). The former owned a house and sometimes *fundi intravillani* (the "internal" part of a serf section). The *subinquilini* possessed neither house nor land, but lived in a serf's or a *zsellér's* house, where they usually had a hearth of their own.

BIOGRAPHICAL REGISTER

BELOW ARE two lists giving the kings and palatines of Hungary in chronological order. These are followed by a register of the principal characters mentioned in this book, including a few men of earlier times who made a direct and significant contribution to the period under discussion.

KINGS OF HUNGARY

HOUSE OF HABSBURG

Ferdinand I, 1526–64 (rival on the throne of Hungary: János Zápolya, 1526–40)

Maximilian, 1564–76

Rudolf, 1576–1608 (as Holy Roman Emperor to 1612)

Matthias II, 1608–19

Ferdinand II, 1619–37

Ferdinand III, 1637–57

Ferdinand IV, 1647–54 (crowned during his father's lifetime, he died before his father and never actually reigned)

Leopold I, 1657–1705

Joseph I, 1705–11

Charles III (VI as Holy Roman Emperor), 1711–40

Maria Theresa, 1740–80

HOUSE OF HABSBURG-LORRAINE

Joseph II, 1780–90

Leopold II, 1790–92

Francis I, 1792–1835

Ferdinand V, 1835–48

Francis Joseph, 1848–1916

Charles IV, 1916–18

PALATINES OF THE KINGDOM OF HUNGARY
(from the Early Seventeenth Century)

György Thurzó, 1609–16

Zsigmond Forgách, 1618–21

Szaniszló Thurzó, 1622–25
Miklós Eszterházy, 1625–45
János Draskovics, 1646–48
Pál Pálffy, 1649–54
Ferenc Wesselényi, 1655–67
Office vacant, 1667–81
   Governor-General: Ferenc Nádasdy, 1667–70
   Governor-General: György Szelepcsényi, 1670–81
Pál Eszterházy, 1681–1713
Miklós Pálffy, 1714–34
Office vacant, 1734–41
   Governor-General: Prince Francis of Lorraine, 1734–41
János Pálffy, 1741–51
Lajos Batthyány, 1751–65
Office vacant, 1765–90
   Governor-General: Prince Albrecht of Saxony, 1765–81
   Lord High Treasurer: Kristóf Niczky, 1781–90
Archduke Alexander Leopold, 1790–95
Archduke Joseph, 1796–1847
   Locum tenens: Archduke Stephen, 1847–48
The office of Palatine was discontinued in 1848.

ALEXANDER LEOPOLD, Archduke (1772–95), the first Habsburg Palatine of the Kingdom of Hungary, a son of King Leopold II. The memorandum that the Archduke prepared after the suppression of the Jacobin movement in Hungary was a charter for reaction. He proposed the introduction of extreme absolutism—advice that his brother, King Francis I, adopted.

ÁNYOS, Pál (1756–84), a prominent poet of the first generation of enlightened Hungarian writers. As a monk Ányos received a doctor's degree from the University of Buda. He became a teacher of philosophy at the *Gimnázium* of Székesfehérvár. His collected works were first published posthumously in 1798 and have appeared in several later editions.

BACSÁNYI (also BATSÁNYI), János (1763–1845), writer and poet of the Hungarian Enlightenment and a founder of the first Hungarian literary magazine, *Magyar Museum* (or *Múzeum*). He was strongly opposed to the Germanizing efforts of Joseph II. Much influenced by the ideas and events of the French Revolution, he penned the first poem in Hungarian in its praise. In other verse he vigorously attacked the dynasty and the Roman Catholic clergy, and championed the cause of the serfs. He was imprisoned in 1795 as a member of the Hungarian Jacobin conspiracy. When Napoleon entered Vienna, Bacsányi joined him and helped to draft Napoleon's Manifesto to the Hungarian Nation in 1809. On the withdrawal of the French, he moved to Paris, where he was seized after Napoleon's fall by the reactionary authorities. He was interned in Linz for the remainder of his life. Notwithstanding this, he was elected to the Hungarian Academy of Sciences in 1843.

BALOGH, Péter, of Ócsa (1748–1818), *Főispán* of Torontál, later of Zólyom, county. A leader and chief political ideologist of the feudal revolt in Hungary in 1790, he opposed the powers of the crown and advocated the idea of popular sovereignty (*népfelség*). Like the majority of the nobility, however, he meant by "the people" the estates, not the whole populace. In the wake of the failure of the feudal revolt, he accepted the Habsburgs' olive branch and, in return for several signs of Habsburg favor including decorations and high office, he became a loyal follower of the dynasty.

BARÓTI-SZABÓ, David (1739–1819), poet and Jesuit monk. In his verse he naturalized the classical Latin metrical system, making a major contribution to the modernization of the Hungarian language. He was a founder of the first Hungarian literary magazine, *Magyar Museum* (or *Múzeum*).

BATTHYÁNY, Cardinal Archbishop Count József (1727–99), Primate of Hungary and adviser to Maria Theresa. A staunch reactionary, he opposed the reforms of Joseph II. When Pope Pius VI visited Vienna, he tried unsuccessfully to mediate between the Pope and Joseph II. During the feudal revolt, he sided with the Habsburgs and was one of those who arranged the 1790 compromise between the court and the estates.

BÉL, Mátyás (1684–1749), a Calvinist minister of Slovak origin and a pioneer of the Latinized Hungarian literary culture. He was also one of the first to try to interpret Hungary's problems by scientific and intellectual methods. His major work, *Notitia Hungariae novae historico-geographica* (1735–42), was never completed. An effort to compile a comprehensive account of all knowledge about Hungary, it affords the best contemporary geographical and historical description of northwest Hungary.

BELNAY, György Alajos (1765–1809), Hungarian historian whose works were written mostly in Latin.

BERZEVICZY, Gergely (1763–1822), progressive writer on political economy. A member of the gentry, he nonetheless was a friend and associate of the Hungarian Jacobins. He advocated freedom of international trade in opposition to Habsburg mercantilist and colonialist policies. One of the first to recognize the economic disadvantages of the feudal system and criticize it, he deplored the servile status of the serfs. He argued that the only road to economic progress was the introduction of a market economy, the prerequisite for which was the emancipation of the serfs.

BERZSENYI, Dániel (1776–1836), writer. A nationalistically minded poet at first, he extolled the national virtues of the gentry in his early writings. Little by little, however, he was won over by enlightened thought and became a sharp critic of the barrenness of the life of the Hungarian gentry. Following Széchenyi's example, he advocated economic and social reforms for Hungary.

BESSENYEI, György (1747–1811), writer. Son of a landed noble family, he became a member of the Hungarian Noble Bodyguard in Vienna in 1765. Inspired by French Enlightenment, he educated himself and, with a group of his fellow Bodyguards, decided to disseminate French civilization and literature in Hungary. He wrote poetry, drama, and prose. The year 1772, when his first work was published, used to be considered the beginning of modern Hungarian literature. In 1773 Bessenyei quit the Bodyguard but stayed on in Vienna as representative of the Hungarian Calvinists. In 1779 he founded Hazafiui Tudós Társaság (the Patriotic Scientific Society), forerunner of the Hungarian Academy of Sciences.

BETHLEN, Gábor (1580–1629), Prince of Transylvania. Born of the lesser nobility, he emigrated to the Ottoman Empire in the early seventeenth century as the Habsburgs began their reign of terror in Transylvania. He was elected Prince of Transylvania with Turkish help in 1613. His ambition was to restore the Kingdom of Hungary's independence from Habsburg rule. For this reason above all others he took part in the Thirty Years' War as a member of the anti-Habsburg coalition. The treaties of Nickolsburg in 1622, Vienna in 1624, and Pozsony in 1626 extended his realm beyond Transylvania to cover most of royal Hungary. He set up a modern state system and a mercantilist economy; he developed education and became a patron of the arts and sciences. Bethlen created a Hungarian national monarchy in Transylvania, which under him became the bastion of Hungarian cultural life.

BOCSKAY, István (1557–1606), Prince of Transylvania after 1605. As a military leader of the Kingdom of Hungary, he started his career a loyal subject of the Habsburgs. Under their flag he led several successful campaigns against the Turks. Habsburg duplicity, however, drove him to head the Hungarian independence movement and, in an alliance with the Ottoman Empire, he swept the Habsburg troops out of all of Hungary not occupied by the Turks. By the Treaty of Vienna in 1606 he secured for Hungary its independent status and the political privileges and religious freedoms of the Hungarian estates. He guaranteed the Székelys their status as freemen and settled and knighted the Hajdus.

CLOŞCA (pseudonym of Ioan Oarga) (d. 1785), peasant leader. He and Horia (q.v.) were the leaders of a serf uprising in Transylvania in 1784. He was executed the following year.

DÉCSY, Sámuel (1742–1816), writer. A physician, Décsy took part in the literary activities of the Hungarian Enlightenment, writing in defense of, and for the development of, a Hungarian literary language.

ÉDES, Gergely (1763–1847), poet. Born in Madar, Komárom County, he became a Calvinist preacher. Édes was a *leoninus* poet, that is, one who wrote verse in ancient hexameter and pentameter form.

ESZTERHÁZY (also ESTERHÁZY), Prince Miklós (1714–90), field marshal in Maria Theresa's army. He built Hungary's Versailles, the rococo castle of Eszterháza (modern Fertőd), and was a patron of the composer Joseph Haydn.

FEKETE, Count János, of Galántha (1741–1803), writer and poet. He wrote in Hungarian, French, German, and Latin in the pure spirit of the Enlightenment, assailing the conservative nobility and the Roman Catholic Church. He corresponded with Voltaire.

FESTETICS, Count György (1755–1819), agronomist. In 1790, as an officer in the Graeven Hussars, he was involved in the protonationalist ferment in the Hungarian regiments of the Habsburg standing army and backed the demands of the feudal revolt in Hungary. He was consequently court-martialed. In 1797 he founded one of the first agrarian colleges in Europe, the Georgicon, in Keszthely. From 1814 to the year of his death he organized the annual Helicon festival in which the foremost scholars, scientists, artists, and writers from all over Hungary took part.

HADIK, Field Marshal Count András (1710–90), soldier and statesman. A son of gentry, he rose through the military and social ranks during Maria Theresa's and Joseph II's wars. During the Seven Years' War he led the Empire's attack on Berlin. He later became the first Hungarian President of the *Kriegsrat*.

HAJNÓCZY, József (1750–95), lawyer and Jacobin. Born into an *honoratior* family, he joined the Freemasons early in his life and became an ardent Josephinist. Joseph II defied tradition by appointing Hajnóczy to be *Alispán* of Szerém County, an office that had always been held up till then by a member of the leading county gentry. The leaders of the feudal revolt had him removed after Joseph II's death. In a number of leaflets he called for the serfs to be emancipated and granted property rights. After 1791 his writings began to favor the ideas and course of the French Revolution and he became more and more radical. He took to advocating the abolition of feudal privileges, the opening of public office to the most talented regardless of their social background, equal taxation for all citizens, and freedom of the press. In short, he demanded the establishment of a liberal state system. He joined the Hungarian Jacobin conspiracy in 1794 and became one of the leaders of the Szabadság és Egyenlőség Társaság (Society for Liberty and Equality). He was decapitated in 1795.

HORIA or HORA, Nicholas (pseudonym of Vasile Nicolae Ursu) (1730–85), peasant leader. He and Cloşca (*q.v.*) led a serf rebellion in Transylvania in 1784. He was executed after its defeat.

KÁRMÁN, József (1769–95), littérateur. Son of the Calvinist preacher, Kármán became a Freemason and frequented the best social circles in Pest. In 1794 he began publishing *Uránia,* a literary magazine mostly for ladies, with the promotion of culture in Hungary as his prime motive. A man of society, Kármán firmly believed in the refining effects of leading a good, cultured social life. He tried to make Pest a mecca of culture.

KAZINCZY, Ferenc (1759–1831), littérateur. Kazinczy's parents were Calvinist gentry of Bihar County. He was educated in the Calvinist college of Sárospatak, and then in the law schools in Kassa, Eperjes, and Pest. In 1784 he joined the Masonic lodge of Miskolc. Two years later Joseph II appointed him superintendent of the primary schools of northern Hungary. He lost this office following the death of his beloved master. In 1788 he was coeditor of *Magyar Museum* (or *Múzeum*), the first Hungarian literary magazine, and became editor of *Orpheus,* another early literary periodical, two years later. In 1795 he was condemned to death in the Martinovics conspiracy, but the capital sentence was commuted to life imprisonment and in 1801 he was pardoned. After 1806 he lived in Bányácska, a small village in the north, which he renamed Széphalom. That name became a concept in Hungarian literature and the village has been justly considered the cradle of modern Hungarian literature and language. Kazinczy was a member of the Hungarian Academy of Sciences but never received the coveted secretary-generalship. In 1831 he fell victim to the plague that swept over northern Hungary in the wake of a wave of refugees from the Polish revolution of 1830.

MARTINI, Baron Karl Anton (1726–1800), Professor of Law at the University of Vienna. He was teacher to many of Hungary's leading statesmen in the late eighteenth century.

MARTINOVICS, Ignác (1755–95), leader of the Hungarian Jacobins. The son of a Serbian merchant in Pest, Martinovics joined the Franciscan Order when he was sixteen. He traveled widely in Western Europe and in 1783 became Professor of Mathematics at the University of Lemberg (modern Lvov). In 1790, in cooperation with Leopold II, the friar began writing to promote liberal ideas in Hungary. After the king's death, he organized the Jacobin conspiracy to counter the rising tide of conservatism. His closest collaborators were János Laczkovics, Ferenc Szentmarjay, Baron László Orczy, Count Jakob Sigray, and József Hajnóczy. The conspiracy was uncovered, however, and its leaders were executed on May 20, 1795.

NAGYVÁTHY, János (1755–1819), economist and agronomist. At György Festetics' invitation, Nagyváthy drew up plans with Sámuel Tessedik for the Georgicon in Keszthely and became the college of agriculture's first superintendent. His writings concentrated on the application of scientific methods to the cure of agrarian problems.

NICZKY, Kristof (1725–87), Lord High Treasurer of Hungary. A personal friend of Joseph II, Niczky was the chief executive official in Hungary while the offices of Palatine and Lord Chief Justice were vacant. As Lord High Treasurer (*Tárnokmester*), Niczky presided *ad interim* over the *Consilium locumtenentiale* and pushed all the Josephine reforms through with scant regard for their constitutionality.

ORCZY, Baron Lőrinc (1718–88), writer. A landlord and professional officer in the Imperial Army, he rose to the rank of cavalry general during the wars of Maria Theresa. After his retirement, he began writing poetry and patronizing other writers. His work is characterized by a blend of the traditional ideas of the gentry and enlightened thought.

PAULY, Carolus, author of *Constitutio rei urbarialis regni Hungariae* (Vienna, 1817), a collection of classic early writings on servile obligations and lordly privileges.

PFAHLER, Carolus, author of *Ius Georgicum regni Hungaricae et partium eidem annexarum* (Keszthely, 1820), a classic collection of manorial records of jurisdictional regulations, serf obligations, and lordly privileges.

PRAY, György (1723–1801), Jesuit monk and historian. After the expulsion of the Society of Jesus, he became chief librarian of the University of Buda. The lasting merit of his work is that he drew the attention of historians to the rich material in the Hungarian archives, where he himself carried out extensive research.

RÁKÓCZI, Ferenc II (1676–1735), Prince of Transylvania and insurgent leader. Rákóczi led a war (1703–11) against the Habsburgs. In 1704 he became Prince of Transylvania and the following year was proclaimed Prince Regnant (*Vezérlő Fejedelem*) of Hungary. After the compromise between the dynasty and the estates was agreed on in his absence, he chose not to return to Hungary. He lived out the rest of his years in France and in the lands of the Ottoman Empire, writing and fostering the struggle for Hungary's independence from the rule of the Habsburgs.

RÁT, Mátyás (1749–1810), newspaper editor. An Evangelical minister born in Győr, Rát studied in the West. He was editor of the first modern Hungarian newspaper, *Magyar Hirmondó*, to which for three years he devoted all his energy and time. While, as he admitted, foreign news was lifted from the foreign press, *Hirmondó*'s home news was supplied by reporters, whom Rát enlisted among the educated men of his day, particularly scholars. The newspaper printed political as well as scholarly articles and gave great space to book reviews, despite the protests of some subscribers. Rát refused to yield to such criticism on the ground that the newspaper's mission was educational. Generally speaking, he set high professional and cultural standards for *Hirmondó*.

SZACSVAY, Sándor (1752–1815), newspaper editor. He was born in the Szekler district, studied in Debrecen, traveled in Germany and France, and joined the Freemasons. Szacsvay was acquainted with Grössinger, Joseph II's secretary, who persuaded him to start publishing the *Magyar Kurir* in Vienna. This Hungarian newspaper, of which he was the editor, became the organ of Josephinism and, later a mouthpiece of the French Revolution. Szacsvay is looked on as the first Hungarian political columnist.

SZALKAY, András (1753–1804). While an officer in the standing army, he was sent at Professor Hoffmann's suggestion to stir up the peasantry in support of the dynasty. So successful was he that he was rewarded with the office of Chancellor to the Palatine of Hungary, Archduke Alexander Leopold.

SZENTMARJAY, Ferenc (1767–95), Jacobin. He was a leader of the Szabadság és Egyenlőség Társaság (Society for Liberty and Equality), one of the Hungarian Jacobins' organizations under Martinovics. He translated J.-J. Rousseau's Contrat Social. He was beheaded in 1795.

TESSEDIK, Sámuel (1742–1820), agronomist and Evangelical pastor of the parish of Szarvas. Tessedik received his primary education in Pozsony and graduated from the Calvinist college in Debrecen. He did postgraduate studies at the University of Erlangen in Germany and traveled widely in Western Europe. In 1767 he accepted the benefice of Szarvas in Békés County. In 1780 he established in Szarvas the Experimental Economic Institute, the first school of economics in Hungary, where he started a model farm system. The Institute's object was to train peasant youths in advanced economic methods by teaching a combination of practical work and theoretical studies. Tessedik popularized vegetable gardening, fruit growing, cultivation of fodder crops, and the production of silk and wool. He proved his ideas by his own work on the land and spread them through numerous writings. The foremost agrarian reformer of his age, he deplored the wretched treatment and status of the serfs and advocated the peasants' "freedom and ownership of the land."

THÖKÖLY, Count Imre (1657–1705), landlord and leading Protestant statesman. In 1678, in the anti-Habsburg tradition of his family, he took over leadership of the malcontents. At the head of his insurrectionary army, he set out from Transylvania and occupied most of Habsburg-controlled Hungary. He allied himself with the Ottoman Empire against the Habsburgs, but the Turks' defeat under the walls of Vienna in 1683 and their subsequent decline doomed his movement also. In 1690 he occupied Transylvania and was elected Prince, but the Peace of Karlovce in 1699 put an end to his political influence in Hungary. He died in exile in Asia Minor.

ÜRMÉNYI, József (1741–1825), Chief Justice (Személynök), later Lord Chief Justice (Országbíró), of the Kingdom of Hungary. He helped to draft Maria Theresa's famous educational-reform edict, Ratio Educationis, in 1777. During the feudal revolt of 1790, he was one of the leaders of the moderates and an architect of the compromise between the estates and the Habsburgs.

VERBŐCZI (also WERBŐCZY), István (d. 1541), jurist and statesman. A typical member of the Hungarian lesser nobility, he became a justice of the Supreme Court in 1505. He was one of those who in 1514 helped to organize the measures used to subdue peasant unrest caused by the Dózsa serf rebellion. His major work was the *Tripartitum,* an exposition of the principles and practices of the fundamental laws of feudal society establishing noble privileges and the servile status of the peasants. The *Tripartitum* was first published in Vienna in 1517 in Latin and republished several times thereafter. He was elected Palatine in 1525, but before the battle of Mohács the following year the king and aristocrats forced him to resign from office. He became the Royal Chancellor of János Zápolya, Ferdinand I's rival as king of Hungary. After the capital fell under Ottoman rule, he continued in his position as Chief Justice of Buda.

WESSELÉNYI, Baron Miklós (1796–1850), landlord and reformer in Transylvania. He was a leader of the gentry's liberal reform group in the diet of Transylvania and later in the Hungarian national diet, and was also a member of the Hungarian Academy of Sciences. During the clash between Széchenyi's reformism and Kossuth's revolutionary line, he sided with Kossuth. He was imprisoned by the Habsburgs' reactionary authorities. He advocated complete emancipation of the serfs, and in his major work, *Balitéletekről* [On Misconceptions], published in 1833, he argued in favor of setting up a liberal system of government.

ZICHY, Count Károly (1753–1826), Lord Chief Justice. He was a leader of the moderates during the feudal revolt of 1790 and helped to frame the compromise between the estates and the Habsburg dynasty.

BIBLIOGRAPHY

THE HISTORY of Hungary in the late eighteenth century has been the focus of attention of a very large number of Hungarian historians, both in the past and at present. These numerous scholars have been outstanding for the quality of their work. To try to give a more or less complete bibliography here would be impossible and to little avail, for several exhaustive bibliographies of the period are in print. Hóman and Szekfü, *Magyar Történet*, Vol. V (1928), contains an impressive bibliography of works in Hungarian as well as in Western European languages. Even more up to date and extensive is Domokos Kosáry, *Bevezetés a magyar történelem forrásaiba és irodalmába*. Volume II offers a historiography of the period up to 1954, while Vol. III lists additional literature published up to 1958; both volumes include critical analyses of the works named. With such comprehensive references on hand, there is no need to offer more than a selective list of the most useful sources.

The following select bibliography was compiled with this order of priority: works of contemporary authors; collections of documents; and the most substantial contributions to work on the period made by noted historians. In the third category a reasonable effort has been made to strike a balance in the number of works relating to the social, intellectual, economic, and political aspects of the period.

UNPUBLISHED MATERIAL

1. Haus-, Hof- und Staatsarchiv, Vienna
    Colloredo Acten. Papers of Count Francis Colloredo, tutor and then cabinet minister of Emperor Francis I (II); he had considerable influence on the monarch.
    Handarchiv Kaiser Franz I.
    Hungarica aus der Privat Bibliotek Seiner Majestät. The secret correspondence of Emperor Francis I (II).
    Hungarica 1789–1791 March, Fasc. 260, 261: "Representationes comita-

tum R. Hungariae ad Franciscum Imp. et Regem ad Palatinum excelsum consilium et corespondentiae ab anno 1790–1830." Contains several instructions of various county assemblies for the deputies to the diet.

* *Privatbibliothek.* The secret correspondence of Emperor Leopold II.

Staatsrat Archiv. (Detailed catalogue in *Inventare Österreichischer Staatlicher Archive,* Vol. V: "Inventare des Wiener Haus-, Hof- und Staatsarchivs," Vienna: Verlag Adolf Holzhausens Nachfolger, 1936.) Lists all the resolutions of the *Staatsrat.*

* *Vertrauliche Akten.* The secret correspondence of Emperor Francis I (II).

2. Kriegsarchivs Schrift Abteilung Wien

Hofkriegsrat Akten (G-9220 ff.). Contains resolutions of the *Hofkriegsrat* as well as documents relating to the protonationalist stir in the standing army in 1790. Also contains correspondence between counties and Hungarian regiments.

Kanzlei Akten (KA), No. 138. Contains a rich collection of documents on the *banderium* movement and on the correspondence of the Hungarian officers of the standing army with the diet and the *bene possessionati* in the counties.

PUBLISHED MATERIAL

Acsády, Ignácz. *A magyar jobbágyság története* [The History of the Hungarian Serfdom]. Budapest: Politzer-féle Könyvkiadóvállalat, 1906.

Adler, S. "Ungarn nach dem Tode Kaiser Josephs II," in *Festschrift zum 100 jährigen Jubileum des Wiener Schottengymnasiums.* Vienna, 1907.

Agárdi, Ferenc, et al. *Társadalmi mozgalmak Magyarországon* [Social Movements in Hungary]. Budapest, 1946.

Ágoston, Péter. *A magyar világi nagybirtok története* [The History of Hungarian Lay Landed Properties]. Budapest: Grill Károly, 1913.

Andics, Erzsébet. *Munkásosztály és a nemzet* [Working Class and Nation]. Budapest: Szikra, 1946.

Andrássy, Gróf Gyula. *The Development of Hungarian Constitutional Liberty.* Translated from the Hungarian by C. Arthur and Ilona Ginever. London: K. Paul, Trench, Trübner & Co. Ltd., 1908.

H. Balázs, Éva. *Die Lage der Bauernschaft und die Bauernbewegung, 1780–1787.* Acta Hungarica Academiae Scientiorum Hungaricae. Budapest: Magyar Tudományos Akadémia, 1951.

—— *Magyarország Története 1526–1790: A késői feudalizmus korszaka* [History of Hungary, 1526–1790: The Era of Late Feudalism]. 3 vols. Budapest: Tankönyvkiadó, 1962.

Ballagi, Géza. *Politikai irodalom Magyarországon 1825-ig* [The Political

* Most of the documents of this group are to be found in the archives of Budapest.

Literature in Hungary up to 1825]. Budapest: Franklin-Társulat, 1888.

Beer, Adolf. *Joseph II, Leopold II und Kaunitz: Ihr Briefwechsel.* Vienna, 1873.

Benda, Kálmán, ed. *A Magyar jakobinusok iratai* [The Papers of Hungarian Jacobins]. Fontes Historiae Hungaricae Aevi Recentioris. 3 vols. Budapest: Akadémiai Kiadó, 1952–57.

Benedek, Marcell. *A magyar irodalom története* [The History of Hungarian Literature]. Budapest: Singer és Wolfner, 1938.

Beőthy, Zsolt. *A magyar irodalom története* [The History of Hungarian Literature]. 2 vols. Budapest: Athenaeum, 1899–1900.

Berlász, Jenő. *A magyar jobbágykérdés és a bécsi udvar az 1790–es években* [The Hungarian Serf Problem and the Court of Vienna in the 1790s]. Budapest: Gróf Teleki Pál Tudományos Intézet, 1941.

Berzeviczy, Gergely. "A parasztok állapotáról és természetéről Magyarországon" [On the Nature and Conditions of the Peasants in Hungary], in Jenő Gaál, *Berzeviczy Gergely élete és művei* [Life and Works of Gergely Berzeviczy]. Budapest: Politzer Zsigmond, 1902.

Biró, Sándor, et al. *A magyar református egyház története* [The History of the Hungarian Reformed Church]. Budapest: Kossuth Kiadó, 1949.

Blum, Jerome. *Lord and Peasant in Russia from the Ninth to the Nineteenth Century.* Princeton, N. J.: Princeton University Press, 1961.

—— *Noble Landowners and Agriculture in Austria, 1815–1848: A Study in the Origins of the Peasant Emancipation of 1848.* Baltimore: The Johns Hopkins University Press, 1948.

—— "The Rise of Serfdom in Eastern Europe," *American Historical Review,* Vol. LXII, No. 4 (1957).

Bóka, László, and Pál Pándi. *A magyar irodalom története* [The History of Hungarian Literature]. Budapest: Bibliotheca, Gondolat, 1957–63.

Bota, László, ed. "*Urak, papok dölyfét, im eleget tűrtük*": *antologia a magyar irodalom antiklerikális hagyományaiból* ["We Tolerated the Haughtiness of Lords and Priests for Too Long": An Anthology of the Anticlerical Heritage of Hungarian Literature]. Budapest: Szépirodalmi Könyvkiadó, 1952.

Concha, Győző. "A 90-es évek reformeszméi és előzményeik" [The Reform Ideas of the 1790s and Their Origins], *Budapesti Szemle,* Vol. XXIX, No. 63 (1882).

Corpus Juris Hungarici Editio Millenaria Memorabilis. Leipzig: Sumptibus, Duncker, und Humbolt, 1902.

Criste, Oskar. *Kriege unter Kaiser Josef II.* Vienna: Verlag von L. W. Seidel & Sohn, 1904.

Cserkey, István. *Die Verfassung Ungarns.* Budapest: Danubia Verlag, 1944.

Dezsényi, Béla. *A magyar hirlapirodalom első százada (1705–1805)* [The First Century of Hungarian Journalism (1705–1805)]. Budapest: A Nemzeti Múzeum Országos Széchényi Könyvtára, 1941.

—— *Az időszaki sajtó története a Dunatáj országaiban* [The History of

Periodicals of the Countries of the Danubian Basin]. Budapest: Gergely, 1947.

Dezsényi, Béla, and György Nemes. *A magyar sajtó 250 éve* [Two Hundred and Fifty Years of the Hungarian Press]. Budapest: Művelt Nép Könyvkiadó, 1954.

Domanovszky, Sándor, ed. *József nádor iratai* [The Papers of Palatine Joseph]. Fontes Historiae Hungaricae Aevi Recentioris. 3 vols. Budapest: Magyar Történelmi Társulat, 1925–29.

—— *Magyar művelődéstörténet* [Hungarian Cultural History]. 4 vols. Budapest: Magyar Történelmi Társulat, n.d.

Éble, Gábor. *Az ecsedi százéves urbéri per története, 1776–1877* [The Hundred-Year Long Urbarial Suit of Ecsed, 1776–1877]. Budapest: Franklin-Társulat, 1912.

Eckhardt, Sándor. *A francia forradalom eszméi Magyarországon* [The Ideas of the French Revolution in Hungary]. Budapest: Franklin-Társulat, 1924.

Eckhart, Ferenc. *Magyar alkotmány és jogtörténet* [History of the Hungarian Constitution and Law]. Budapest: Politzer Zsigmond és Fia, 1946.

Elkán, László. *Ungarn im Zeitalter der französichen Revolution und die Krise des Feudalismus.* Leipzig: Druckerei der Werkgemeinschaft, 1929.

Ember, Győző. *A magyar királyi helytartótanács gazdasági és népvédelmi működése III Károly korában* [The Economic and Popular Welfare Activities of the Hungarian Royal Viceregal Council During the Era of Charles III]. Budapest: Athenaeum, 1933.

Faragó, Ede. *Szociális Magyarország, a magyar szociálpolitika törvény és adattára* [Social Hungary, the Compilation of Laws and Facts of Hungarian Social Policy]. Budapest: Athenaeum, 1943.

Féja, Géza. *A felvilágosadástól a sötétedésig: A magyar irodalom története 1772-tól 1867-ig* [From Enlightenment to Darkness: History of Hungarian Literature from 1772 to 1867]. Budapest: Magyar Élet, 1942.

Felhő, Ibolya, and Antal Vörös. *A Helytartótanácsi levéltár* [Archives of the *Consilium locumtenentiale*]. Budapest: Akadémiai Kiadó, 1961.

Fraknói, Vilmos. *Martinovics Élete* [The Life of Martinovics]. Budapest: Athenaeum Irodalmi és Nyomdai R. T., 1921.

Gaál, Jenő. *Berzeviczy Gergely élete és művei* [The Life and Works of Gergely Berzeviczy]. Budapest: Politzer Zsigmond, 1902.

Gárdonyi, Albert. "A Vármegye es a város társadalma" [The Society of County and Town], in Sándor Domanovszky, ed., *Magyar Művelődéstörténet* [Hungarian Cultural History]. Budapest: Magyar Történelmi Társulat, n.d.

Gragger, Robert. *Preussen, Weimar und die ungarische Königskrone mit dem Faksimile eines Goethe-Briefes.* Berlin: Walter de Gruyter & Co., 1923.

Gróf Hoffmansegg utazása Magyarországon 1793–1794-ben [The Travels of Count Hoffmansegg in Hungary in 1793–1794]. Translated and introduced by István Berkeszi. Budapest: Magyar Kőnyvtar, 1887.

Grünwald, Béla. *A régi Magyarország, 1711–1825* [Old Hungary, 1711–1825]. Budapest: Franklin-Társulat, 1888.

Gulyás, Pál. *Magyar irók élete és munkái* [Life and Work of Hungarian Writers]. 6 vols. Budapest: Magyar Könyvtárosok és Levéltárosok Egyesülete, 1939–44.

Hadrovics, László. *Parasztmozgalmak a 18. században* [Peasant Movements in the Eighteenth Century]. Budapest: Művelt Nép Könyvkiadó, 1951.

Hankiss, János. *Európa és a magyar irodalom: A honfoglalástól a kiegyezésig* [Europe and Hungarian Literature from the Settlement to the Compromise]. Budapest: Singer és Wolfner, 1939.

Hankiss, János, ed. *Antologie de la prose hongroise.* Paris: Editions du Sagittaire, 1938.

Hermann, Egyed. "A vallásos ember a barokk korban" [The Religious Men in the Baroque Era]. in Sándor Domanovszky, ed., *Magyar művelődéstörténet* [Hungarian Cultural History]. Budapest: Magyar Történelmi Társulat, n.d.

Hetényi, János. *Robot és Dézsma* [Robot and Tithe]. Budapest: Tankönyvkiadó, 1947.

Hóman, Bálint. *A magyar történetirás új útjai* [New Trend in Hungarian History]. Budapest: Magyar Szemle Társaság, 1931.

—— *Történetirás és forráskritika* [History Writing and Analyses of Sources]. Budapest: Magyar Történelmi Társulat, 1938.

Hóman, Bálint, and Gyula Szekfü. *Magyar történet* [Hungarian History]. 5 vols. Budapest: Királyi Magyar Egyetemi Nyomda, 1935–36.

Horváth, Jenő. *Modern Hungary, 1660–1920.* Budapest: Magyar Külügyi Társaság, 1922.

Horváth, Mihály. *Huszonöt év Magyarország történetéből 1823–1848* [Twenty-five Years of Hungary's History, 1823–1848]. 3 vols. Pest: Ráth Mór, 1868.

—— *Az ipar es kereskedés története Magyarországban a három utolsó század alatt* [The History of Commerce and Industry in Hungary During the Last Three Centuries]. Buda: A Magyar Királyi Egyetem, 1840.

Illésy, János. *Az 1754–55 évi országos nemesi összeirás* [The National Census of the Nobility in the Years 1754–55]. Budapest, 1902.

Jászai, Rezső. "A francia forradalom első másfél esztendejéről szóló egykoru hirlapirodalmunk kritikai méltatása" [A Critical Analysis of Our Contemporary Journalism on the First One-and-one-half Years of the French Revolution], in *Szegedi Piarista Gimnázium Értesitője.* Szeged, 1897.

Jászi, Oszkár. *A nemzeti államok kialakulása és a nemzetiségi kérdés* [The Evolution of National States and the Nationality Problem]. Budapest: Grill Károly, 1912.

Jenny, Ilona. *Sopron úrbéri falvainak viszonya a városhoz 1765-től 1836-*

280 BIBLIOGRAPHY

ig [The Relation of the Urbarial Villages of Sopron to the Town, 1765–1836] Pécs: Dunántul Könyvkiadó és Nyomda, 1930.

Kann, Robert A. *A Study in Austrian Intellectual History from Late Baroque to Romanticism.* New York: Frederick A. Praeger Publishers, 1960.

Kató, István. *"Tépjétek le a sötétség bilincseit": A XVIII. századi magyar röpiratok a feudális egyházról* ["Shake Off the Yoke of Darkness": Leaflets on the Feudal Church in the Eighteenth Century]. Budapest: Akadémiai Kiadó, 1950.

Kazinczy, Ferenc. *Kazinczy Ferencz levelezése* [The Correspondence of Ferenc Kazinczy]. 23 vols. Budapest: Magyar Tudományos Akadémia, 1890–1960.

—— *Pályám emlékezete* [Memoirs]. Budapest: Singer és Wolfner, n.d.

Kecskeméti, Károly. *Notes et rapports français sur la Hongrie au XVIIIème siècle.* Fontes Rerum Historiae Hungaricae in Archivis Extraneis. Brussels: Institut Imre Nagy de Sciences Politiques, 1963.

—— *Témoignages sur la Hongrie à l'époque de Napoléon 1802–1809.* Fontes Rerum Historiae Hungaricae in Archivis Extraneis. Brussels: Institut Imre Nagy de Sciences Politiques, 1960.

Kemény, Báró Zsigmond. *"Erdély közélete, 1791–1848"* [The Public Life of Transylvania, 1791–1848], in *Báró Kemény Zsigmond Munkáiból* [From the Works of Baron Zsigmond Kemény]. Edited by Pál Gyulay. 32 vols. Budapest: Franklin-Társulat, 1905.

Keresztesi, József. *Krónika Magyarország polgári és egyházi közéletéből a XVIII–dik század végén* [Chronicle of the Lay and Church Public Life in Hungary at the End of the Eighteenth Century]. Pest: Ráth Mór, 1868.

Keresztury, Dezső, and Andor Tarnai. *Batsányi János 1763–1845* [János Batsányi, 1763–1845]. Budapest: Akadémiai Kiadó, 1953.

Kerner, Robert Joseph. *Bohemia in the Eighteenth Century: A Study in Political, Economic, and Social History, with Special Reference to the Reign of Leopold II, 1790–1792.* New York: The Macmillan Co., 1932.

Klaniczay, Tibor, et al. *History of Hungarian Literature.* London: Collet's, 1964.

Klaniczay, Tibor, ed. *Hét évszázad magyar versei* [The Hungarian Poetry of Seven Centuries]. Budapest: Szépirodalmi Könyvkiadó, 1954.

Kohn, Hans. *The Idea of Nationalism: A Study in Its Origins and Background.* New York: The Macmillan Co. 1945.

Komróczy, György. *A magyar kereskedelem története* [The History of Hungarian Commerce]. Budapest: Magyar Szemle Társaság, 1942.

Korda, Miklós, ed. *A magyar felvilágosodás breviáriuma* [The Breviary of Hungarian Enlightenment]. Budapest, 1918.

Kornis, Gyula. *Hungary and European Civilization.* Washington, D. C.: American-Hungarian Federation, 1947.

—— *Ungarische Kulturideale, 1777–1848.* Leipzig: Quelle, 1930.

Kosáry, Domokos. *Bevezetés a magyar történelem forrásaiba és irodalmába*

[Guide to Sources and Historiography of Hungarian History]. 3 vols. Budapest: Művelt Nép Könyvkiadó, 1954–58.

Kovacsics, József. *A történeti statisztika forrásai* [Sources of Historical Statistics]. Budapest: Közgazdasági és Jogi Könyvkiadó, 1957.

—— *Város és községstatisztika* [Rural and Urban Statistics]. Budapest: Statisztikai Kiadó Vallalat, 1954.

Kovacsics, József, ed. *Magyarország történeti demográfiája: Magyarország népessége a honfoglalástól 1949-ig* [Historical Demography of Hungary: The Population of Hungary Since the Settlement (of Hungarians in Hungary) up to 1949]. Budapest: Közgazdasági és Jogi Könyvkiadó, 1963.

Kropatschek, Joseph, ed. *Handbuch aller unter der Regierung des Kaisers Joseph II. für die K. K. Erbländer ergangenen Verordnungen und Gesetze.* 18 vols. Vienna, 1784–90.

K. U. K. Kriegsarchives. *Geschichte der Kämpfe Österreichs: Kriege die Französiche Revolution 1792–1797.* Vienna, 1905.

Lányi, Károly. *A magyar egyház történelme* [The History of the Hungarian Church]. 2 vols. Esztergom: Horák Egyed, 1866–69.

Link, E. Murr. *The Emancipation of the Austrian Peasant, 1740–1798.* New York: Columbia University Press, 1949.

Máday, Pál. *Az 1735 évi békésszentandrási parasztfelkelés* [The Peasant Uprising of Békésszentandrás in 1735]. Békésszentandrás: Községitanács 1960.

Magyar nemzeti bibliográfia [Hungarian National Bibliography]. Budapest: Országos Széchenyi Könyvtár, 1947–61.

Magyar Tudományos Akadémia. *Munkák és folyóiratok tartalmának betürendes czimjegyzéke, 1889–1910* [A Catalogue of Books and Periodicals]. Budapest: Magyar Tudományos Akadémia, 1911.

Mályusz, Elemér. *A türelmi rendelet: II József és a magyar protestantizmus* [The Toleration Patent: Joseph II and Hungarian Protestantism]. Budapest: Magyar Protestáns Irodalmi Társaság, 1939.

—— "A magyarországi polgárság a francia forradalom korában" [Hungarian Burghers in the Era of the French Revolution], in *A bécsi magyar történeti intézet évkönyve* [The Yearbook of the Hungarian Historical Institute of Vienna]. Budapest, 1931.

Mályusz, Elemér, ed. *Sándor Lipót főherceg nádor iratai 1790–1795* [Papers of Palatine Archduke Alexander Leopold, 1790–1795]. Fontes Historiae Hungaricae Aevi Recentioris. Budapest: Magyar Történelmi Társulat, 1926.

Marczali, Henrik (Henry). *Hungary in the Eighteenth Century.* Cambridge: The University Press, 1910.

—— *Magyarország története II József korában* [History of Hungary in the Era of Joseph II]. Budapest: Magyar Tudományos Akadémia, 1881–88.

—— *Magyarország története III. Károlytól a bécsi kongresszusig (1711–1815)* [The History of Hungary from Charles III to the Congress of

Vienna (1711–1815)], in Sándor Szilágyi, A magyar nemzet története [The History of the Hungarian Nation]. Vol. VIII. Budapest: Athenaeum, 1898.

—— Ungarische Verfassungsgeschichte. Tübingen: Mohr, 1910.

—— Az 1790/91-diki országgyűlés [The Diet of 1790–91]. Budapest: Magyar Tudományos Akadémia, 1907.

Mérei, Gyula. Magyar iparfejlődés, 1790–1848 [The Development of Hungarian Industry, 1790–1848]. Budapest: Közoktatásügyi Kiadó vállalat, 1951.

—— Mezőgazdaság és agrártársadalom Magyarországon, 1790–1848 [Agriculture and Agrarian Society in Hungary, 1790–1848]. Budapest: Teleki Pál Tudományos Intézet, 1948.

Mérei, Gyula, and György Spira, eds. Magyarország története 1790–1849: A feudalizmusról a kapitalizmusra való átmenet korszaka [History of Hungary, 1790–1849: The Era of Transition from Feudalism to Capitalism]. Budapest: Tankönyvkiadó, 1961.

Meszlényi, Antal. A Jozefinizmus kora Magyarországon 1780–1846 [The Era of Josephinism in Hungary, 1780–1846]. Budapest: Stephaneum Nyomda, 1934.

Mezei, Márta. Történetszemlélet a magyar felvilagosodás irodalmában [Interpretation of History in the Literature of the Hungarian Enlightenment]. Budapest: Akadémiai Kiadó, 1958.

Miskolczy, Julius. Ungarn in der Habsburger-Monarchie. Vienna: Verlag Herold, 1959.

Mód, Aladár. 400 év küzdelem az önálló Magyarországért [Four Hundred Years of Struggle for an Independent Hungary]. 7th ed., rev. Budapest: Szikra, 1954.

Molnár, Erik, editor in chief. Magyarország Története [A History of Hungary]. 2 vols. Budapest: Gondolat Könyvkiadó, 1964.

Morvay, Győző. Galánthai gr. Fekete János [Count János Fekete of Galántha]. Magyar történelmi életrajzok [Hungarian Historical Biographies Series]. Budapest: Magyar Történelmi Társulat, 1903.

Nagy, Ernő. Werbőczi és a felvilágosodás [Verbőczi and the Enlightenment]. Szeged, 1941.

Niederhauser, Emil. A jobbágyfelszabaditás Kelet-Europában [The Emancipation of Serfs in Eastern Europe]. Budapest: Akadémiai Kiadó, 1962.

Nyiri, Sándor. A nagybirtok vallásügyi magatartása a 18. században [The Relation of Great Landed Estates to the Church in the Eighteenth Century]. Budapest, 1941.

Oszetzky, Dénes. A hazai polgárság társadalmi problémái a rendiség felbomlásakor [The Social Problems of the Indigenous Burghers During the Dissolution of Feudalism]. Budapest: Királyi Magyar Egyetemi Nyomda, 1935.

Palmer, R. R. The Age of Democratic Revolution: A Political History of

Europe and America, 1760–1800. Princeton, N. J.: Princeton University Press, 1959.

Pamlényi, Ervin, ed. *A Magyar nép története* [The History of the Hungarian People]. Budapest: Müvelt Nép Könyvkiadó, 1954.

Pintér, Jenő. *A magyar irodalom története* [The History of Hungarian Literature]. 2d ed. 2 vols. Budapest: Bibliotheca, 1942.

—— *A magyar irodalom története Bessenyei György fellépésétől Kazinczy Ferencz haláláig (1772–1831)* [The History of Hungarian Literature from the Debut of György Bessenyey to the Death of Ferenc Kazinczy (1772–1831)]. 2 vols. Budapest: By the author, 1913.

Rácz, István. "Parasztzenditő röpiratok a Felső-Tisza vidékén 1790-ben" [Leaflets for the Inciting of Peasants in the Upper Tisza Region in 1790], in István Szabó, *Agrártörténeti tanulmányok* [Essays on Agrarian History]. Budapest: Tankönyvkiadó, 1960.

Raichle, Walter. *Das ungarische Zeitungswesen: Seine Entwicklung bis zum Jahre 1938*. Berlin: Walter de Gruyter & Co., 1939.

Révai, József. *Marxizmus, népiesség, magyarság* [Marxism, Populism, the Hungarians]. Budapest: Szikra, 1948.

Révész, Imre. *Esquisse de l'histoire de la politique religieuse hongroise entre 1705 et 1860*. Budapest: Akadémiai Kiadó, 1960.

—— *Magyarországi protestántizmus történelme* [History of Protestantism in Hungary]. Budapest: Magyar Történelmi Társulat, 1925.

—— *Sinai Miklós és Kora: Adalékok a XVIII. szazadvégi magyar társadolom történetéhez* [Miklós Sinai and His Era: Data on the Hungarian Society at the End of the Eighteenth Century]. Budapest: Akadémiai Kiadó, 1959.

Révész, Imre, and J. Stephen Kováts. *Hungarian Protestantism: Its Past, Present and Future*. Budapest: Gábor, 1927.

Riedl, Frigyes. *A History of Hungarian Literature*. New York: D. Appleton & Co., 1906.

Sayous, E. *Histoire des Hongrois et de leur littérature politique de 1790–1815*. Paris: Germer-Baillière, 1872.

Schlitter, H. *Briefe der Erzherzogin Marie Christine Statthalterin der Niederlande an Leopold II*. Fontes Rerum Austriacarum. Diplomataria. Vienna: Carl Gerold's Sohn, 1896.

Schöpflin, Aladar. *Magyar irók: Irodalmi arcképek és tollrajzok* [Hungarian Writers: Literary Biographies and Essays]. 2d ed. Budapest: Nyugat, 1919.

Silagi, Denis. *Jakobiner in der Habsburger-Monarchie: Ein Beitrag zur Geschichte des aufgeklärten Absolutismus in Österreich*. Vienna: Verlag Herold, 1962.

Skerlecz, Miklós Báró. *Művei* [Works]. Translated from the Latin original by Pál Berényi. Budapest: Grill Károly, 1914.

Soós, Imre. *Az urbéri birtokrendezések eredményei Sopron megyében* [The Results of Urbarial Arrangements in Sopron County]. Sopron, 1941.

Spira, György, ed. *Tanulmányok a parasztság történetéhez Magyarországon,
1711–1790* [Essays on the History of Peasantry in Hungary, 1711–
1790]. Budapest: Akadémiai Kiadó, 1952.
Strada, Ferenc. "Izdenczy József, az allamtanács első magyar tagja"
[József Izdenczy, the First Hungarian Member of the Staatsrat], in
A Bécsi Magyar Történeti Intézet Évkönyve [The Yearbook of the Hun-
garian Historical Institute of Vienna]. Vol. X. Budapest, 1940.
Sugar, Peter F. "The Influence of the Enlightenment and the French Revo-
lution in Eighteenth Century Hungary," *Journal of Central European
Affairs,* Vol. XVIII (1958).
Szabad, György. *A tatai és gesztesi Eszterházy-uradalom áttérése a robot
rendszerről a tőkés gazdálkodásra* [The Transition from Serf Labor to
Capitalist Economy in the Eszterházy Estates of Tata and Gesztes].
Budapest: Akadémiai Kiadó, 1957.
Szabó, Dezső, ed. *Magyarországi úrbérrendezés története Mária Terézia
korában* [The History of the Urbarial Regulations in the Era of Maria
Theresa]. Fontes Historiae Hungaricae Aevi Recentioris. Budapest:
Magyar Történelmi Társulat, 1933.
Szabó, István. *A magyar parasztság története* [The History of the Hun-
garian Peasantry]. Budapest: Magyar Szemle Társaság, 1940.
—— *Tanulmányok a magyar parasztság történetéből* [Essays on the His-
tory of the Hungarian Peasantry]. Budapest: Teleki Pál Tudományos
Intézet, 1948.
Szádeczky, Lajos. *Iparfejlődés és a czéhek története Magyarországon
okirattárral, 1307–1848* [The History of Guilds and Industrial Develop-
ments in Hungary, with Collection of Documents, 1307–1848]. 2 vols.
Budapest: Ranschburg Gusztáv, 1913.
Szántó, Imre. *A parasztság kisajátitása és mozgalmai a Gróf Festeticsek
keszthelyi ágának birtokain 1711–1850* [The Expropriation and the
Movements of the Peasantry on the Estates of the Keszthely Branch of
the Counts Festetics, 1711–1850]. Budapest: Művelt Nép Könyvkiadó,
1954.
Szeberényi, Lajos. *A parasztság története* [The History of the Peasantry].
Budapest: Gergely R. Könyvkereskedése, 1937.
Székely, Ottokár. "Az egyházi nemesség" [The Church Nobility], in *A gróf
Klebelsberg Kunó Magyar Történetkutató Intézet évkönyve* [The Year-
book of the Count Klebelsberg Kunó Hungarian Historical Research
Institute]. Budapest, 1935.
Szekfü, Gyula. *Etat et Nation.* Paris: Les Presses Universitaires de France,
1945.
—— *Három nemzedék egy hanyatló kor története* [Three Generations,
the History of a Declining Era]. Budapest: "Élet" Irodalmi és Nyomda
R. T., 1920.
Szekfü, Gyula, ed. *Mi a magyar?* [What Is the Hungarian?] Budapest:
Magyar Szemle Társasag, 1939.

Szerb, Antal. *Magyar irodalomtörténet* [Hungarian Literary History]. Budapest: Magvető Könyvkiadó, 1958.

Szilágyi, Sándor, ed. *A Magyar nemzet története* [The History of the Hungarian Nation]. 10 vols. Budapest: Athenaeum, 1895–98.

Tessedik, Sámuel. *Der Landmann in Ungarn, was er ist, und was er seyn könnte, nebst einem Plane von einem regulirten Dorfe.* N.p.: By the author, 1784.

Thirring, Gusztav, *Magyarország népessége II József korában* [Population of Hungary in the Era of Joseph II]. Budapest: Magyar Tudományos Akadémia, 1938.

Timon, Ákos. *Magyar alkotmány- és jogtörténet: Tekintettel a nyugati államok jogfejlődésére* [History of the Hungarian State and Law: In Comparison with the Development of Western Legal Systems]. Budapest: Hornyánszky, 1903.

Townson, Robert. *Travels in Hungary with a Short Account of Vienna in the Year 1793.* London: G. G. and J. Robinson, 1797.

Trócsányi, Zsolt. *Az erdélyi parasztság története, 1790–1849* [The History of the Transylvanian Peasantry, 1790–1849]. Budapest: Akadémiai Kiadó, 1956.

Ungár, László. "A magyar nemesi birtok eladósodása 1838 előtt" [The Indebtedness of the Landed Property of the Nobles Prior to 1838], *Századok*, 1935, pp. 46–60.

Valjavec, Fritz. *Geschichte der abendländische Aufklärung.* Vienna: Verlag Herold, 1961.

—— *Der Josephinismus: Zur geistigen Entwicklung Österreichs im achtzehnten und neunzehnten Jahrhundert.* Munich: Verlag M. Schick, 1945.

—— "Zu den Richtlinien der ungarischen Aufklärungsforschung," in *Ungarische Jahrbücher.* Berlin, 1932.

Verbőczi, István. *Hármaskönyve Tripartitum.* Pest: Magyar Tudós Társaság, 1844. (First published in Vienna, 1517.)

Waldapfel, József. *A magyar irodalom a felvilágosodás korában* [Hungarian Literature in the Era of Enlightenment]. 2d ed. Budapest: Akadémiai Kiadó, 1957.

Wandruszka, Adam. *Leopold II: Erzherzog von Österreich, Grossherzog von Toskana, König von Ungarn und Böhmen, Römischer Kaiser.* 2 vols. Vienna: Verlag Herold, 1965.

Wangermann, Ernst. *From Joseph II to the Jacobin Trials: Government Policy and Public Opinion in the Habsburg Dominions in the Period of the French Revolution.* London: Oxford University Press, 1959.

Warriner, Doreen, ed. *Contrasts in Emerging Societies: Readings in the Social and Economic History of South-Eastern Europe in the Nineteenth Century.* Bloomington: Indiana University Press, 1965.

Wellmann, Imre. *Tessedik Sámuel* [Sámuel Tessedik]. Budapest: Művelt Nép Könyvkiadó, 1954.

—— "Az udvari ember" [The Courtier], in Sándor Domanovszky, ed.,

Magyar művelődéstörténet [Hungarian Cultural History]. Budapest: Magyar Történelmi Társulat, n.d.

—— "Mezőgazdaság történet-irásunk uj utja" [New Roads of Our Agrarian History], in *Domanovszky emlékkönyv* [Book Published to Commemorate Domanovszky]. Budapest, 1937.

INDEX

Acsády, Ádám, 22n
Agriculture, 9–10; productivity of serf
  holdings, 136–37; introduction of
  new methods, 140–41; experimenters
  and reformers, 141–47; activities of
  Tessedik, 142, 143–47, 270, 272; Ex-
  perimental Economics Institute, 144–
  45; Georgicon Academy, 145–46, 269,
  270; see also Land; Serfs
Albrecht, Prince of Saxony, 93n, 266
Alexander Leopold, Archduke, 93n,
  229–30, 260, 266, 272
Almássy, Ignácz, 180
Almássy, Pál, 218
Althan, Cardinal Mihály F., 120n
Amadé, Count Antal, 142, 143
Ányos, Pál, 30–31, 266
Aristocrats, 15, 25–32, 82, 87, 94, 131,
  177; Hungarian Noble Bodyguard,
  11, 29, 156, 268; and Enlightenment, 149–50; see also Lords; Nobles
Army, 181, 183–84; standing, establishment of, 7, 8, 103, 106, 110,
  184; and taking of 1788 census, 16;
  Generalkommando, 17, 103, 184,
  198, 256; number of soldiers in 1788
  census, 19 (table); insurrectio (duty
  of nobles to bear arms), 70, 183–84,
  260, 261; Hofkriegsrat, 77n–78n,
  185, 187, 256, 257, 259; Kriegsrat,
  92, 97, 103–4, 181, 187; composition, 104; commissariatus provincialis (országos bizottság), 104, 254;
  commissarii districtuales, 105; periods
  of service, 105; regulamentum (accounting for supplies), 106, 261;
  taxes for support, 106; supply, 106–
  7; portio (supply system), 106, 107,
  215, 220, 260–61; deperdita (prices),
  106, 261; domus annonaria (surplus
  food storehouse), 107, 255; participation of units in feudal revolt, 187–
  90; Civil Guard, 198
Árpád dynasty, 78, 79

Bacsányi, János, 158–59, 266–67
Balitéletekről (Wesselényi), 273
Balogh, Péter, 32n, 161, 178–79, 180,
  193, 195n, 235, 267
Bánság of Temes (Temesi Bánság), 137
Barco, General, 184–85
Barkóczy, Ferenc, 32n, 121, 151n
Baróti-Szabó, Dávid, 158, 267
Batthyány, Count Ferenc, 121
Batthyány, Cardinal Archbishop Count
  József, 32n, 124, 173, 237, 267
Batthyány, Prince Lajos, Palatine, 22n,
  28, 30n, 32n, 266
Batthyány family, 193
Beck, Pál, 193
Békés County peasant revolt, 212–15
Bél, Mátyás, 48, 49, 120, 267
Belnay, György Alajos, 267
Beőthy, Imre, 32n, 180
Berzeviczy, Gergely, 142, 267; quoted,
  138–39
Berzsenyi, Dániel, 31, 267–68
Bessenyei, György, 148, 268; quoted,
  88, 108–9
Bethlen, Prince Gábor, 115n, 268
Bétsi Udvari Deárium (Wiener Dia-
  rium, court bulletin), 156
Bezerédy, Ignácz, 32n, 180
Bocskay, István, 52, 258, 268
Boráros, János, 207
Bossányi, Ferenc, 39
Buda, 25n, 28n, 44, 45, 46, 48, 99,
  115n; as royal capital, 45, 80n, 95,
  173, 177, 184, 198, 200–1
Burghers, 4, 5, 37–38, 79, 82, 136, 178;
  number in 1788 census, 19 (table);
  number in 1782, 43; as fourth estate, 43–50; and Enlightenment, 151–
  52; organization to combat feudal
  revolt, 196–211; Civil Guard, 198,
  210; proposed oath, 203–4, 205

Calvinists, 116; number of parishes in
  1788 census, 22; members in 1788